THE PRESS
AND
POLITICAL
CULTURE
IN GHANA

THE PRESS AND POLITICAL CULTURE IN GHANA

JENNIFER HASTY

INDIANA UNIVERSITY PRESS

Bloomington & Indianapolis

This book is a publication of

Indiana University Press
601 North Morton Street
Bloomington, Indiana 47404-3797 USA

http://iupress.indiana.edu

Telephone orders 800-842-6796
Fax orders 812-855-7931
Orders by email iuporder@indiana.edu

The paper used in this publication meets the minimum
requirements of American National Standard for Information
Sciences—Permanence of Paper for Printed Library
Materials, ANSI Z39.48-1984.

Manufactured in the United States of America

Library of Congress Cataloging-in-Publication Data

Hasty, Jennifer.
  The press and political culture in Ghana / Jennifer Hasty.
    p. cm.
  Includes bibliographical references and index.
  ISBN 0-253-34524-3 (alk. paper) — ISBN 0-253-21748-2 (pbk. :
alk. paper)
  1. Press and politics—Ghana. 2. Government and the press—
Ghana. 3. Political culture—Ghana. I. Title.
  PN5499.G4H37 2005
  070.4'493209667—dc22
                                    2004018269

1 2 3 4 5 10 09 08 07 06 05

Kwan war a owie abow ano.

However long the distance, it ends at the door.

—Fante Proverb

CONTENTS

PREFACE

In 1995, I first came to Ghana to check out the feasibility of my dissertation project on news media. I had originally planned on fieldwork in Nigeria—and had just defended my qualifier thesis on the press and politics in Lagos. At that time Nigerian journalists were embroiled in conflict with the Abacha government, staging a series of marches and protests to criticize the continual harassment, arrest, and detention of journalists by the state. In addition, the Ogoni activist Ken Saro Wiwa and eight of his companions were under prosecution by a military-appointed tribunal and subsequently sentenced to death, sparking a massive outcry in the oppositional media.

A few days before my scheduled departure for Lagos in late June, my visa application was returned to me in the mail. The Nigerian consulate was unable to issue me a visa, the accompanying letter explained, because of the potential dangers involved in my project. In addition to the points of contact I had already made with editors and journalists in Nigeria, I would need to establish a stronger set of relationships with media scholars, practitioners, and institutions before I would be allowed in the country. Of course, in times of political turmoil, such contacts can be difficult to consolidate unless one is already in the country. Rehearsing this argument in various tones of confidence, supplication, and urgency, I finally gave up with the consulate. I then spent several hours, head in hands, ruing my fate.

Rather frantic at my predicament (plane ticket and grant money in one hand, rejected visa application in another), I devised a plan to fly initially to Ghana and then make my way to Nigeria from there. Changing my ticket from Lagos to Accra, my somewhat dubious but remarkably resourceful airline consolidator miraculously produced a Ghanaian entrance visa for me in a mere forty-eight hours. So off I went, consulting *The Lonely Planet* for Twi phrases and scheming for a way to get myself to my field site in Nigeria as soon as possible.

Arriving in Accra, I began to make arrangements for my transit to Nigeria. I quickly made my way to the Nigerian Embassy, only to be spurned with the same set of concerns and stipulations. In the midst of further head-hanging and ruing, I started buying all the local newspapers and reading the intense debate over the sudden resignation of President Rawlings' popular and reputedly brilliant finance minister, Kwesi Botchwey, engineer of Ghana's structural adjustment program in the early 1980s. Botchwey had quit in disgust, charging allegations of corruption in the Ghana National Petroleum

Corporation. The state press deflected these allegations of corruption while the private press chastised Rawlings for losing such a brilliant tactician with such strong global links. Although the Ghanaian news media certainly hadn't captured the same international reputation as Nigerian journalism, the complex political passions of this debate impressed me with the vibrancy and openness of news discourse in Ghana.

One afternoon shortly after my arrival I met a local young man hanging out in the foyer of my hotel who told me he knew the editor of the best-selling newspaper in Ghana and would be happy to introduce me. Somewhat suspicious of my new friend I nonetheless took him up on his offer, and the next day we went to the Graphic compound where we checked in at the gate and were ushered to a spacious, air-conditioned office. I noticed with some surprise that the walls were oddly decorated with labels from Chicken of the Sea cans. After a brief wait, in walked a rather stout and ruddy white man who introduced himself as the manager of "Graphic." Befuddled by his whiteness, as well as his choice in office decor, I introduced myself and explained my interest in news media. "Oh," he replied amiably, "you've come to the wrong man, I'm the manager of Graphic Corporation. We print labels for local products like tuna and beer," he said, gesturing to his handiwork on the walls. "You want to meet the editor of *Daily Graphic*, Elvis Aryeh. Let me call him for you." (At this point, my young friend took the opportunity of leaving for some business in town.)

Minutes later I found myself in the office of the editor in chief of *Daily Graphic*, with a long row of local newspapers archived along the wall. An extroverted Ghanaian, Elvis Aryeh greeted me effusively, questioned me on my project at length, and then insisted on taking me and his secretary out for a leisurely lunch at the poshest place in town, the restaurant at the Labadi Beach Hotel. By the end of the day he had invited me to come to work for his newspaper the following year, encouraging me to abandon my plans for Nigeria and relocate my project in Ghana.

Seriously considering this notion, I began interviewing the editors of the major newspapers in Accra. A cosmopolitan group, they all spoke the transnational language of political liberalism, emphasizing the centrality of the press to the democratic process and the obligation of the journalist to act as a watchdog in the public interest. As an editor for the state-funded *Graphic*, Aryeh stressed the importance of responsibility and the commitment of his newspaper to the national interests of unity and development. Editors of the private newspapers dismissed the sycophantic journalism of the state press and voiced their own set of commitments to editorial independence, freedom of speech, and human rights. I was fascinated by these two contradictory interpretations of the democratic functionality of the press. Furthermore, I was continually surprised by the welcome access I received at nearly every newspaper office in town. Editors assured me that I could easily work for state and private news organizations without any concerns about state harassment or visa problems. "This is Ghana, nobody will worry you," I heard again and again.

Convinced that Ghana was indeed the place I could freely pursue such a controversial political topic, I went back to Duke, explained the situation to my dissertation committee, and wrote my project proposal on the press and politics in Ghana.

In September 1996, I returned to Accra to begin my dissertation field-work. I arrived in September, just as the campaign season was heating up in anticipation of the presidential and parliamentary elections scheduled for December 7. Just five years earlier, Ghana had adopted a democratic consti-tution after ten years of military rule under the charismatic populist Flight Lieutenant Jerry John Rawlings. Shortly after the ratification of the 1991 constitution, Rawlings and his ruling party, the National Democratic Con-gress (NDC), were elected to power in the controversial elections of 1992, decried by the opposition as "the stolen verdict" even as the international observers declared the process "free and fair." Much was at stake in the elec-tions of 1996, not only the perpetuation of the NDC or the viability of the fragmented opposition but the very future of popular participation in polit-ical discourse and decision making. When I arrived in September I could sense the simmering of national anticipation for the political rituals of vot-ing and counting, complicated by anxieties of chaos and coups should the results go the wrong way.

These national political passions were expressed and intensified in the news media. Since television and radio were still largely controlled by the state, newspapers became the crucible of political contest during the 1996 campaign, juxtaposing the inspirational development rhetoric of the ruling party with the spirited allegations of corruption and illegitimacy leveled by the opposition. The state media churned out pro-government rhetoric daily and blanketed the front page with color photos of the president in various stances of political heroism and development activism. Against this bias, the private press took up the cause of the opposition, launching investigations to expose government corruption, portraying the president as a violent drug addict, and continually celebrating the slogan of the opposition presidential candidate J. A. Kufour, who advised Ghanaians to "*Hwe wo asetena mu na to aba paa*" (Examine your living standards and vote accordingly).

With my basic training in journalism, I had imagined I might start out by serving as some kind of apprentice or office assistant, perhaps copyedit-ing or simply proofreading for spelling and grammar. However, when I presented my proposal to the editor of the privately owned *Ghanaian Independent*, Kabral Blay-Amihere, he immediately welcomed me onboard and introduced me to his staff as an anthropologist who would be working as a journalist for the newspaper. Moreover, in a strategic and extroverted maneuver, the paper then ran a picture of me on the front page, announcing my internship to the readers of the newspaper.

I worked for the *Independent* throughout the campaign season, writing political and cultural stories along with the occasional editorial and a brief guest stint on the editor's own political column. I then moved on to the premier state paper, the *Daily Graphic,* in January where I went out on daily "invited assignments" to cover the development initiatives of the state. Pausing for a few months of interviews and archival research at the J. B. Danquah collection of newspapers at Legon, I then went to work for the investigative newspaper *Ghanaian Chronicle* in the summer of 1997. I returned to North Carolina for a Mellon Fellowship at Duke in 1997–98 but traveled back to Ghana again the summer of 1998 to work for the state-funded Ghana News Agency. On subsequent research visits every summer, I have continued to interview journalists and editors, conduct research in the archives, work for news organizations, and collect contemporary newspapers.

This book is based on my experiences as a journalist and researcher over this seven-year period of democratic renewal and consolidation in Ghana from 1995 to 2002. Without the hard work of Ghanaian journalists throughout this period, the celebrated political renaissance of Ghanaian democracy would never have been possible.

My father is a disc jockey, now retired. One of the most exhilarating experiences of my childhood in Springfield, Missouri, was a visit to KWTO, the radio station where he worked for a few years in the 1970s. Leaning against his knee in the control room, I vividly remember looking out over the vast, complicated array of buttons and levers on the control panel, trying hard to observe his serious admonishment that my brother and I should keep quiet when the little red light signaled, "On the Air." Hearing my own father's voice deepen and broaden into his "radio voice" narrating the news, I felt that electric sense of publicity, at once intimate and alienated, channeled through my father's body through the microphone and into some shared, imagined space of the city. At other times, while eating breakfast or driving somewhere with the radio on, I have experienced the odd sensation of suddenly recognizing the familiarity of my father's voice in the background noise, then inclining my head to hear if it really *is* my father, speaking not to me but to this shared imagined space of listeners.

So many years later, walking home from a hard day's work at the Ghana News Agency, I was worrying over some troubling episode in my everyday life as a journalist in a state-owned news organization, when I sensed the sound of vaguely familiar words in the background. A booming radio somewhere was tuned into Radio GAR, the state-owned radio station, and the commentator was reading out a local news story. Suddenly recognizing the familiarity of my own "official" turn of phrase, I stopped in my tracks and inclined my head to identify the news story I had just written a few hours ago with my partner at GNA read out verbatim to the audience of my unsuspecting neighbors. Projecting from the immediacy of my neighborhood, I thought of all the radios tuned into GAR throughout Accra, creating the shared, imagined space of public discourse at that very moment. Somehow conspicuous yet completely anonymous, I felt again that mysterious sense of publicity, both intimate and alienated, channeled through my own corporeal experience of going out on assignment that day, sifted through the shared mental work of narrative production, passing through my fingers on the computer keyboard—and then released into the world to find the community that must be there to hear it.

ACKNOWLEDGMENTS

This book is based on my dissertation, completed in the Department of Cultural Anthropology at Duke University in 1999. My appreciation goes out to this stellar department, full of enthusiastic scholars doing fascinating work. I am especially grateful for the support of my adviser at Duke, Charles Piot. Since the emergence of this project in 1995, Charlie has been a motivating source of scholarly advice and critique, conveying his enthusiasm for African studies as well as his subtle and rigorous understanding of contemporary issues in the field. I am lucky to have had such an inspiring adviser. Ralph Litzinger and Orin Starn also provided insightful criticism on the dissertation as well as collegial advice and support since my graduation. Jan Radway and Jan Ewald also served on my dissertation committee, raising important issues that might otherwise have been neglected. Fellow graduate students at Duke, Clare Talwalker and Nilgun Uygun, helped me to think through issues of postcoloniality and globalism over many games of gin rummy and cups of tea.

Funding for the research and write-up of this project was provided by a Mellon Predoctoral Fellowship in Transnationalism and Public Culture as well as two travel grants from the Duke Center for International Studies. Follow-up research was carried out with funding from two Regency Advancement Awards from Pacific Lutheran University (PLU), where I have taught since 1999.

In the final stages, the manuscript was polished off with support from a postdoctoral membership at the Institute for Advanced Study (IAS) in Princeton, New Jersey, in 2002–2003. Many thanks to Michael Walzer, Clifford Geertz, Adam Ashforth, Joan Scott, and Albert Hirschman for a wonderful year of writing and scholarly sociality at the Institute. I would also like to thank fellow members and colleagues at IAS that year, including Rachel Neis, Madeline Kochen, Rasma Karklins, Brenda Chalfin, Dan Smith, Neil Englehart, and Melissa Miller. IAS staff Linda Garat and Ame Dyckman were masters of cheerfully adept office support throughout the year. Robin Clark, mathematical linguist from the University of Pennsylvania, shared many ideas about language, meaning, structure, and stress reduction that have stimulated progress on this book.

This book has benefited from many discussions with colleagues and mentors in African studies. In particular, Jean Allman and Birgit Meyer have contributed excellent suggestions, feedback, and advice throughout the project. Tom McCaskie, Lynne Brydon, John Parker, Natasha Gray, and Amy Settergren have all sat around with me at one time or another in Accra, sharing their perspectives on politics and news media over a table full of Ghanaian newspapers. I wish to convey my appreciation to Emmanuel Akyeampong at Harvard, Alan Howard at Rutgers, Birgit Meyer at the Amsterdam School of Social Research, and Ann Anagnost at the University of Washington for invitations to present versions of this work at their respective universities. Ato Quayson has also provided stimulating feedback. Between conferences in the Netherlands one summer, I finished the prospectus for the book at the Afrikastudiecentrum at the University of Leiden, in the office of Rijk van Dijk who graciously allowed me to use his computer while he was out of town. In Seattle, discussions with historian Lynn Thomas at the University of Washington regarding notions of African modernity, media, gender, and interdisciplinarity have sharpened my understanding of these issues. At PLU, archeologist Kevin Vaughn and his wife Dawn have provided comments, friendship, vegan cakes, and good wine that have all contributed to the completion of this project. Warm thanks to my editor, Dee Mortensen at Indiana University Press, for her excellent support and advice throughout the publication process. Copyeditor Rita Bernhard put the manuscript in shape in the final stages.

In Ghana, I owe a huge debt of gratitude to the many journalists and editors who contributed directly and indirectly to the book. Thanks especially to everyone at the *Ghanaian Independent*, the *Ghanaian Chronicle*, the *Daily Graphic*, the Ghana News Agency, and *Public Agenda* for their cooperation, collegiality, and friendship. In particular, Kabral Blay-Amihere and Elvis Aryeh have made crucial contributions to this book, answering my endless questions and opening doors of access into the realm of Ghanaian journalism. While in Ghana, Mrs. Emily Asiedu provided a comfortable home and the feeling of family, as well as interesting dinnertime commentary on my various daily adventures. My good friend Isabella Gyau-Orhin was a constant source of cultural and professional insight as I carried out my field research.

This book is dedicated to my mother, Mary June Hasty, an elementary school principal, now retired. She has always emphasized the centrality of study and learning, giving so many kinds of support to my brother and me through so many years of university studies. From my brother, Jeff Hasty, a physicist in the Biomedical Engineering Department at the University of California–San Diego, I have learned many lessons valuable to the accomplishment of this project (regarding, for instance, creativity, perseverance, loyalty, rambling, wistfulness, and political absurdity). My grandmother, Peggy Hasty, a self-taught painter and musician, encouraged me to write stories and poems throughout my childhood. She always wanted to write a book herself, and I hope she would be proud of this one.

ABBREVIATIONS

AFRC	Armed Forces Revolutionary Council
BNI	Bureau of National Investigations
CHRAJ	Commission for Human Rights and Administrative Justice
CIB	Castle Information Bureau
EC	Electoral Commission
ECOWAS	Economic Community of West African States
EPA	Environmental Protection Agency
ERA	Economic Recovery Program
EU	European Union
FES	Friedrich Ebert Stiftung
GIJ	Ghana Institute of Journalism
GJA	Ghana Journalists Association
GNA	Ghana News Agency
GNPC	Ghana National Petroleum Corporation
IFJ	International Federation of Journalists
MP	Minister of Parliament
NDC	National Democratic Congress
NEC	National Electoral Commission
NMC	National Media Commission
NPP	New Patriotic Party
PCP	People's Convention Party
PRINPAG	Private Newspaper Publishers Association of Ghana
PRO	Public Relations Officer
TUC	Trades Union Congress
UP	United Party
USIA	United States Information Agency
USIS	United States Information Service
WAEC	West African Examinations Council
WAJA	West African Journalists Association

THE PRESS
AND
POLITICAL
CULTURE
IN GHANA

Introduction

Waking up in your house any morning in the bustling Ghanaian capital of Accra, you are immediately drawn in to the local discourse of news. The first sound you may hear in the morning, after the soft sweeping of needle brooms on the compound floor, is the chattering of disc jockeys on the radio, discussing the fresh news of the morning from the pages of the *Daily Graphic* or the *Ghanaian Independent*. As you get ready to go out in the morning, a friend or two might stop by to say hello, adding, "My friend, have you *heard* what they're saying about the president's wife?" or "Can you *believe* what they found in the finance minister's closet?"

Stepping out of your house, the source of this discourse comes into view as you spot groups of young men tending kiosks or striding along the roadside, proffering an impressive array of daily and weekly newspapers. Winding through traffic and hissing inquisitively, roadside vendors display the day's headlines to passersby in a dramatically colorful palette, artfully arranged on one arm, while deftly leafing and selling with the other. At neighborhood markets and most major intersections, crowds gather every morning and afternoon to peruse and compare the lead stories of all the newspapers currently for sale, hung in a vibrant collage across the frames of the wooden kiosks that sell them. Top stories from the major newspapers are reported and analyzed on the morning shows of many television and radio stations. People who buy newspapers often read out the stories to those around them, punctuating the news with their own editorial comments, drawing their listeners into the collective exercise of interpretation. Once read, a paper is never thrown away but passed around for others to read, reaching as many as ten readers who may relay that news to a network of hundreds.

Whether you walk, take a taxi, or ride the bus to work, someone around you is reading, listening, or discussing the news, usually adding context and commentary and inviting your own participation. And when you get to work (or school or the market or wherever you're going), you meet up with friends, colleagues, and customers throughout the day, engaged in intermittent yet ongoing commentary on local, national, and global events. In some form or another, news is nearly always within earshot in Accra, heard in nearly every taxi and most public offices, emanating from chop bars and drinking spots, blasting from domestic patios as women sew, do laundry, and look after little children. Combining the "formal" genres of mass media with "informal" modes of social communication, news discourse is embedded in a complex circuit of social knowledge that combines a diversity of sources and audiences, all engaged in exchanges of official information, unofficial leaks, scholarly analysis, popular commentary, rumors, and jokes. The daily drama of national news stimulates the flow of information through this circuit, continually conjuring political imagination and compelling popular fascination.

Newspapers form the nexus of this news discourse in Ghana. The most provocative and influential news stories circulating through mass media and into the public sphere are produced by the state and private press. While newsworthy events are also covered by radio and television, newspapers constitute the very terms of local news discourse: identifying the main characters, the important local events, and recurring themes—subsuming all in an ongoing narrative frame of national news. In Ghana, as in other postcolonies, news discourse is divided into two distinctive genres, the state press and the private press. In my year of fieldwork, the two state-funded newspapers, the *Daily Graphic* and the *Ghanaian Times,* were publishing stories designed to amplify the inspirational rhetoric and development policies of the government in their distinctive coverage of national events. These conservative stories were frequently accompanied by flattering color photos of the president himself, wielding a pickax or driving a bulldozer to demonstrate his personal commitment to development projects throughout the country. This benevolent and charismatic portrayal of the state was countered in the private weekly and biweekly newspapers with stories of drug abuse, violence, irrationality, and rampant corruption among government officials, particularly the president and his wife. Often the front-page stories of the private press featured a sinister photo of the president in a threatening pose, dressed in military fatigues and mirrored sunglasses, sneering at some perceived threat to his authority. The most popular private papers published exposés on the lavish lifestyles of government officials and the mismanagement of government affairs, thereby pointing out multiple hypocrisies in the rhetoric of national development. Whereas the stories in the state press were based on the printed speeches and official statements of government ministers, private journalists were excluded from these sources, forced to articulate with the flow of unofficial information through circuits of popular rumor, anonymous tips, and oppositional commentary.

1. Candidate Rawlings, the patron-populist. This front page of the premiere state newspaper, appearing in the midst of the presidential campaign of autumn 1996, is dominated by a color photo of President Rawlings (in a working-man's smock) wielding a pick-ax to break ground for a state-funded market at Mankessim in the Central Region. While the lead story conveys a message of peace from the King of Asante ("Otumfuo" Opoku Ware II), that story is discursively framed by the Mankessim story above and the ruling party advert to the right. Note the complete absence of news on the opposition candidate. *Courtesy of the* Daily Graphic, *November 30, 1996.*

2. Chairman Rawlings, the violent revolutionary. The front page of this popular private newspaper depicts the menacing, agitated figure of young Rawlings, in fatigues and dark sunglasses, crouching as if to attack the reader. The accompanying story reports a threat by Rawlings to stage a revolt if the opposition should win the elections, reenacting the revolutionary violence of his first military coup in 1979. The unrelated story below reports on an unprovoked police attack against peaceful demonstrators, underlining the theme of state violence. *Courtesy of the* Independent, *November 6, 1996.*

Situated at the interstices of politics and popular culture, the combined discourse of state and private newspapers constitutes an intensely dialogic and hotly contested public sphere, constructing the authoritative social imaginary of the government while equipping oppositional groups with a means of discursive challenge and political re-signification. While punctuated with social and cultural controversy, this public sphere of political contest is crucial to the cohesion of the nation-state in the new dispensation of democracy in Ghana.

This book explores the production of news discourse in Ghana during this crucial period of political contest, liberalization, and democratic consolidation, the late Rawlings period of 1995–2000. While focusing the crucial role of newspapers in the consolidation of democracy, I came to understand Ghanaian journalism in a broader historical and cultural context as an apparatus for the production and reconfiguration of distinctive forms of African modernity, postcolonial nationalism, and global articulation. Fundamental to the current globalizing agenda of democratization and civil society, the ideals and institutions of print journalism may seem to bear the universal logic of liberal modernity. However, the everyday practices of journalism in Ghana are profoundly particular, shaped by historicized cultural understandings of political authority and resistance as well as notions of African sociality and discursive propriety. As journalists in Ghana increasingly position themselves globally to define and defend their professional vocation, the seemingly universal discourses of political liberalism come into conflict with durable forms of cultural and historical locality embedded in practice. This ethnography of the state and private press in Ghana sets out to illustrate the historical and cultural particularity of Ghanaian journalism while demonstrating how Ghanaian journalists actively grapple with the contradictions that continually emerge among globalizing discourses and localizing practices.

Working as a journalist for the Ghanaian press, I was continually struck by the complicated ways that African political and discursive forms dramatically shape the seemingly universal practices of journalism. The daily work routine, relationships with sources, criteria of newsworthiness, narrative techniques—all are locally determined by Ghanaian standards of discourse and sociality. Local notions of authority and patronage structure a cultural context for daily assignments and beats. Local aesthetics of representation and discursive propriety establish a distinctive set of conventions for political speech and news writing. Local histories of colonial authoritarianism, anticolonial nationalism, and postcolonial instability inform the terms and techniques of political contest between the state and oppositional groups, an antagonistic discourse played out in the public sphere between the state press and the private press.

Ghanaian journalists recognize their professional practices as both cosmopolitan and culturally distinct. While the "difference" of Ghanaian journalism is continually reinscribed in social relations and local circumstances, the cosmopolitan nature of journalism has been enhanced by the increase in global ties to professional organizations and human rights groups as well as the proliferating opportunities for professional travel to conferences and programs abroad. So while journalists are embedded in an adversarial drama of national politics pitched in local cultural terms, at the same time they position themselves professionally in larger global narratives of free speech and democratization. The result is a set of contradictions emerging in discourse, text, and practice as journalists articulate their professional vocation through the global discourses of development and human rights while deploying their journalistic practices in a local environment shaped by local cultural, historical, and material circumstances. While contemporary global discourses of political liberalism situate Ghanaian journalists as heroic "watchdogs" of emergent civil society and democratization, deeper forces of colonial history, postcolonial nationalism, and cultural identity have shaped the institutions and practices of news media in Ghana for well over a century, recruiting journalists into processes of hegemony and resistance in a constantly shifting political field.

Newspapers, Civil Society, and the "African Renaissance"

In the 1990s a wave of democratization swept across Africa in response to widespread popular demands for representation and human rights, and supported by the political and economic imperatives of the International Monetary Fund (IMF) and the World Bank (Zartman 1995; Young 1994; Widner 1994; Herbst 1993; Klein 1992; Wiseman 1991). Following two decades of political chaos, authoritarian rule, and economic collapse throughout Africa, political transitions and reforms in Zambia, South Africa, Mozambique, Tanzania, Uganda, Ghana (and elsewhere) transformed the political sphere with more liberal leaders, democratic constitutions, multiparty systems, elections, and deliberative legislative bodies combined with the development of voluntary associations outside the state, such as unions, professional associations, churches, political advocacy groups, and organizations of farmers, women, and students. The widespread transformation in the structure of African governance from authoritarianism to democracy has been hailed as the blossoming of African "civil society," the emergence of new institutions designed to mediate state-society relations while establishing new rules for the popular negotiation of power (Bratton 1994; Harbeson, Rothchild, and Chazan 1994; Calhoun 1993; Fatton 1992; Migdal 1988; Bayart 1986). As Harbeson explains, "Civil society stands between society and government and is distinct from yet engaged with both" (1994, 287). Crucial to the mediating function of civil society is the establishment of a free and inclusive public sphere of discourse, bringing the institutions of state and society into dialogue with each other. The engineering of consensus in this realm of discourse is key to the popular legitimacy and stability of the new dispensations. Thus the scholarship on political renewal in Africa emphasizes the agency and expressivity of these civil institutions in the public sphere, functioning to empower subaltern voices and facilitate popular participation.

The reemergence of the press as a critical public sphere of political discourse in Ghana has occurred in the larger context of this "African Renaissance." Throughout the 1980s then military leader J. J. Rawlings relied heavily on the state media to construct his charisma and define the political legitimacy of his regime in terms of development patronage. Condemned as enemies of national unity and development, private newspapers were repressed and harassed to near extinction. With democratization and the new constitution, the newspaper licensing law was lifted and a slew of private papers suddenly appeared, representing a plurality of popular and political voices outside the state (Hasty 2001). Relying on a discourse of democratization and human rights, the angry discourse of the private press gave vent to years of repressed opposition, challenging the arbitrary abuses of power of the Rawlings regime and asserting the new rules of the political order.

Situated at the interstices of state and society, newspapers frame the very context for discursive mediation and popular legitimacy, thus constituting both a central institution of civil society and the very conditions of possibility of the public sphere. In his seminal study of the emergence of bourgeois civil society in Western Europe, Habermas refers to the news media as "the public sphere's preeminent institution" (1989, 181). Curious, then, that the celebratory scholarship on African civil society has virtually ignored the role of the news media (with few exceptions: Monga 1995, 1996; Agbaje 1993). The reasons for this egregious oversight would seem to be rooted in the liberal assumptions of the scholarship as a whole. As a means of discourse, newspapers might seem to be merely superficial discursive representations of preexisting social facts and perspectives, adjunct to politics but not constitutive. For political scientists working on the state and civil society, scholars with a heavy methodological reliance on newspapers as raw data, the news media ideally ought to reflect political reality according to their proper function in the liberal imaginary, informing citizens of current political and economic affairs so that all might ostensibly participate in the public sphere. In this view, newspapers can be assessed according to the transparency of reflection and neutrality of useful information. So riven with political passions and vivid personalist narratives, African newspapers would not seem to measure up to liberal standards of "objectivity" and transparency. Failing to perform their proper liberal function, African newspapers might seem to be irrelevant to the processes of democratization (and maybe even regressive) and thus tend to drop out of the celebratory discourse on the emergence of civil society in Africa.

Yet another curious silence in the scholarship on African political renaissance is the lack of critical attention to new forms of power and privilege operating within the emergent institutions of the public sphere. It is indeed surprising that a scholarship so centered around the Gramscian notion of civil society virtually ignores the role of civil institutions in the accomplishment and maintenance of hegemony (Gramsci 1971). Just as the institutions of civil society, liberated from authoritarian control, allow for the free expression of political opinions and agendas, they also provide the means for the strategic organization of public consensus and the consolidation of power in the new democratic dispensation (Mbembe 2001; Comaroff and Comaroff 1999, 2001; Apter 1999; Ferme 1999; Mamdani 1995). For the discourse of news media not only reflects an already existing social reality, this discourse strategically imagines a total social order in the interests of a certain class, excluding or subordinating the voices of marginalized groups (as irrelevant, outdated, or simply unrecognizable). And beyond merely informing the citizenry, news media actually constitute the very political subjects they purport to serve, interpolating those subjects into the social reality they redundantly invent.

This is nothing new, of course. Since the mid-nineteenth century, locally produced news media have formed politicized spheres of public discourse in Africa, constructing strategic versions of reality and inculcating specific forms of political subjectivity. While the recent triumph of democracy over authoritarianism in so many parts of Africa is an accomplishment to be celebrated by citizens and scholars alike, a rather longer historical gaze at the discursive content and maneuverings of power in the realm of news media dramatically illustrates an enduring dynamic of repressive domination and expressive resistance in the civil institutions of the public sphere. While the liberal scholarship on African political renaissance celebrates the globalizing resistance to local forms of tyranny and kleptocracy, news media in Africa emerged as expressive local forces of indigenous resistance against the globalizing forces of colonial repression and exploitation. Subsequently appropriated in processes of "nation building," news media as expressive tools of resistance were quickly transformed into the means of discursive domination and control by postcolonial elites. While celebrating the new freedoms of democratization and civil society, historical context suggests the importance of critically examining the operations of power in the revived institutions of civil society, discerning the lineaments of new forms of consensus, consolidation, marginalization, and exclusion. Moreover, history overturns the contemporary equation of empowerment and globalization, calling into question the essentially liberating nature of global political and economic forces against African political cultures so often essentialized as pathologically repressive and backward.

National Narratives: Discourse and Practice

The first newspapers in West Africa were published by colonial authorities in Sierra Leone (1801) and the Gold Coast (1822), representing an official voice of colonial policy while circulating commercial and regional news (Jones-Quartey 1975). By the middle of the century groups of mission-educated African elites in Ghana, Sierra Leone, and Nigeria began publishing their own newspapers, aimed at an educated African readership. Early African journalists recognized in this imported form of mass-circulated discourse a means of circumventing traditional political authority, crafting a new social identity as African elites, and striking up a gentlemanly conversation with colonial officials over local government affairs. If the early West African press constituted a public sphere in the liberal sense, this discursive space was certainly dominated by the voices of a privileged few Anglophiles discursively positioning themselves to inherit the authority of the British.

By the early twentieth century African elites had become frustrated with the lack of opportunity for participation in government and civil service; therefore their criticism of colonial administration became much harsher, losing its mannered gentility in populist vents of anticolonial outrage. West African newspapers thus became the crucible of African nationalism and anticolonialism (Asante 1996). Benedict Anderson (1983) argues for the crucial role of "print capitalism" in the sociocultural transformation from vertical and diffuse forms of affiliation (the feudal dynastic realm) to horizontal and territorially bounded identities (the modern world order of nation-states). Similarly the politically motivated project of Gold Coast newspapers to galvanize popular support for independence through the liberation of a colonially defined territory provided for the spread of a fundamentally national postcolonial imaginary.

Then leader of the oppositional Conventional People's Party, Kwame Nkrumah was a newspaperman himself, using his *Accra Evening News* as a blatant propaganda tool in the popular struggle for independence in Ghana. Shortly after independence Prime Minister Nkrumah nationalized the media, redefining its role from anticolonial opposition to national integration and development. Nkrumah was critical of the liberal function of the media as a marketplace of ideas, asserting that a liberal media could easily be hijacked by divisive, factional interests, particularly the regressive "tribalistic" interests of the elites who opposed him. Over time, he harassed and outlawed the private press out of existence (with one exception) as he consolidated his authority in a one-party state. Thus, just as they were liberated and empowered by the retreat of colonial forces, news media were immediately co-opted into the service of the state, reflecting not so much the domination of an economic class of bourgeois elites but instead the domination of a political class in the form of the state. Thus news media did not become a marketplace of ideas representing the semblance of ideological struggle but instead became an institution of propaganda representing the semblance of national unity and cooperation in the pursuit of a common destiny.

If print capitalism is key to the founding of the national imaginary, then newspapers take part in a national "system of signification" (Bhabha 1990) that brings into being a "hegemonic topography" (Malkki 1995), an ambivalent, contested order of social categories situated in time and space. This categorical order is set in motion through a range of national narratives—situating the nation locally, nationally, and globally (Anagnost 1997, 1993). Thus the national imaginary of print capitalism not only constructs an ontology of political reality but also a narrative that positions a hypothetical set of actors in relation to one another (be they classes, ethnic groups, regions, or personalities) and organizes the historical logic of their engagement and ongoing interaction. In her work on television serials Mankekar (1999) discusses the challenges facing the newly independent state in India and the deployment of the state television station, Doordarshan, by Nehru in the pursuit of national unity, modernity, and development. Thus media work at establishing the primacy of the national as political while subsuming all other social categories and modes of affiliation (i.e., Hindu, Muslim, regional identities) in the common pursuit of a secular, material, and social agenda. As Mankekar's analysis reveals, claims of national representation obscure a prevalent northern Hindu bias at the heart of Indian nationalism, indicating that Doordarshan functions as a "hegemonic state apparatus" through the national narratives of development and modernity (see also Eickelman and Anderson 1999; Rofel 1994; Abu-Lughod 1993).

Anderson's discussion of print capitalism illustrates how news media provide a means of imagining the community of the postcolonial nation (1983). Largely left out of his analysis is an examination of the actual practices through which the national imaginary is achieved and maintained by the state. News media not only produce a set of strategic texts for imagining the nation but also structure a set of strategic everyday practices that organize relationships among state officials, journalists, and the diverse groups that make up the audiences of news. These practices orchestrate the production, circulation, reading, and recirculation of information.

The newly independent state of Ghana relied heavily on the nationalized "state media" to integrate a diversity of ethnic and regional identities, political factions, and economic interests through a superordinating narrative of national integration and development. In the state press the modern project of development is primarily portrayed as material progress, a continual process of socioeconomic cultivation, accumulation, and distribution under the "benevolent" leadership of the state. The form of journalism that evolved to articulate the national narrative every day in the newspapers (as well as radio and television) came to be called "development journalism" (Fair 1989; Boafo 1985; Domatob and Hall 1983; Rogers 1976) and entailed the routinization of a set of practices of discursive production unique to its cultural and historical context.

While journalists with the state press profess a strong commitment to the national interests of unity and development reminiscent of the political project of the state in the 1960s and 1970s, the neoliberal rhetoric of democracy and human rights embraced by private journalists represents a more recent, competing version of postcolonial nationalism, less invested in state patronage and more oriented toward global articulation and market competition. Positioning themselves against the state media, private journalists rely on a global rhetoric of liberal vocation, identifying themselves as watchdogs in the public interest, free from state control and ideological manipulation. This self-portrait is reflected and reinforced by scholarship on the African press that emphasizes the expressive, democratic functions of independent media in contrast to repressive, ideological domination in the state media (Geekie 1994; Ogbondah 1994; Asare-Addy 1992; Ekpu 1992; Mbachu 1992). This narrative of struggle against the state is rehearsed again and again in so many journals (the *Index on Censorship,* the *IPI Report,* the *Africa Report*) and in scholarly analyses of African news media (Lardner 1993; Faringer 1991). However, the private press is just as deeply implicated in ideological processes as the state media. As Arjun Appadurai has recently observed, "There is some reason to worry about whether the current framework of human rights is serving mainly as the legal and normative conscience—or legal-bureaucratic lubricant—of a neoliberal, marketized political order" (2001, 25). With celebrations of charismatic oppositional politicians and entrepreneurs, coupled with the push for an inviolate sphere of private accumulation free from state control, the private press contains the seeds of liberal domination with a global rhetoric of human rights, individualism, and free speech supporting the interests of a local rising elite.[1] While private journalists may claim to be the objective watchdogs of liberal discourse, in their everyday practices they are necessarily and routinely implicated in a political culture of power and privilege that straddles both public and private spheres. This "reciprocal assimilation of elites" (Bayart 1993) emerges in the journalistic practices of the private press.

Despite their rhetorical commitments to competing versions of the national imaginary, both state and private journalists participate in a common political logic grounded in African notions of authority, political legitimacy, sociality, and discursive propriety. While transnational discourses shape the professional rhetoric of journalism, this local logic shapes the texts, practices, and institutions of news media in Ghana. According to this logic, political legitimacy is defined in the ability of a strong and statesmanly leader to organize the project of material accumulation and benevolent distribution while avoiding the temptations of corruption and self-interested abuse of power (Schatzberg 2001; Durham 1999). Informed by the ideology of chieftaincy, these local notions are carried into the state press as depictions of the president as a legitimate accumulator with global ties to foreign capital, and also the moral and benevolent director of state distribution to his loyal and grateful subjects throughout the regions. The private press does not criticize this rhetoric as parochial or patrimonial per se; rather, it frequently uses the very same cultural logic to deconstruct these heroic portrayals of the president, depicting him as an ineffective manager whose policies have resulted in economic hardship rather than accumulation, a weak leader whose political machine has become thoroughly corrupt, and a haphazard executive whose ability to distribute state wealth has been compromised by this corruption as well as by ethnic bias and personal favoritism. The agonistic and frequently militaristic style of this critique closely resembles the oppositional rhetoric of young men against southern chiefs whose contamination by colonial cooperation and exploitation inspired popular efforts to depose them in the early twentieth century. This local logic of power, embracing both authority and resistance, goes beyond the discursive into the realm of everyday practice. Both state and opposition parties, as well the state and private press, are problematically involved in the social practices associated with this logic of power (political oratory, professional mediators, prestation, a divide between official and unofficial forms of discourse). The examination of the relations between journalistic rhetoric and practice in this book demonstrates the disjoint between global and local that results from the juxtaposition of the discourses of global liberalism with local practices grounded in this local political logic. Participating in global associations and travel for conferences and programs abroad, both state and private journalists in Ghana are becoming increasingly cosmopolitan, confronted more and more frequently with the contradictions between the commonsense logic of power at home and the professional discourse and practices of political liberalism elsewhere.

Universalism, Localism, and the Ambiguities of Opposition

Contradictions between the globalizing rhetoric of liberal democracy and the historically situated dynamics of local political culture were dramatically played out in the campaign season of 1996. As elections neared in late November I was working for the private newspaper the *Independent*. For months I had been going out on assignment, writing stories, chatting with other journalists, and reading the newspapers every day—and still I wasn't sure exactly what I was supposed to be doing as a journalist for the private press. Against the pro-Rawlings bias of the state media, the private press seemed blatantly oppositional, bent on exposing government corruption and portraying the president as a violent, tyrannical "smallboy," lacking the wisdom and good judgment of a legitimate leader. In contrast, the managing editor of the *Independent* consistently wrote admiring accounts of the opposition presidential candidate in his weekly political column, reporting massive enthusiastic support for the opposition coalition throughout the country. Everyone in the office of the *Independent* vocally and continuously demonstrated their allegiance to the opposition in their everyday conversation. The stories I wrote in solidarity with the opposition were generally well received by the managing editor (and published), while the more neutral or ambivalent stories I wrote were ignored or rejected. I was tempted to conclude that our private newspaper was primarily a mouthpiece of the opposition, just as many claimed that the state media was a mouthpiece of the government.

Absolutely not so, according to my boss, the editor in chief. Whether working for the state or private press, all journalists should be objective and free from partisan bias, he maintained. I took his opinion very seriously, as he was not only my boss but had also become a good friend of mine. At press events and social occasions, or just running errands around town, we talked at length about local politics and the role of journalism in Ghana's emergent democracy. With his cosmopolitan commitment to free speech and human rights, he believed that journalists should inform and educate the public on important issues of the day, acting as independent "watchdogs" in the public interest. He criticized other newspapers for their blatantly partisan editorial policies: the widespread use of flashy and misleading headlines, unbalanced coverage of political parties, and editorializing on the front page.

One month before the elections both the editor in chief and the managing editor serendipitously left the country for professional programs abroad. Before leaving, the editor in chief showed me an article from *Time* magazine comparing the political agendas of candidates Clinton and Dole in the ongoing presidential campaign in the United States. Issues were listed and the candidates' positions compared in two parallel columns. "This is what we should be doing," the editor told me, "not just partisan reporting." In his absence he instructed the *Independent* staff to take such a comparative approach throughout the newspaper, in the various sections on politics, business, and the environment.

In order to compare and contrast political platforms we would need to collect the printed "manifestos" of the main political parties. As I began my work with another journalist on this assignment, naively I assumed that our allies in the opposition would respond promptly to our request while the ruling party would surely balk and frustrate us. However, at the headquarters of the most popular opposition party, an official barely paused between bites of fried yam to coldly inform us that the manifesto would be out next week. If we needed more immediate information, we would just have to purchase the party newsletter for 400 cedis (at that time, 2,000 cedis = $1.00). My partner insisted that as journalists (and comrades, I would have added), we should get one for free. No luck with this argument—I had to buy the newsletter for us.

To further defy my expectations, at ruling party headquarters we were very warmly received. We asked for their manifesto and the public relations officer promptly handed it over, jibing us with a devious grin, "What do you want it for, to twist it around and distort it?" Returning this jovial banter, my partner smugly protested that our newspaper was the most objective in Ghana, criticizing both sides equally (I could not corroborate). He continued: The *Independent* criticized the opposition to such an extent that some people actually accused us of taking money from the ruling party. Suddenly, in the confused moment that money was mentioned, the ruling party official quickly opened a drawer at his desk and produced an envelope, handing it over to my partner who swiftly tucked it away in a bag. "For your travel expenses," the official said mischievously. When we got back to the car, my partner opened the envelope to discover 12,000 cedis, easily six times the taxi fare back to the office (we had our own car that day anyway). Jubilant at our windfall, my partner split the money three ways between himself, me, and our driver. Laughing, he explained to me that such a gift, called "soli," is no sin but we shouldn't mention it to our editor. If the editor found out, he would only tease us.

Well, I certainly didn't tell him but I was impressed by the complexity of the whole episode. While professing the contemporary rhetoric of independent watchdogs, private journalists are historically positioned against the state and therefore animated by discursive enthusiasm for the politics of opposition. However instrumental to the cause, we were nonetheless belittled and dismissed as insignificant smallboys by elite officials of the opposition party. In contrast, we were warmly welcomed into the personalized sociality of the ruling party by the public relations officer who clearly recognized our inferior status as a strategic opportunity. The gifts of cash and party ideology represented an attempt to suspend our historical oppositionality by culturally repositioning us in hierarchical relations of reciprocal obligation. In the short run at least, the attempt was unsuccessful: the special "comparative" edition of the paper still favored the opposition. In the long run, however, both the cold reception of the opposition and the charismatic hospitality of the ruling party reinforced the practical priority of circumstances understood to be distinctively "local," over and against global abstractions. As global liberalism is replicated and universalized in a constellation of institutions devoted to democracy and human rights, the global logic of those very institutions simultaneously motivates the production of alternative forms of identity, sociality, and cultural locality against the universal dominant. Neither global ideals nor local determinations can be taken for granted in this context; both are now products of ambivalent engagement, negotiation, and struggle (Appiah 1992).

Modernity, Alternative Modernity, Subaltern Globalism

The newspaper, like the novel (Lukacs 1971 [1916]), originally emerged in Western Europe as a literary genre establishing and reinforcing the phenomenological parameters of modern reality. Elaborating on the role of newspapers in the imagination of spatially "disembedded" national communities, Anderson describes how newspapers juxtapose a daily array of global events on the front page, uniting spatially disparate experiences in the "calendrical coincidence" of homogenous empty time (1983, 33). Depicted on the front page, the disembedded and calendrically synchronized world order ritually envisioned in the newspaper is a geopolitical reality divided into distinct nation-states whose relations are fundamentally organized according to the logic of liberalism (Giddens 1990). The more national a newspaper becomes, the more its content comes to embody this liberal logic.

Exemplified in such American one-day best-sellers as the *New York Times* and the *Washington Post,* news discourse divides its daily dose of information into a hierarchy of knowledges. While the liberal imaginary privileges the causal primacy of political and economic fields, the news media privileges objective "hard news" concerning the state and the market in its depiction of world and national events on the front page and throughout the leading section of the newspaper. Front-page stories narrate how national entities articulate in global networks of cooperation, competition, opposition, and conflict. In the modern political paradigm of news, generally speaking, world news is relevant insofar as it takes place between, among, or against nation-states, or potential nation-states (i.e., Palestine). Among nation-states, political events are recognizable and meaningful in the activities of state representatives who are made to express and pursue the situated (rational, individualized) "national interests" of states and constituent populations, either well or badly (i.e., Saddam Hussein, Robert Mugabe, etc.). Even transnational figures like Osama bin Ladin and the rhizomatic networks of global terror are largely interpreted within the context of this national order—response to 9-11 became a war against Afghanistan, and Bush's "axis of evil" came to identify a list of enemy nation-states.

Economically speaking, world news is meaningful and relevant insofar as it participates in the global market and makes sense within the naturalized laws of competition, profit, and growth. The activities of transnational or infranational citizens' groups are recognizable only in relation to recognized nation-states or the global market—that is, they become newsworthy only when they enter into the national arena (politically) or the transnational arena (economically). The contracts and treaties of national governments, the proclamations of international organizations, the intrigues of divestiture and hostile takeover among transnational capitalists, all are deemed worthy of our attention not only because they potentially impact our own lived reality (mostly they don't) but, more importantly, because they are made to seem as if they participate in a globalized logic of liberalism, whether by achievement or failure. Similarly the social totality of national news is imagined as an array of self-interested and competitive organizations, primarily political parties, voluntary citizens' groups, and capitalist institutions of civil society. Thus, both in world news and national news, the logic of institutional relationships reflects an undergirding liberal framework based on notions of representation, interest, and rationality.[2]

In the postcolonial context, the institutions of media not only are national in the historic and political sense described in the previous section but also are profoundly modern in this epistemic and ontological sense. The political newspapers produced in Accra assume the political ontology of the nation-state, participating in the very constitution of the disembedded, imagined space of the national community of citizens. As representatives of the state, the daily state newspapers ritually conjure the homogenous empty time of this national community, in contrast to the weekly interval of opposition newspapers. However, the logic of political representation and self-interested social relations reflected in Western news is confuted by the themes, linguistic styles, and interdiscursive qualities of Ghanaian news discourse.

At the level of practice, the form of political modernity embodied in Ghanaian journalism is shaped by particularly local historical processes and contemporary circumstances. Historically, local journalistic practice is shaped by the discursive methods of mediation and representation in Akan politics as well as the oppositional struggles of anticolonial nationalism in the first half of the twentieth century and the integrative ideological program of postcolonial state-building in the second half. Moreover, the modernity of Ghanaian news media is fundamentally shaped by the subjectivities and positionalities of those who practice it—the class status, regional origins, gender identities, and typical age of those attracted to the field of journalism, as well local forms of recruitment and training that make those novices into Ghanaian journalists and the common career paths they pursue.

Contemporary Ghanaian journalism is largely a "second choice" vocation of local young men (and increasingly women) from the regional secondary schools of southern Ghana, those denied admission to the university. Their original aspirations set aside, students with an aptitude for English and an interest in politics may apply instead to the Ghana Institute of Journalism (GIJ) in Accra, established and funded by the government. Nearly all practicing journalists in Ghana are graduates of GIJ, holding a two-year vocational degree. Upon graduation, GIJ graduates are hired by local state or private media organizations, mainly in Accra. While state journalists are somewhat better off than their colleagues in the private press, the typical salary of a journalist on staff (as opposed to "stringers" who are paid by the story) is so meager that most continue to live with extended family, deferring plans for marriage and independence until their financial situation improves. As junior journalists sent out on business and political assignments, they come into daily contact with a broader Ghanaian public sphere dominated by elite professionals with advanced degrees from prestigious universities in Ghana and abroad. Because class status in this postcolonial context depends heavily on educational credentials (as well as on the conspicuous consumption made possible by discretionary income), the status differential among journalists and their sources carries important consequences for their professional reputations, relationships, and practices. A journalist requesting assistance from an official source is nearly always encountering a person of superior status, a situation that summons common notions of patronage, manifest in a set of deferred and highly euphemized exchanges of benevolent largesse and loyal diligence. Many journalists, considering the subordinated status, low pay, and limited opportunities for advancement in the profession, consider journalism to be only a short-term profession while in their twenties and early thirties, just until they can position themselves for better employment in public relations, government, or a nongovernmental organization (NGO). While relying on well-placed politicians and businesspeople as regular sources of news, they may also consider the value of those connections for future career possibilities. Thus journalists are stigmatized by a common assumption that their work is not a "serious" profession but rather a kind of parasitic scheme practiced by conniving, obsequious "smallboys." Front-page representations of patronage (or its scandalous abrogation) reflect the interpolation of journalists themselves in relations of appeal, prestation, and obligation with their own sources, frequently the "bigmen" of the Ghanaian public sphere.

At the discursive level, the localized form of political modernity expressed in Ghanaian newspapers is evident in quite particular understandings of newsworthiness and narrative content. Considered fairly irrelevant in the Western paradigm of news, stories based on donations of money and material goods among various local and foreign groups are prevalent in the pages of the state newspaper, the *Daily Graphic*. Often the economic impact of these gifts is fairly small (a few cartons of minerals, a few boxes of biscuits), so the newsworthiness of such prestations must derive from the logic of social relations represented in such stories. In contrast to themes of development and prestation in the state media, the private press is fixated on the pronouncements and activities, both beneficent and nefarious, of prominent local figures, the "bigmen" of Accra society. Frequently front-page stories in the private press depict the "shocking" behavior of political officials, how a politician slipped and fell in public or failed to pay the school fees of his illegitimate child, reflecting alternative notions of political representation. Ignoring the self-abnegating pretense of journalistic objectivity, these sensational exposés on the outrageous behavior of Ghanaian bigmen frequently mix "fact" with emotionally charged personal opinion, speculation, and editorial positioning.

Anthropologists have used the term "alternative modernity" to describe the cultural mutations of modernity as a universalizing form (Schein 1999;

Nonini and Ong 1997; Appadurai 1996; Ivy 1995; Gilroy 1993). In her ethnography of Japanese hostess clubs, Anne Allison (1994) describes how the institutions of monopoly capitalism are mediated by institutions of "conviviality" and deferred sexuality, identified by patrons and hostesses as distinctly Japanese. Mayfair Mei-hui Yang (1994) describes how the modern bureaucracy of the Chinese state is mediated by a complex gift economy, *guanxixue,* similarly embraced as culturally distinct. Both examples illustrate how modernity is conceived as purely instrumental and culturally empty, motivating a set of humanizing and localizing practices to make it worth living. While in the West, the "existential experience of alienation and despair associated with living in a disenchanted world" motivated a "cultural modernity" centered on humanistic liberation of the self (Goankar 1999), the cultural response to the sinister side of modernity outside the West has often involved repudiation of the isolation of modern subjectivity in favor of more relational identities and modes of resistance. Against the universal pretensions of modernity, a resistant antimodernity is configured as a local response, summoning notions of common history and cultural intimacy. Both Allison and Yang recognize, however, that these cultural practices, while frequently essentialized by their practitioners, are not somehow previous to or outside modernity but rather are adjunct to it. Hostess clubs and gift networks might challenge the cold rationalism of modern institutions, but these local practices also fortify the modern state and corporate institutions by fulfilling modernity's lack, reproducing the workforce and greasing the gears of exchange. Moreover, the material and psychological components of these "alternative" practices are actually derived from the institutions of modernity, creating a kind of ambivalent symbiosis.

While news media constitute a modern epistemic regime deriving from Western Europe, both the practices of Ghanaian journalism and the strategies of representation in Ghanaian news media are shot through with local influences, recognizable to anthropologists and Ghanaians alike as culturally distinct though certainly a complex product of cosmopolitan engagement. Since news media both reflect and manifest the dominant social relations of political and economic realms, the predominance of themes of prestation (in the form of donorship) and material distribution (in the form of development) in the news stories of the state press not only point to the subordinated status of journalists, but also reflect the larger cultural context of a primarily agrarian though thoroughly modern postcolonial society. At the discursive level, historical dynamics of dependency and extraversion (Bayart 1993) that structure relations between Africa and the West are narrated in an idiom of magnanimous gift giving and loyal gratitude, a portrayal that idealizes and legitimizes the roles of both. Moreover, the relational identities frequently associated with segmentary societies and the personalism and patronage associated with chieftaincy shape the compositional styles of news text as well as the journalistic routines of informational and material exchange.

These features seem to define a culturally distinct alternative modernity of Ghanaian news media, a localized form of political modernity blending African and Western forms. There is a danger to this approach, however. As Ghana has become identified as a promising context for the consolidation of democracy on the African continent, Ghanaian journalists have become a target for a profusion of programs, seminars, and workshops organized by foreign governments and transnational NGOs specializing in human rights and democracy. All too often the message at such events is that Africans in general, and Ghanaian journalists in particular, fall short of their idealized role in processes of democratization and development largely because they are too mired in regressive and unenlightened practices of local culture, such as "solidarity" and patronage, even as such practices are recognized as local efforts of accommodation with the forces and institutions of modernization. Once chastened for a lack of modernity, it seems that Africans will now be hassled for culturally overcompensating. Similarly, in media studies, the prevailing normative approach is aimed at overcoming the local cultural contaminants of journalism so that the public sphere of news media might function as it was institutionally intended, according to the liberal model. For instance, Louise Bourgault (1995) describes the discursive features that distinguish Nigerian journalism from its Western prototype, narrative styles mired in empathy, participation, agonistic tone, traditionalism, and redundancy. She then concludes with a set of recommendations for African journalism training aimed at overcoming these distinctive features. Similarly appropriating anthropological accounts into policy analysis, liberal policy makers might view the ritual and magical features of politics in Nigeria (Bastian 1993; Apter 1992), Togo (Piot 1999), Cameroon (Geschiere 1997), Liberia (Ellis 1999), and Sierra Leone (Ferme 1999) as local stumbling blocks to the achievement of a fully modern form of liberal democracy—even if those cultural features are understood as historical and cosmopolitan.

But what if there is no "real" or "essential" local culture to blame for the pathologies of postcolonial authoritarianism, political instability, and other forms of postcolonial difference? What the normative appropriation of alternative modernity misses is the very constructed nature of both terms in the operative binaries: local and global, indigenous and foreign, tradition and modernity. Much policy-oriented analysis of the institutions of democracy and civil society in Africa tends to assume the preexistence of a consensual, shared, and relatively bounded local African culture, conceptually and experientially delineated from the variable, contested, dynamic, and historically mobile forces of Western modernity. But if this delineation was strategically forged in the colonial encounter, then all the binaries are themselves a product of translocality and the normative equation has it all backward. To the point: it is misleading to assume that local culture and imported institutions syncretize in the production of alternative modernity in the postcolonial context. Alternative modernity is not a product of syncretism of these opposed forces; rather, both local culture and modernity are themselves products of the syncretic processes of translocality, colonial and postcolonial (Piot 1999). Just as Gold Coast intellectuals strategically invented a rarified model of traditional political leadership in early genres of "native" ethnography, contemporary Ghanaians (and Nigerians) creatively construct notions of local African culture through the discourses and practices of news media. These notions of culture and locality are not singular, static, and subconsciously shared, but rather are self-consciously crafted, multiple, and highly contested in the public realm.

This points to the potential weakness of the notion of alternative modernity—the cultural essentialism (i.e., of "African culture") transcended by the syncretic and cosmopolitan connotations of this concept is too easily recouped into a naturalized essentialism of locality—so that we might identify an African, Indian, Chinese, or Japanese "version" of modernity, whether in the sympathetic depictions of anthropologists or the critical evaluations of policy makers. Universalizing in "democratization," "good governance," "development," or "economic growth," the meaning of modernity itself would seem to be held constant while culture, the "alternative," becomes a localized adaptation, a way of dealing with local consequences. Intending to replace the modernist narratives of backwardness and lack, the concept of alternative modernity leaves open the possibility of reinscribing a pathology of difference as local cultural determinism. This way of thinking parallels the portrayal of liberalism as a universal struggle for freedom and human rights, threatened by the regressive ideological domination of local (or national) culture.

Such is the logic of Empire. Michael Hardt and Antonio Negri (2000) describe the emergent world order of globalized liberalism as the organization of a decentered and deterritorialized Empire, eroding national boundaries and ideologies, naturalizing and eternalizing the conditions of liberal domination by declaring "a perpetual and universal peace outside of history" (xv). Earlier theories of postmodernity tended to suggest (at least diagrammatically) that the conditions of late capitalism were transforming the cultural logic of postindustrial societies at the same time that institutions of modernity took root in the Third World in the form of sweat shops, commoditization, coercive national institutions, and the development of mass media (Jameson 1991; Harvey 1989). Negri and Hardt demonstrate, however, how the regime of modernity itself has been transformed into a rhizomorphic and hybridizing transnational force—everywhere at once. Drawing on Deleuze and Guattari (1987, 1977) and the later Foucault, they argue that the cultural logic of Empire appears in a constellation of transitions from the repressive institutions of discipline to the productive institutions of control. While the disciplinary apparatuses of schools, prisons, factories, asylums, and (one might add) national news media command the vertical imposition of a regime of rules that habitually constrain and ideologically normalize (bodies, minds, discourses, etc.), the institutions of control such as transnational corporations and global media operate horizontally and "democratically," directing flows of capital, information, identity and affect through bodies and across boundaries. These flows not only normalize and homogenize (in fact, they do not do this at all), they rather continually produce the very differences that compel and organize flow—material and structural differences (differentials in wealth) as well as differences in culture, ethnicity, religion, locality, and other forms of identity.

> What needs to be addressed ... is precisely the *production of locality,* that is, the social machines that create and recreate the identities and differences that are understood as the local. The differences of locality are neither preexisting nor natural but rather effects of a regime of production. Globality similarly should not be understood in terms of cultural, political, or economic *homogenization.* Globalization, like localization, should be understood instead as a *regime* of the production of identity and difference, or really of homogenization and heterogenization. (Hardt and Negri 2000, 45)

While disciplinary apparatuses operate primarily through localized and nationalized forms of ideological domination (an Althusserian view of homogenizing domination that suggests a sort of localized cultural determinism), the global institutions of control continually produce the transnationally contested terms of liberal hegemony (a more Gramscian view that suggests the argumentative and heterogenizing production of culture and locality).

In line with this insight, theorists of globalization have insisted that cultural configurations everywhere are now less locally defined and disciplined within cultural and national boundaries and instead are more structured by the control of global flows of trade, aid, people, ideas, and technologies. Like their Gold Coast predecessors, Ghanaian journalists strategically craft notions of indigeneity and locality through their professional training and practices at home and their increasing access to cosmopolitan associations and experiences abroad. As they carry distinctively "local" discursive forms and practices into the field of Ghanaian news media, they simultaneously carry distinctively "global" discursive forms and practices (from professional organizations and human rights groups) into that very same realm. Instead of alternative modernity, we might speak of alternative postmodernity or pretermodernity or, perhaps, subaltern globalism. Rather than creating an essentially Ghanaian *version* of a universal institution, the contradictions of the discursive and practical juxtaposition of local and global elements constitute instead an intense ongoing *argument* over the sort of political locality that is being produced through these discursive practices. Journalists are not immersed unawares in local culture, modern or traditional, but rather, as cosmopolitans, position themselves ambivalently and strategically at the nexus of so many local, national, and global flows. It is through these flows that they continually produce contradictory and adversarial notions of African culture, African politics, and African journalism—notions fashioned in an ongoing struggle (Roseberry 1996) over the hegemonic terms of commonsense reality, national identity, and political legitimacy.

Immersed in the Inky Fraternity

African news media is both a producer and product of these pretermodern struggles, continually appropriating and churning out a constellation of global, national, and local discourses while embodying the contradictions of culture and history in localized, everyday practice. While political scientists, media scholars, journalists, NGOs, and diplomats all herald the forces of political renaissance in contemporary Africa, most are methodologically constrained by a normative focus that tends to assume the self-evident transcendence and universality of notions of democracy, human rights, free speech, representation, and the public sphere—held against the regressive local and cultural forces of authoritarianism, secrecy, oppression, political instability, and corruption. While describing the local "difference" of Ghanaian journalism, my objective in this book is to move beyond the *pacifist* depiction of "alternative modernity" to demonstrate how journalists for both the state and private press in Ghana actively and strategically produce *argumentative* distinctions between universal ideals and local realities, charting how those distinctions continually emerge in a contradictory interplay of discourse and practice. As with democracy, civil society, environmentalism, feminism, or any other universalist discourse, the "difference" of Ghanaian journalism does not signify local lack or failure to achieve global ideals but rather a resistant and self-defining engagement of the local against the global, a process that continually reconstructs both terms.

Necessary to understanding this pretermodern experience in the field of African journalism is a method that not only charts the cultural and historical particularity of local practices, but also engages with articulated controversies over the very meanings of global and local while tracing the productivity of those contradictions among discourse and practice. Participant-observation as a working journalist for both state-owned and private newspapers gave me experience in the everyday practices of news media, while interviews with journalists and close readings of the texts that they routinely produce provided two angles of entry into the articulated discourses surrounding, reflecting, and contradicting those practices.

In fifteen months of fieldwork between 1995 and 2002 I worked as a junior reporter for various news organizations in Accra, conducted interviews and archival research, participated in the conferences and programs of the Ghana Journalists Association, and attended classes at the Ghana Institute of Journalism. My rationale for working as a journalist was not only that I wanted to observe Ghanaian journalists at work; I also hoped to place myself in a position to learn something of what they know about news production and how that knowledge is embodied in practice. In addition, I found myself subject to the political, social, and cultural forces that constitute the contradictory positionality of African journalists, experiencing the pressures and possibilities they face everyday. As a white foreigner, I also observed how and why everyday routines could be suspended to accommodate or capitalize on my alternative identities.

In total, I worked for five news organizations in Ghana. In my year of fieldwork I worked first for a privately owned paper, the *Independent;* then the premiere state-owned paper, the *Daily Graphic;* and next the privately owned investigative paper, the *Ghanaian Chronicle.* Returning the following summer, I worked for the state-owned news agency (GNA). Finally, in the summer of 2002, I worked for the private, NGO-funded *Public Agenda.* Following this serendipitous itinerary, I traversed the fault lines of Ghanaian political culture time and time again, variously interpolated as discursive agent for the state and the opposition, writing published stories that supported either conservative or antagonistic political agendas. For instance, just three months into my fieldwork, the editor of the oppositional *Independent* appointed me as a guest columnist for his own political column while he was traveling during the campaign season. As a political news writer, I was also assigned to cover the movements of the opposition candidate, John Agyekum Kufour, as he campaigned throughout the country. Taking up such a partisan role at such a crucial moment in Ghanaian politics, I became publicly and professionally associated with the political agenda of the opposition. However, just a little over a month later, I found myself a conciliatory guest at state ceremonies every day, reproducing the rhetoric of government officials as a journalist for the state paper, the *Daily Graphic*. My editor at *Graphic* seemed to assume that I had merely been duped and exploited by the private press, and he generously paved the way for my rehabilitation at his own paper.

It is rare for any local journalist to work for both state and private news organizations under the same government, although some private journalists shift across the great divide to work for the state when a sympathetic political party comes into power, and all too often state journalists for one regime are made redundant under the next, forced to change vocation or seek employment with the private press. Although it is more likely that GIJ students alternate between the state and private media in their period of practical attachments to local media organizations, most tend to focus their aspirations on either one, positioning themselves for future employment by arranging all their practical attachments at either state organizations or private ones. As a foreigner writing a book on Ghanaian journalism, I seemed largely exempt from the pressure to establish such a coherent political and professional identity. Indeed, arriving at any new attachment, new colleagues always welcomed me into the fold, eager to diversify and complicate my experience of Ghanaian news media. While Ghanaians so graciously accommodated my unusual trajectory, I myself experienced a troubling sense of professional, political, and personal dissonance as I skipped from paper to paper. Working together under difficult conditions, writing in support of a common project, colleagues at each news organization develop a unique perspective on the political field and a distinctive sense of solidarity and intimacy. As an anthropological "witness" to the lifeworld of Ghanaian journalism, I was drawn into the positionality of journalists at each news organization, experiencing the centrifugal and centripetal forces that similarly shape the subjectivities of colleagues and form a common habitus for the practice of journalism at any particular paper. Though I know as a foreigner that my experiences in Ghanaian journalism were often exceptional, participating with Ghanaians closely and daily in the generation of news at each paper gave me the opportunity not only to observe, but to feel some sense of the political passions that animate each news organizations, the popular memories and historical narratives that summon and reinforce their identities, the everyday experiences of inclusion and exclusion in their interactions with politicians, the state, and the public.

Both Liisa Malkki (1997) and Frank Pieke (1995) refer to fieldwork as a form of anthropological "witnessing," a process of immersion in alternative positionalities that carries an ethnographic responsibility to faithfully and carefully document the experience. Motivated more by empathetic engagement than scientific objectivity, the anthropological witness is far more concerned to form a deep and complex connection with the people in the field —not as sources of "data" but as fellow human beings in unique and frequently precarious circumstances. Since I am not a Ghanaian journalist, I can only claim partial understanding of the lifeworld of journalism at any Ghanaian news organization—surely there is much more to tell, and I hope to encourage further study in this rich and little examined field. The goal of ethnography, then, is not to give an exhaustive report or even to meticulously describe what happened in the field but rather to "affirm one's own connection to the ideas, processes, and people one is studying (Malkki 1997, 96). Further, ethnographic witnessing means relaying that connection to colleagues and students at home, wherever that might be for the anthropologist, recognizing the larger forms of meaning and mutuality made possible by fieldwork and acting as a conduit for ongoing social and political articulations.

One could argue, however, that the intensity and partiality of witnessing may lead to one-sided accounts of complex events, processes, and structures. Drawing from his fieldwork on Argentina's "dirty war," Antonius Robben (1995) describes how both victims and perpetrators of violence attempted to "seduce" him into ethnographic complicity by summoning common social and moral commitments, drawing him into the truth claims and sociality of their own lifeworlds. His conscience and criticality pulling him in different directions, Robben finally concludes, "I could only subvert seduction by playing along with it and grasp its meaning from the inside" (1995, 98). Similarly, over the course of fieldwork at different news organizations, I was (quite willingly) "seduced" into the positionality of each newspaper, not only through professional commitment but also through various relationships of political camaraderie, bosom friendship, antipathetic rivalry, and unrequited love. For this reason, although key to my overall fieldwork strategy, I found it difficult to leave one paper and go to work for another, and my own social world became increasingly complicated as time went on. While the ambivalence and divided loyalties of "serial seduction" in this anthropological sense are certainly confusing and uncomfortable to experience, the result, I believe, is stronger and more important ethnography. The shield against one-sided ethnography is not the maintenance of "analytical distance" but quite the opposite: the willingness to take up a specific positionality, participate in the practices of those who serve there and listen to what they have to say—and then, crucially (precariously, sometimes regretfully), withdraw and reposition at an alternative point in the social field, becoming interpolated in the discourses and practices of that positionality. While the deliberate naiveté and seeming erasure of personal political agenda might appear disingenuous from the point of view of activist anthropology, what Ghanaian journalists seem to find most useful about my work thus far is *not* my dedication to any particular political agenda but rather the representation of multiple perspectives, relaying forms of knowledge and practice inaccessible to them given the political and professional boundaries of Ghanaian society. Which is to say, since I will never actually *be* a Ghanaian journalist, as an outsider it is much more useful to capitalize on what I *can* do as an anthropologist practicing journalism in Ghana—to develop multiple connections and convey alternative points of view.

Given the focus on the news production and texts, the equally important realm of reception and interpretive practices of audiences is largely left out of this study. This does not reflect any theoretical commitment to privileging any particular moment in the circuit of social knowledge but rather indicates the most likely beginning of a thorough understanding of this form of political discourse (see also Boyer 2000; MachLachlan 2000; Wolfe 1997; Denkabe and Gadzekpo 1996; Shope 1995; and Ebo 1988). Participant observation in the organized field of production was far easier to conceptualize than any systematic and participatory method in the spatially and temporally dispersed practices of audiences.

I certainly heard a lot of talk about the news, everywhere I went in Ghana, and have attempted to convey some sense of that popular engagement throughout this study. For a scholarly account of popular reading practices in Ghana, Stephanie Newell's 2002 study of the rise of literary culture in colonial Ghana describes the appropriation and recrafting of reading practices in the colonial period, showing how Gold Coast readers used texts to form networks of shared meaning, constructing and expressing new identities and desires in the complex socioeconomic context of colonial society. Similarly, although I have not conducted systematic research on practices of reading news media in contemporary Ghana, my impression is that news discourse is not merely a source of political information and ideology for Ghanaian readers but rather a means of maneuvering in discursive networks of power and meaning, constructing interpretive communities and positioning emergent identities in the dynamic dispensation of neoliberal Ghana (see also Karikari and Ansu-Kyeremeh 1996).

Mapping Contradictions: Rhetoric, Text, and Practice

This study examines Ghanaian journalism at three levels: rhetoric, text, and practice. Taking up the contradictory professional commitments in the rhetoric of African journalism, I locate the primary authors of each rhetorical position at the local level and attempt to explain the sources and motivations behind that rhetoric. Furthermore, in each section I draw on interviews with journalists at state and private newspapers to see how these rhetorical terms are ambivalently deployed (and often reinterpreted) in their own professional talk. Then I take a look at news texts in state and private newspapers, examining both the narrative structure of these texts and how they participate in certain hegemonic or counter-hegemonic projects. Comparing news texts with the discursive rationales of the journalists that produce them, I identify the contradictory relationship between text and rhetoric, and trace the contradictions into the realm of practice.

Ghanaian journalists recognize a deep divide separating the practices of journalism at state and private newspapers. State and private journalists articulate different forms of professional rhetoric, deploy different tactics of newsgathering, negotiate different political pressures, and enjoy different forms of compensation and reward for their work. Reflecting this divide, I have structured this book as two separate case studies, the first on the state press and the second on the private press. Each section addresses a common set of issues, exploring the articulation of rhetoric, the structure of texts, and the deployment of practices in both the state and private press. Chapter 1 discusses the rhetoric of state journalism, and chapters 2 and 3 illustrate the practices of textual production at the state press. Chapter 4 describes the reemergence of the private press, relying on discourses of human rights and democracy, and chapter 5 analyzes the operationalization of these commitments in the texts and practices of private journalists. By separating the case studies, I emphasize the differential positioning of state and private journalists in the political field and demonstrate how issues of rhetoric, textual form, and practice intersect in two distinctly different problematics.

The questions that motivate this book revolve around the relation between discourse and practice in a context of discursive production dense with historical and cultural determinations, political and popular inflections, and local and global flows. Throughout this book I attempt to trace how these contradictory forces traverse the practices and subjectivities of Ghanaian journalists, producing notions of culture and politics that are at once distinctly African and assertively cosmopolitan.

PART I THE STATE PRESS

1

National Discourse and the State Apparatus

During my internship with the state-owned *Daily Graphic* I went out one day on assignment with Kweku Tetteh,[1] a junior reporter. We had been called by the Trades Union Congress (TUC) to the opening of a workshop for the writers of the TUC newspaper. Like most invited assignments, this event consisted primarily of a series of speeches, the main one delivered by the TUC Secretary General, Mr. Appiah Agyei. The speech was basically a pep talk for the TUC writers, encouraging them to educate the public about the policies of the TUC and boost circulation of the TUC newspaper. Usually journalists receive a photocopy of speeches delivered at official assignments, but this time the speech was not available so we would have to rely on our notes to write the story.

Later, snacking on cakes and Fanta with the rest of the state press corps (compliments of TUC), I wondered how this "event" could possibly be newsworthy. On invited assignments, state journalists adhere faithfully to the printed speeches of public officials, structuring the lead of the story around some particularly poignant utterance, usually about development or popular initiative. So where was our angle on this story? When we had finished our snack, TUC arranged for a car to take the state journalists back to our newspaper offices.

Back at *Graphic,* Tetteh and I sat down at a computer to compose the story. "Now for the lead," he said, looking at me inquiringly. Confused, I looked back and said nothing. Resting his hands on the keyboard for a moment, he seemed a bit anxious. Then he typed:

"The Secretary-General of the Trades Union Congress (TUC), Mr Christian Appiah Agyei, has called on workers to contribute harder than before to enable the country to achieve its developmental target for this year."

Tetteh sat back in his chair, appraising this sentence and giving me time to read it. Then he looked me in the eye and asked, "Is that not so?"

Suppressing my amazement, I nodded.

He went on typing:

"He said effective contribution to the implementation of government policies and objectives would improve the living conditions of the people."

Tetteh turned to me again, asking, "Is that not so?"

Again I nodded, wondering if I might have dozed off and missed this inspiring kernel of national rhetoric in Agyei's speech. Or were we even at the same assignment?

He went on typing:

"Mr Appiah made the call when he opened a five-day workshop for stringers of the TUC newspaper, the *Ghanaian Worker.*

The workshop, organized by the TUC, is aimed at equipping the participants with the skills to educate the members of the general public on the activities of the congress."

Consulting my notes on this point, I found that it was so (although I saw no mention of developmental targets or improved living conditions). To be helpful I shared a few other observations from my notes, and Tetteh and I went on to write the rest of the story, highlighting the main points of the speech.

The next day our routine and rather insignificant story appeared in the upper-right-hand corner of the front page of the *Daily Graphic.* Since the little stories I worked on were frequently carried on the front page, I was not surprised that *Graphic* had once again deployed the symbolic capital of my American name, there in the byline with Tetteh's name. Seeing our questionable lead cheek-to-jowl with the masthead, I wondered if Mr. Appiah might call in to complain that he had been misquoted. He never did.

During my internship at *Graphic* I wrote several stories with Tetteh and many other stories with various *Graphic* reporters, and never encountered another situation quite like that one. We had been sent on an official assignment of questionable news value, consisting of a speech directed at a very limited audience. Faced with the task of molding this event into the iconic narrative preferred by *Graphic,* we were actually lucky not to have the usual copy of the speech.

Many of the regular news stories carried by the *Daily Graphic* are based on the speeches and statements of public officials, usually delivered at invited assignments to meetings and ceremonies. Journalists for the *Daily Graphic,* sent out on these invited assignments, hear this rhetoric every day and faithfully reproduce it in the leads and quotes of their news stories. Mr. Agyei may well have said that bit about working harder and national development. Public officials on invited assignments usually do (although in this case I am sure I did not hear it). The point is not that Tetteh or state journalists in general regularly fabricate the news. Rather, the drive to reproduce this kind of rhetoric can be so compelling that, in the absence of it, journalists can spontaneously produce it themselves.

Journalists for the state press become quite adept at culling the developmental themes from routine assignments. Proud of their responsibility to a progressive national agenda, they rely on a specific professional rhetoric of state journalism to inform and organize their professional ideals. Through a public rhetoric of state journalism grounded in the discourse of national development, journalists for the state press are rhetorically summoned into the hegemonic project of the state and positioned to reproduce its daily ceremonies of legitimacy and consensus. The rhetoric of state journalism, however, submerges the practical experiences of this positionality, creating instead an abstract and idealized position for journalists, emphasizing public responsibility and the national interest. Journalists themselves wrestle with this rhetoric, incorporating it into their own accounts of their work while attempting to modify and reconcile it with contradictory experiences.

Nationalism and the State Information Apparatus

The two daily papers in Accra, the *Daily Graphic* and the *Ghanaian Times,* are both owned by the state.[2] The *Daily Graphic* was started in 1950 by the Daily Mirror Group headed by British newspaper magnate Cecil King (Asante 1996). Daily Mirror started sister papers in Nigeria and Sierra Leone. At the time, other newspapers in Ghana (the *Accra Evening News,* the *Ashanti Pioneer*) were backed by political parties and focused primarily on national news. Since those papers were set by hand, production was rudimentary and circulation limited. The Daily Mirror papers were founded on a policy of vigorous neutrality and constructive criticism (Hachten 1971), using rotary printing presses for mass circulation and air transport for broad distribution. Although the Daily Mirror papers were staffed by African reporters and editors, the papers initially faced boycotts by Ghanaians and Nigerians who suspected a neocolonial agenda (Faringer 1991). Gradually, through its technical expertise and coverage of international news, the *Daily Graphic* won the largest readership of all Ghanaian newspapers and boosted the professional standards of Ghanaian journalism (Ainslie 1966).

Kwame Nkrumah was released from detention to become the prime minister of Ghana in 1951. Six years later Ghana achieved independence from the British, and Nkrumah began to consolidate power in a one-party African socialist state. Recognizing the inferior technical and professional quality of his own newspaper, the *Accra Evening News,* Nkrumah set up Guinea Press, Ltd., with funding from the state and local businessmen. In

1958 Guinea Press began publishing the *Ghanaian Times,* a serious morning newspaper designed to compete with *Graphic* in news coverage, professional quality, and circulation.

Although he came to power through his own nationalist and defiantly oppositional press, Nkrumah became a vocal critic of private newspapers, believing that capitalist competition interfered with the sanctity of the truth and the project of national development (Asante 1996). Facing growing intimidation by the state, Cecil King finally approached Nkrumah with an offer to sell the *Daily Graphic.* Arranging for an independent trust to oversee operations (now a board of directors), Nkrumah made *Graphic* a state paper in 1962. Trustees included King, Ghana's chief justice, and the attorney general.

In his effort to control the flow of information in the national interest, Nkrumah established a network of coercive and partisan institutions, including the Ghana News Agency, the Ministry of Information, the Press Secretariat, the Kwame Nkrumah Ideological Institute, and the Ghana Institute of Journalism—all exerting direct or indirect control over the news content and editorial policies of the two state newspapers, *Graphic* and *Times.* In addition, the government summoned the legal system to fortify this apparatus, passing a series of repressive laws allowing for censorship, deportation, preventative detention, and imprisonment for such crimes as false reports, sedition, or publication of material "contrary to the public interest." Through a newspaper licensing law, the state reserved the right to allow or prohibit the publication of any newspaper. When the *Ashanti Pioneer* was finally banned in 1962, only *Graphic* and *Times* remained.

The logic governing this apparatus was the national fixation on development. The press was assigned the task of galvanizing popular consent for government policies by explaining those policies as part of the benevolent and revolutionary project of national development. Newspapers were meant to foster unity and loyalty to the common cause by publicizing the progressive activities and optimistic pronouncements of government officials. Criticism was considered regressive, divisive, and neocolonial.

Through these rhetorical, institutional, and legal means, Nkrumah's complex system of information control established the functional role of the state dailies in constructing and reinforcing the representational authority of the African socialist state. Since Nkrumah was deposed by a coup in 1966, Ghana has been ruled by nine governments, five military and four democratic. Each time a new faction assumes power the editorial staff of the state newspapers is shuffled or replaced, and the editorial positions of the papers are transformed, sometimes overnight, to reflect the personal and ideological commitments of the new government. Not surprisingly, the military regimes (especially under Ankrah, Acheampong, and Rawlings) have tended to exercise outright control over the press, through repressive decrees and other institutional arrangements. The presidents of Ghana's republics (Busia, Limann, Rawlings, and Kufuor) have been somewhat more tolerant of criticism, granting more freedoms to the press and encouraging journalistic independence, at least rhetorically.

Scholarship on the press in Ghana, in line with the human rights orientation of journalism discourse in general, is largely preoccupied with the dynamic relationship between the government and the press, measured by the amount of freedom, tolerance, and access to information granted by each leader. This relationship is narrated through the unusually provocative actions and incidents that distinguish one regime from another. Histories and contemporary appraisals of the news media in Africa gravitate toward this narrative of repression and oppositional struggle (Asante 1996; Blay-Amihere and Alabi 1996; Ziegler and Asante 1992; Faringer 1991; Hachten 1971; Barton 1966). What scholars and journalists seem to overlook is the remarkable structural durability of the state information apparatus constructed by Nkrumah and the degree to which the *Daily Graphic* and the *Ghanaian Times* actually function within the state and not exterior to and responsive to state control. Excepting the Ideological Institute, the other institutions of the information apparatus remain linked in a complex network heavily dependent on state support. Within this structure, the production and dissemination of daily news is organized through social relations and everyday practices that reinscribe this dependency and the functional role of the state press.

Under the Fourth Republic Rawlings repealed many of his own prohibitive decrees and stressed the need for an objective and responsible press. As part of the project of political liberalization, state and private newspapers began to enjoy unprecedented freedoms in the 1990s. Repressive actions were directed mainly at the private papers, which were confronted with constant public harassment and libel suits by offended state officials. The state press, admittedly partisan in the revolutionary 1980s, became allegedly independent of editorial direction from the state. The 1992 Constitution set up a National Media Commission specifically designed to insulate the state press from government control. *Graphic* editors and reporters frequently insist that their paper is completely objective and free from state bias.

However, throughout the 1990s the content of both *Graphic* and *Times* was dominated by the development rhetoric of government officials while editorials encouraged unity, loyalty, and popular initiative in the national quest for development. How can journalists reproduce this rhetoric every day and still maintain a commitment to nonpartisan objectivity? Are they

3. Waist-deep in it: Rawlings shovels "silt" from an open gutter as part of a "massive clean-up exercise" in the township of Ashaiman. This performance, reminiscent of the revolutionary "self-help" campaigns of the early 1980s, was intended to launch the celebration of Ghana's fortieth anniversary of independence. *Courtesy of the* Daily Graphic, *March 3, 1997.*

lying? Although the practice and rhetoric of state journalism are completely contradictory, the prevalence and earnest assertion of the rhetoric and the tendency to compartmentalize practice as apolitical both suggest a different interpretation. Rather, journalists are so embedded in naturalized social structures and normalized social behavior that the production of state-biased social reality becomes a matter of professional competence and social propriety. As a Ghanaian journalist for the state press, Tetteh was just doing his job—in accordance with the implicit expectations of his editors and his news sources.

Objectivity and Responsibility: The Public Rhetoric of State Journalism

The journalist's task is to ensure that the people are regularly provided with accurate, truthful, factual, and unbiased information, objectively assembled and analysed to enable them to make informed decisions.

> —Yaw Boadu-Ayeboafoh, "Our Constitution and the Media."
> *Daily Graphic,* January 8, 1998

Journalism is not just the provision of information and entertainment, it is more importantly the pursuit of education and development-support communication. Where one aims at informing and entertaining, one is not so much bothered about content of media products as much as their packaging. However, if the objective is to educate and stimulate development or qualitative change, then one has to be cautious in the selection of news and their presentation.

In our setting, culture is very predominant and fundamental to development. Any strategy that discounts the relevance of culture could lead to anomie, alienation, or social discord. Issues must be put in their proper perspectives and their dimensions established for the necessary programmes to effect change.

> —Yaw Boadu-Ayeboafoh, "The Role of Women in Journalism,"
> *Daily Graphic,* September 10, 1996

When I first began reading Ghanaian newspapers, I was struck by the amount of newsprint devoted to the subject of journalism itself. Most newspapers cover the frequent journalism conferences and professional events of the Ghana Journalists Association, often in front-page stories, and publicize any noteworthy travel or award accomplished by their own journalists. At least once a month the *Daily Graphic* devotes a long features article, strategically situated next to the editorial, to media issues. Such articles are often very formal and highly rhetorical essays on the ideal role of the journalist in Ghanaian society. Throughout the 1990s most of these articles were written by an intriguing and controversial *Graphic* journalist, Yaw Boadu-Ayeboafoh. As formal public statements of journalistic philosophy, Ayeboafoh's essays demonstrate how state journalists understand their craft and publicly justify their practices. The disjuncture between this idealized professional rhetoric and Ayeboafoh's own complicated and ambivalent position within the *Daily Graphic* exemplifies the way that journalists commonly segregate their journalistic philosophy from their everyday practices.

Ayeboafoh, associate editor of news and public affairs at *Graphic,* writes very serious and well-documented statements, studded with international quotes by journalists and politicians, on the constitutional rights and moral responsibilities of the Ghanaian journalist. Ayeboafoh was originally hired by former chief editor Sam Clegg and weathered the political battles at *Graphic* during periods of intense resistance to state manipulation followed by conservative reform under the new editor, Elvis Aryeh. Because of his previous work as part of a resistant editorial staff, many believe that the position of associate editor was created for Ayeboafoh to marginalize him from major editorial decision making and thwart the possibility of confrontation with Aryeh who may be intimidated by him. Although his role at *Graphic* is now somewhat mysterious, Ayeboafoh remains a strong and well-respected force in Ghanaian journalism. Small in stature, his distinctively high-pitched voice consistently delivers careful and reasoned remarks at the frequent conferences and lectures sponsored by the Ghana Journalists Association (GJA). So valued are his contributions to professional debates that Ayeboafoh was voted GJA "Journalist of the Year" in 1996, even though he never writes news stories (at least not with a byline). According to former *Graphic* editors Clegg and Oakley, Ayeboafoh frequently writes the conservative and highly rhetorical daily editorial. Despite this, Clegg admires him greatly and hopes that "one day he will run the place."[3]

In his features on Ghanaian journalism Ayeboafoh's style is formal and deliberate. His language is calculated and somewhat learned, with complex sentences and political terms deployed with the self-consciousness of someone whose very authority depends on his diplomatic proficiency in this official political language. His introduction to "Our Constitution and the Media" (cited above) is a good example.

> The media in any society must serve as the bulwark to safeguard the fundamental human rights of the citizens to give meaning to the rule of law. The media must aim at protecting the governed from any

abuse by those in all manner of leadership, including political, religious, and traditional as well as commercial and economic interests.[4]

He introduces his topics with rhetorical statements so abstract and widely held that seemingly no one in his audience could disagree—and then slowly leads them into more contentious territory. On particularly sensitive issues he backs up every single point with a quotation or legal documentation, preferring these over personal examples or observations. No mention is ever made of his personal experiences as a journalist at *Graphic*. Rather, his narrative subjectivity is evacuated and replaced with an international chorus of statesmen, judges, media scholars, and journalists. The heavy use of secondary sources to make his points serves to situate his controversial arguments in local, national, regional, and international discourses on journalism and politics.

As the above excerpts indicate, Ayeboafoh's features ply a politically precarious course between the constitutional rights and moral responsibilities of the Ghanaian journalist. In general, state journalists stress their moral commitment to development, stability, and "the national interest," while private journalists summon human rights discourse and constitutional guarantees to defend their antagonistic stance toward the state. As a state journalist, Ayeboafoh emphasizes the responsible role of the journalist in national development, but he also makes a solid case for alternative responsibilities, mandated in the 1992 Constitution, to democratic pluralism and political accountability. Through his essays on these professional responsibilities, Ayeboafoh positions the Ghanaian journalist between political society and the Ghanaian people, constructing a vision of both in the process and subtly setting a more progressive course for journalists in the state press.

In Ayeboafoh's political imaginary of Ghanaian society, the ideal journalist merely acts as a vehicle for transporting information back and forth between political institutions and the people so that all may perform their constitutional functions efficiently.

> Political parties provide the platform for linking social groups with governance. The parties need information to perform effectively and that requires dynamic, daring and assertively independent media willing to ferret vital information to keep the parties, government and parliament on their toes. The electorate must be well informed since an ill-informed people cannot hold their elected representatives accountable to the mandate.[5]

In this vision, political and social groups are vertically and horizontally discrete. Situated at the vertical boundary, the political parties integrate the disparate groups in a total, politically charged system. Although vital to the functional stability of this system, journalists are located somehow outside it, tending to the maintenance of social cohesion through their professional duties of information transfer. This vision, crucial to the rhetoric of journalistic neutrality, obscures the obvious fact that journalists actually do occupy significant positions in the social totality, positions that vary according to their own social and political affiliations and those of their media houses. Ayeboafoh must know this from personal experience.

In September 1996, just as campaigns were getting under way for the December 7 presidential and parliamentary elections, Ayeboafoh ushered in the political season with a feature on "Reporting Politics." Summoning the Constitution, the GJA *Code of Ethics*, and the National Media Commission's *Guidelines for Political Reporting*, the article exhorts journalists to "relate fairly and equitably to all the established political parties without pandering to the interests of any." Implicit in this call for journalistic neutrality are the reciprocal accusations of bias between the conservative state media and the oppositional private press, together with the ongoing controversy over the proper role of the state press. Following the controversial 1992 elections, the New Patriotic Party (NPP) took the Ghana Broadcasting Corporation (GBC) to court, alleging a breach of the new constitutional guarantee to equal coverage in the state-owned media. Reviewing the campaign coverage, the court found in favor of the NPP, and GBC was strongly reprimanded (although the NPP has yet to collect the awarded damages). And still, as late as 1995, *Graphic* editor Elvis Aryeh publicly made the claim that the state press should function as the partisan mouthpiece of the government. Aryeh made that statement at the taping of a talk show for the state-owned television station, GTV. So scandalous were those remarks that the show was never aired. Several journalists told me, shaking their heads, how the editor had spoken badly and embarrassed himself on that occasion.

Confronted with allegations of state bias at *Graphic*, Aryeh often makes the counter-claim that journalists in the private press serve the political agendas of their publisher-editor masters. Briefing the journalism students on practical attachment to *Graphic*, Aryeh stressed that *Graphic* is the most objective newspaper in Ghana. Those private papers, he said, are run by self-interested publishers aspiring to public office, using their newspapers to launch their political careers. (Oddly the only journalists who ever admitted political ambitions to me were reporters, not publishers, and some of them worked at *Graphic*.) Journalists in the state press point out that private journalists are always aligning themselves with one faction or another in their sensational coverage of any dispute, from the "Guinea Fowl War" in the

North to conflicts between the Asantehene and the Ashanti Regional Minister as well as parliamentary and presidential campaigns.

Avoiding any reference to the highly controversial events that actually frame the context of his call for neutrality—in fact, avoiding any explicit mention of the upcoming elections at all—Ayeboafoh's article points to research on American news media that suggests unintended bias toward Israel in reporting on crises in the Middle East. This example identifies political bias as a professional problem, not reducible to party politics in general or isolated in the Ghanaian political sphere in particular. Only then can Ayeboafoh refer to the problem of bias in the Ghanaian news media. Even then his "indictment" of bias in both state and private papers is made secondhand through the report of a fellow Ghanaian journalist who observed that state and private journalists at the same event picked out certain details and ignored others in order to represent their given political positions. And where does this indictment lead him?

> There is a serious need for a new orientation and education among Ghanaian journalists to enable us to appreciate our relevance to our society. For as has been argued by Jaawant S. Yadava in *Politics of News,* it is "the solemn responsibility of journalists to help in spreading consciousness among the masses to enable them to understand the forces at work, those that help social advance and those that impede it."[6]

Thus the divisive problem of state and private media bias is preemptively depoliticized and immediately transformed into a collective problem of professional responsibility. Substantive solutions become unnecessary as the problem of bias is resolved in rhetorical appeals to "uphold the provisions of the Constitution" and "give vent to the aspirations and interests of all political parties."[7]

Ayeboafoh's article is itself a good example of this rhetorical solution to media bias. The objective authority constructed in "Reporting Politics," typical of Ayeboafoh, conceals the taint of his embodied and structurally positioned experiences as a Ghanaian journalist working for a state newspaper. Certainly it is those experiences, and not the abstract introductory ruminations on "constitutional injunction" and "multiparty democracy," that actually motivate the article. Ayeboafoh's objective authority is achieved by first lifting himself free of his lived conditions and then using the linguistic capital of official English and the social capital of international elites to construct an abstract professional subject position in place of actual experience.

Bias and the National Interest: The Professional Talk of State Journalists

Like Ayeboafoh, most state journalists overlook their practical relationship to the state and earnestly profess commitments to both "safeguarding human rights" and protecting the "national interest." Juxtaposing these two commitments, state journalists conclude that their journalism is far more balanced than that of the private newspapers, seen as oppositionally biased and disproportionately committed to exposing government scandals and human rights abuses. Furthermore, state journalists contend that those sensational exposés are not only politically but also professionally irresponsible, often based on rumor and speculation rather than on established fact.

> It's the role of the paper to be the watchdog over office holders, state officials. So if state funds are diverted or dissipated, that's not in the interest of the entire nation, and we should come out with it. But where the report is inaccurate and full of exaggerations, that is where I beg to differ. I'm in favor of trying to unearth people who are trying to embezzle state funds. That is a worthwhile effort, worthy of commendation. (Franklin Botsio)

Arguing that such stories stir up controversy and "create confusion in society," state journalists claim a more responsible approach aimed at promoting social cohesion and stability.

> We say we must be very responsible. We don't want to create confusion in society so we don't take an issue and bandy it about and say that this is happening. . . . Some people think that the state media is trying to please one master or another. I don't see it as that. I see it as trying to play a careful role in such a way that it doesn't degenerate into something else. (Isaac Opoku)

Echoing Aryeh's argument that the private press is merely a tool of the opposition in a strategy to topple the ruling party, state journalists say that only *Graphic* rises above party politics to represent the national interest and public safety.

> *Graphic* is a public paper and does not belong to the NDC [National Democratic Congress]. So it should take a balanced view, representative of the population. The ruling party has papers (referring to *Palaver, Democrat*) and they can do their propaganda for them but *Graphic* should not be a mouthpiece of the ruling party. It should chart the national course but should be responsible enough not to sabotage government no matter what party is in power. The government of Ghana is more important than what party is in power. I would not expect *Daily Graphic* to report like *Chronicle* because it has the national interest to protect but also I would not expect it to report like *Palaver* and *Democrat* because it is not any party's newspaper. (Maxwell Appenteng)

Steering clear of either "sabotage" or "propaganda," state journalists assume a "careful role," paternalistically concerned with providing information to protect the public.

> *Graphic* is state-owned and has to take into consideration the national interest and national security. So there are certain things they should make the public aware of so that they can take the necessary precautions. (Sebastian Kwesi Mensah)

In this conservative interpretation of the national interest, *Graphic* journalists are dedicated to reinforcing the legitimacy and authority of the state (and not necessarily the party, though at that time in Ghana the two were inextricable). As the state hinges its legitimacy on benevolent paternalism, *Graphic* participates in the paternalistic appeal as one particularly crucial instrument in the larger state apparatus.

While vocally committed to this "responsible" role and highly critical of the "irresponsible" journalism of the private press, state journalists are also quick to claim the role of "watchdog" of the public interest against injustices and abuses of public office. They maintain that *Graphic* is not so concerned with protecting the image of the government that journalists are discouraged from writing such critical stories.

> If you really look out for objectivity, there's an element of objectivity in what they do. Because if a state functionary is not living up to expectations, they'll be the first people to come out with it. *Graphic* will come out with it. (Franklin Botsio)

> JH: What do you think about these stories in the private press about ministers having big houses? Are those stories in the public interest?

> Mensah: The public should know if that is true or not. When such a thing happens, *Graphic* publishes it.

When a state official falls out of favor with the president or the ruling party, *Graphic* will, in fact, be the first to come out with the story. Contrary to Botsio's interpretation, such strategic reporting would seem to disprove the element of pure objectivity. When rumors begin to circulate about the kleptocratic practices of NDC favorites and Rawlings' closest allies, however, *Graphic* remains notoriously silent as the private press breaks the story and continues with ongoing investigations. *Graphic* only seems to recognize the newsworthiness of the controversy when popular accusations are formalized in court or before the Commission for Human Rights and Administrative Justice (CHRAJ). At that point a *Graphic* journalist is assigned to sit in on the daily hearings, and stories are structured around the testimony of witnesses, often emphasizing the defense of accused ministers.

This insistence by some state journalists that *Graphic* breaks critical stories (when, in fact, it does not) indicates a deeper contradiction between their professed commitments to both constructing and challenging state authority. Recognizing that *Graphic* strenuously avoids direct criticism of the government might suggest that *Graphic* is actually controlled by the government, a conclusion state journalists are reluctant to admit. Rather, the professional identity of state journalists depends on their image as balanced and objective reporters operating outside the boundaries of state influence. On the other hand, *Graphic* journalists alternatively position themselves as part of the legitimate and responsible authority of the state itself. *Graphic* journalists enjoy the prestige attached to their role as journalists in the state media. Their exclusive contacts with state officials and the "professional quality" of a state-supported daily press contribute to their privileged professional identity.

In the midst of these competing commitments, the journalistic ideal of balance becomes a problem of profound contradiction. Often, my questions about the controversial role of the state press elicited long and extremely ambivalent responses. A particularly subtle and eloquent thinker, Franklin Botsio delivered a protracted speech on the subject, beginning with a denial of direct state influence, and then vacillating from one position to the other, until finally concluding with the strength of state influence in the state media.

> Personally, if it is a state paper, you are talking of where the government is funding the media outfit. I don't know but I think that the government no longer provides it. *Graphic* is supposed to do other things to sustain itself. But when you have the long arm of the government in your establishment, a situation where the editor is appointed by the government, I mean it's like that in all Third World countries. And so it's likely that the state media project the image of a particular government in power. I'm not only talking of the NDC government. I'm even referring to succeeding or past governments. That has been the role of the state media all along. But then if you really look out for objectivity, there's an element of objectivity in what they do . . . [see above quote]. But sometimes people don't seem to . . . in Ghana in particular we have a politics of division. If I don't belong to who you belong to then I don't even need to associate myself with you—which is bad. . . . They say we seem to praise government but don't talk about the negative side. Then we are all human beings. I don't control where I work. I feel there is an element of objectivity in what goes on there. If it is a state-owned paper, the likelihood of state influence is very pronounced. (Franklin Botsio)

As Botsio articulates the contradiction, journalists in the state press are torn between their professional commitment to objectivity and their more "human" fidelity to the state apparatus. Botsio implies that *Graphic* journalists actually "belong to" the current government, his way of explaining the contingency and inevitability of bias in the state media.

This recognition is a troubling one for state journalists, threatening their professional ideals of journalistic independence. Like Botsio, state journalists are generally well aware of the widespread allegations of state bias and many, when pressed, admit that *Graphic* tends to avoid criticizing the government or the ruling party. They insist, however, that they are not themselves biased or censored by their editors or representatives of the state.

> People have the idea that you work for the state media and you have this kind of pressure on you. But there is no invisible hand manipulating you. You do the thing your own way. I should say that, there is a house style. You are there for a long time and you realize that this is the kind of style the house wants, the policy they are pursuing. You develop an unconscious habit writing stories in that manner. (Isaac Opoku)

Ingeniously both Botsio and Opoku transform the problem of state bias into an aestheticized notion of market niche, restoring a kind of business professionalism to the biased positioning of the state media. In this way state journalists attempt to preserve their sense of themselves as independent while admitting that the newspaper (like any other) has its slant. For Botsio, the process of professionalization in the state media is less unconscious and more strategic.

> First and foremost, any newspaper or organization has its own ideology or mission statement so when you find yourself there you work to suit that work environment, that mission statement that the corporation or newspaper has, provided there will be job security and the possibility that the paper has a future.

This insistence that their form of journalism is not censored or coercively controlled by the state seems to satisfy state journalists as a response to allegations of bias. If the state is not personally and coercively interfering with the production of news, then apparently the paper itself has chosen its representational slant as a business strategy. As journalists contribute to this slant, they are then merely working in the interests of the newspaper and not in the interests of the state necessarily.

This reasoning completely obscures the prominent role of the state in the history and structural positioning of the newspaper. *Graphic* was, after all, appropriated by the state and fashioned as a representational tool in the larger state apparatus. In the past the state interfered directly with editorial decisions at *Graphic* through the regular interventions of the Ministry of Information. Former editor Sam Clegg recalls the frequent visits of deputy ministers, laying stories across his desk for publication and arguing with any critical or controversial news coverage. Faced with Clegg's repeated resistance to these forms of intimidation, the ministry strategized to alienate and finally replace him. Since the ratification of the Constitution in 1991, such direct intervention with the staff and daily functioning of the state press has been prohibited. As mentioned, *Graphic* is now overseen by a "nonpartisan" Board of Directors and "insulated from state control" by the Media Commission.[8] However, throughout the 1990s, many *Graphic* editors who were handpicked by the state during the revolutionary period (including the main editor) remained on the editorial staff, exercising considerable control over the paper. Furthermore, during the period of my fieldwork, the constitutional repositioning of *Graphic* did not change the daily practices of *Graphic* journalism, crucially shaped by nearly thirty years as a state-owned paper. *Graphic* journalists were still enjoying both a steady supply of invited assignments to state functions and privileged relationships of mutual cooperation with state sources. If the state no longer interferes directly in the production of state news, similar results are nevertheless achieved through the structural overdetermination of these practices along with the daily decisions of editors with deep obligations to the state. Through both journalistic practices and editorial decisions, the structural bias of *Graphic* is subtly actualized in the "house style" of the newspaper.

2

"Who-Leads" and Who Follows: House Style at *Graphic*

Under President J. J. Rawlings, the premier state newspaper, the *Daily Graphic*, articulated and reinforced a specific logic of state hegemony: political legitimacy based on state accumulation, populist morality, and benevolent patronage. Participation in the hegemonic project of the state distinguishes the *Daily Graphic* as a strategic node in the larger "ideological state apparatus" (Althusser 1971) designed to construct and reinforce an official national imaginary. In the pronouncements of state officials, the form of state hegemony specific to Rawlings' regime was conveyed in the ritual celebration of state plans and accomplishments as so many milestones on the developmental path to prosperity. The style of journalism practiced at *Graphic* throughout the 1990s (the "house style" referred to in the previous chapter), was designed to explain government policies and illustrate the positive impact of development projects on grateful communities, generally ignoring political controversies and popular criticisms.[1] Thus, in the state media, dissent is suppressed and oppositional voices are rendered "unqualified" in the narrative frame of *Graphic* journalism. This house style results in a daily construction of the state as a legitimate, benevolent, and unified authority at the helm of national affairs.[2]

As demonstrated in the previous chapter, *Graphic* journalists are reluctant to recognize their participation in the hegemonic project of the state. Rather, state journalists earnestly profess their commitments to the public as well as the state, identifying themselves as both "watchdogs in the public interest" and responsible spokespersons of the benevolent state. Focusing on their own professional intentions and their freedom from outright state censorship, *Graphic* journalists point out that the democratizing reforms of 1991 have abolished overt state control, allowing state journalists the freedom to pursue all sides of a news story with distinctive fairness and objec-

4. In the driver's seat: The lead story of the *Daily Graphic* declares the launching of a government project to protect the Keta coastline from erosion. The photo depicts President Rawlings driving a bulldozer to clear away a heap of sand and concrete, signaling the beginning of work on the project. While the lead story portrays destructive leveling in preparation for development, note the complementary image of developmental construction in the ruling party advert in the lower right. *Courtesy of the* Daily Graphic, *November 18, 1996.*

tivity. *Graphic* journalists tend to overlook the persistence of state influence in everyday practices and relationships that have remained essentially unchanged in the new democratic dispensation. These practices are historically shaped by the positioning of *Graphic* as a strategic representational tool in the larger state information apparatus, still largely intact. Through these journalistic practices, the structural bias of *Graphic* is subtly actualized in the house style of the newspaper.

House style refers to a specific textual frame for shaping the narrative of most news stories at *Graphic*. This frame structures a set of preferences for highlighting certain elements of an event while de-emphasizing or even obscuring certain other elements (van Dijk 1991). Focusing on the pronouncements of "newsmakers," house style at *Graphic* foregrounds the elegant rhetoric of state officials at invited assignments, essentially echoing the interpretive frame of the state in both the selection and representation of newsworthy events.

Who-Leads

At the Ghana Institute of Journalism, as in journalism schools worldwide, students are taught how to organize the six essential elements of a news event into a leading paragraph, or "lead." Identifying who, when, what, where, why, and how the news happened ("the five Ws and one H"), the journalist chooses the most provocative element and uses it to contextualize the entire story, preferably highlighting that element in the first few words of the story. Since the structure of the lead is driven by the nature of each news story, newspapers typically feature a wide variety of leads emphasizing compelling events, actions, places, and people. In American newspapers, leads are commonly structured around an important event, relevant action, or new discovery. Leads emphasizing personalities, times, and places are less common, followed by explanations of how and why something occurred—elements usually left to the body of the story.

In the pages of *Graphic*, however, around half the stories are designed to highlight personalities, with leads that quote the public comments of an authoritative "who." *Graphic* leads often open with a quote by the most senior official at the assignment, identifying him by name and title. The following paragraph (the "neck") then elaborates on the quote, and the third finally explains the occasion of his speech. This structure is so routine that it has become nearly formulaic at *Graphic*. To illustrate the preponderance and uniformity of this kind of lead, I quote a sample of leads from a single edition of the *Daily Graphic*, October 10, 1996:

From the front page:

President Jerry John Rawlings has called on Ghanaians to ensure that their political differences do not degenerate into actions that will disrupt the country's development.

He said no matter how strong the differences are, they should remain at the level of words and not acts of vandalism and violence.

President Rawlings made the call when he met the chiefs and a cross-section of the people of Sunyani at the palace of the Sunyani-hene, Nan Bosoma Nkrawiri II, yesterday. . . .[3]

Dr Emmanuel Evans-Anfom, past chairman of the West African Examinations Council (WAEC), has stressed the need for people in leadership positions and those who seek to lead, to understand that the concept of leadership is one of service.

"To be called upon to lead means to be given the opportunity and privilege to serve.

"The leader should therefore be a servant of his people rather than a master who will lord it over all," he stated.

He said that many leaders fail in their endeavors because they refuse to observe certain cardinal principles of leadership such as consultation and communication with their people.

Dr Evans-Anfom was speaking at the opening of the fourth William Ofori-Attah memorial lectures on the topic "When leaders lead: some reflections on leadership" in Accra on Tuesday. . . .[4]

From page 3 (page 2 is international news):

The First Lady, Nana Konadu Agyeman-Rawlings, has advised supporters of the Progressive Alliance to remain resolute and turn out in their numbers on the polling day to cast their votes.

She asked them not to be deterred by present intrigues by those who want to wrestle power from the NDC from exercising their franchise on December 7.

Nana Konadu who is also the President of the 31st December Women's Movement gave the advice when she interacted with a cross-section of members of the alliance comprising the NDC, EGLE Party and DPP at James Town in Accra on Tuesday. . . .[5]

Mr D.S. Boateng, Minister of Employment and Social Welfare, has stressed the need for a continuous and comprehensive review of legislations and strategies that provide for the protection of the health and safety of workers.

He noted that with the rapid expansion in the application of science and technology workers are increasingly being exposed to potential hazards from the development and use of these new gadgets and equipment.

Mr Boateng was opening a workshop on protecting the Ghanaian workforce and eliminating work hazards in Accra yesterday....[6]

Of twenty-seven national news stories carried in the *Daily Graphic* that day, twelve were structured around the public statements of authoritative figures. In all twelve of these stories the structure of the lead is nearly identical: a lengthy opening quote and identification of the speaker in the first paragraph (the "who" of the story), elaboration of the quote in the second paragraph, and finally an explanation of the occasion and context for the remarks in the third paragraph (filling in the remaining four Ws and one H).

Graphic journalists call this kind of lead the "who-lead" and recognize it as a distinctive feature of news writing at *Graphic*. They point out that the *Ghanaian Times,* the other state newspaper, more often uses the "occasion-lead," foregrounding the "what" or the "where" of an assignment. Quick to emphasize that they do not really "play up the personality too much" (Isaac Opoku), *Graphic* journalists reason that who-leads are so common for *Graphic* stories because officials are the real newsmakers at any assignment—that is, they make the most important statements. This logic is not merely circular, but rather also indicates a complex array of notions involving discursive authority, performativity, propriety, and public interpretation.

Most invited assignments involve the public comments of several official speakers, representing different ministries or various ranks within the ministries or both. In addition, the Public Relations Officer (PRO) of the host ministry often greets journalists with an informal briefing on the proceedings of the assignment, telling them where to go and what to expect. Often, while waiting for an assignment to begin, journalists from the various state media houses share their relevant information about the assignment, including rumors and speculation about the actions of the ministry. If a secretary or other lower-level state worker is nearby, journalists may strike up a chat and ask about certain off-the-record details. From this array of voices, state journalists piece together the context and relevance of the assignment. Since their interactions with busy ministers can be very brief and restrictively formal (with important exceptions, explored in the next chapter), journalists often obtain the most useful information from their informal conversations with PROs, lower-level officials, and one another.

In *Graphic* who-leads, however, the important contributions of all other participants in an invited assignment are subordinated to the public statements of the most senior state official at the assignment.

> Every newspaper has its style. *Graphic* wants something new. The person making the news should be an authority. You can't just say the Ministry of Employment and Social Welfare is going to embark on labor enterprises and attribute it to the Public Relations Officer in the ministry. To us, that is a misplaced source of the story. You have to attribute it to authority, someone in a position to make such a pronouncement to the entire nation. That is why we concentrate on the personality. It's not so much the personality but what they are saying and who made the statement. (Franklin Botsio)

Ideally the minister himself actually makes the most detailed and provocative news in his speech, but often these public speeches are vague and rhetorical. Even when the speech has relatively little to do with the substance of the assignment, *Graphic* journalists feel compelled to open the story with the most authoritative voice. Journalists reason that other sources are simply not qualified to make important public statements on national affairs. Even if the minister is not speaking directly to the topic at hand or conveying any relevant details, his rhetorical statements lend credibility and authority to the rest of the story. Thus the opening quote by a state official not only promulgates the state rhetoric of development or national unity, but it also positions the *Graphic* news story as a certain type of official national text.

In "The Discourse on Language" (1972) Foucault describes how official knowledge is ordered through the disciplinary practices of discourse. A particularly effective mode of discursive regulation, qualification specifies who may enter the discursive field and speak with what specified authority (224). Qualification requires not merely the necessary certification but also the ritual skills necessary to reproduce the appropriate behavior, gestures, and "the whole range of signs that must accompany discourse; finally, it lays down the supposed, or imposed significance of words used, their effect upon those to whom they are addressed, the limitation of their constraining ability" (225). Along with rules of exclusion, notions of qualification mediate the conceptual boundaries of official discourse, dividing reason from folly and truth from falsity (216).

Similarly journalists with the state press recognize official news when it is pronounced by officially qualified sources in specifically qualifying contexts. Without the official qualification, the truth is simply not newsworthy. Franklin Botsio describes the rationale for this sort of discursive regulation.

> If an ordinary economics teacher gets up and makes a contribution that inflation is high and we must embark on. . . . Who is he to talk of managing the

economy? He's not even employed as an economist in the state to make that pronouncement. Though what he said may be true, the right thing, the source of such a story becomes a problem. Not that we are highlighting personalities so much but we have to make the story credible. It's not as if you are playing, it has to be a serious issue of national concern. If left to anybody, then we'd all be standing around in a circle making pronouncements. Because we are also Ghanaians and it concerns us. So we can just take up microphones and be making blah blah blah in the street.

With credibility reserved for state sources, popular and dissenting voices are deemed unqualified and largely irrelevant. Bourdieu (1984/85) describes how state officials deploy a discursive qualification that derives ultimately from a "ventriloquist" paradox of political representation. Through their public speeches, state officials wield their exclusive authority to constitute the very social phenomena they are meant to represent (i.e., "the needs of the people," "the country's development," "the national interest"). Concealing this power is crucial to their legitimacy as servile representatives of the "will of the people." By routing their public discourse through the state press, state officials can disguise their self-referential discursive power, "speaking and yet making it appear that it is someone else who speaks, speaking for those who give one the right to speak, who in fact authorize one to speak" (63). The stories in the *Daily Graphic* are, after all, written not by state officials, but by journalists, the representative "watchdogs" of the people sent to witness the activities of the state. The *Daily Graphic* is more than a mere mouthpiece; it functions as the primary tool of symbolic violence through which the state speaks not only *on behalf* of the people but *instead* of the people.[7] Note how closely Botsio's reasoning is echoed by Bourdieu,

> If I, Pierre Bourdieu, as a single individual and speaking only for myself, said it is necessary to do this or that, overthrow the government, or refuse Pershing missiles, who would follow me? But if I am placed in statutory conditions such that I am able to appear as speaking "in the name of the masses," or better "in the name of the masses and of science, of scientific socialism," then this changes everything. (63)

For Botsio, qualification is a matter of "seriousness"; for Bourdieu, this "seriousness" is achieved through misrecognition.

How do state journalists learn the rules and regulations implicit to this regime of state news? At the Ghana Institute of Journalism, where nearly all working journalists in Ghana are trained, students are not specifically schooled in the discursive regulations of state journalism, even though the state media employ more journalists than do all the private media combined. In fact, GIJ instructors can be quite critical of house style at both state and private press houses. In a weekly class exercise during the fall term of 1996 one GIJ instructor used close readings of current Ghanaian newspapers to point out the journalistic flaws in the leads of private and state news stories. A lecture in early December focused on the front page of the *Daily Graphic*. The instructor took issue with the lead of a prominent story, a story concerning the emergence of FM radio stations in the Central Region. Opening with a conventional who-lead, this story was framed in the self-congratulatory rhetoric of the president, commissioning the new state-supported local FM station. "Who commissions the project is not important," the instructor insisted. "The most important issue is simply that the Central Region now has FM," a development with important implications at local, regional, and national levels. Obscuring the real news with the authoritative comments of the president, the writer left out basic information such as how to tune into the new FM frequencies, a vital piece of information for audiences in the Central Region. This critical commentary sparked a lively discussion in class:

> Student: But the president is the leader of the country and people may feel that what he says should lead.
> Student: But then, every day J.J. is commissioning some project.
> Instructor: Somebody said that if someone puts up his own house and invites J.J., he will come and commission it (laughter). The journalist for this story should rather have talked to companies, advertisers, and listeners in the Central Region to get their views on this FM station.
> Student: It is an open secret that *Graphic* is an NDC [ruling party] paper. It is possible that the editor likes that kind of story so the reporter writes it to please the editor.
> Instructor: One journalist went with the Secretary of State to a construction site in Accra for a story on women workers. The journalist wrote the story about the workers with only two lines on the minister. The minister became very angry because he brought the reporter to the story and financed the trip. This kind of preconceived bias is destroying the profession.

This surprisingly critical perspective in a state training institution puts many GIJ students in a curious position when they go on practical attachment to the state press houses in their second year at GIJ. When I came to work at *Graphic*, I joined a new group of students coming for their "practicals." In our first week there the editor, Elvis Aryeh, called us into his office for a group meeting to introduce himself and welcome us to the paper. After a speech on hard work and professional dedication, Aryeh asked us if we had any questions.

Hesitating, one young woman politely raised her hand. "Sir," she said, "we have learned that things are somewhat different here than what we have been studying at GIJ. It seems we are not using the five Ws and one H in our leads."

"Oh, but you should always use the five Ws and one H," Elvis objected. "We always use them in our leads at *Graphic.*" Aryeh then went on to give a lesson on the inverted pyramid, stressing that journalists must stick to that format for their news stories.

After some time working at *Graphic,* most journalists eventually reason that what they learn at GIJ is just "theory" and not always adequate to the practical demands of the situation.

Chain-Quoting

After the lesson on leads, students at GIJ learn to organize the information for a story in descending order of relevance, structuring the news story in the form of an "inverted pyramid." The inverted pyramid is designed in the interests of both readers and editors. When stories are structured this way, readers can get the most relevant information without necessarily reading all the way to the end of the story. Editors prefer the inverted pyramid form because they can easily cut off the end of a story to fit an allotted space on a page without worrying about losing the most vital elements of the story. Since *Graphic* stories are so often focused on the commentary of public speakers, the inverted pyramid organizes a chain of quotes roughly in descending order of authority, and not necessarily relevance. Or, rather, the relevance of public commentary is not so much in the substantive content, but more in the rank of the speaker, the performative function of his message, and the assimilation of his rhetoric in the larger narratives of state hegemony. These rules of hierarchical quoting are not hard and fast; journalists may exercise their best judgment when lower-level speakers make more informative statements at assignments. However, statements by the president, his wife, or one of his ministers will trump any other informative comments at an assignment.

> At certain times, you go for an assignment, the minister may not make the big news and the reporter will try and get something from him to start the story. . . . The newsmaker is the best person to be used, his name. But if you use another person—who is this? When you use the minister, it's attractive. I went to Press Freedom Day, Mahama was there, the Deputy Minister of Communications, but the General Secretary of Ghana Journalists Association seemed more touching as far as press freedom but I wrote, I had to use . . . I wanted to write two stories, one about how PRINPAG [Private Newspaper Publishers Association of Ghana] would sanction journalists who violate the GJA *Code of Ethics.* The editor says that the minister makes the news, so try and get something to open from the minister and then bring in what the GJA man said. (Geoffrey Yakubu)

While the who-lead sets an authoritative frame (subsuming the content of any story in the narrative of state beneficence), the common practice of *chain-quoting* (my term) often structures the rest of the story according to the comments of other official participants at an assignment, in descending order of formal authority and relevance. Sometimes an assignment features a minister making an appearance at a public function, such as a school graduation. Since the actual event is dominated by the minister, the resulting story is consequently dominated by several paragraphs from the minister's speech while the comments of other officials receive only brief and cursory treatment at the end of the story. Other assignments feature a variety of authority figures whose contributions are organized according to their rank and the "newsworthiness" of their comments. An example of this prevalent practice of chain-quoting is found in an article on the launching of an environmental project, appearing in the center spread of *Graphic* on May 6, 1997.

The Minister of Environment, Science and Technology, Mr J. E. Afful, has reiterated the ministry's mandate to help identify and find solutions to the pressing environmental problems affecting the country.

Mr Afful said this when he launched the PACIPE-Ghana program in Accra yesterday.

PACIPE is the French acronym for Regional Technical Assistance Programme for Awareness and Information on the Protection of the Environment.

It is aimed at protecting the environment in six West African countries, namely Benin, Cote d'Ivoire, Ghana, Guinea, Guinea-Bissau, and Togo.

Dr Kwabena Osei-Bonsu, National Director of PACIPE, said it is funded by the European Development Fund and coordinated by a secretariat in Cotonou, Benin.

He said it is not designed to duplicate any existing information dissemination programme in the country, but to support national and local initiatives in the area of environmental education and information.

Dr Osei-Bonsu said the goal of PACIPE is to effect positive change in people's attitudes and behaviors towards the environment.

He said PACIPE has identified four projects for intervention and support.

Dr Peter Acquah, Executive Director of the Environmental Protection Agency [EPA], said the aims and objectives of PACIPE are consistent with what the EPA hopes to achieve through its educational programmes.

He said PACIPE can therefore support the EPA to provide training in information and education for its regional staff, as well as organize environmental campaigns to encourage pupils and students to participate in programmes to address community issues, among others.

In a speech read on his behalf, Mr Javier Puyol, Head of the European Union [EU] Delegation in Ghana, said under the EU budget, a number of projects are currently being considered by the commission.

He said these include a government proposal on forest certification and an NGO request for support to raise the awareness for the protection of a sensitive lagoon and coastal ecosystem from further degradation.

Mr Alexander Dzogbenuku of Impact Art Limited was presented with CFA 100.000 for designing the PACIPE logo.[8]

The semiotic implications of who-leads and chain-quoting emerge in a close examination of the structure and content of this story. The lead is a typical who-lead citing the honorable minister. A strikingly empty quote with very little relevance to the substance of the assignment, the lead quote is quickly abandoned as the reporter skips to the elaborated "neck" of the quote, placing the context of the speech in the second paragraph. Next we find some background information that seems to emanate from the National Director of PACIPE, whose comments follow. In comparing his relatively substantive and relevant input to the Minister's quote, the real function of the who-lead becomes obvious. If the story is about the launching of an environmental program, why would a reporter not foreground the program director's explanation of the proposed projects of the new program? Or is that really the news here? After the PACIPE director makes a few points, the Director of the EPA emphasizes that PACIPE, an NGO, is working in coordination with the government, to "support" and "provide training" and "organize campaigns." Thus the EPA director demonstrates the firm and productive alliance of the state with this foreign source of aid while simultaneously subordinating the work of the NGO to the effective development apparatus of the state. The comments of the EU representative add further detail to this theme, mentioning EU support for both government and NGO initiatives. Since Puyol failed to show up, his comments are placed at the end of the story even though he is indeed a bigman. Finally, the logo designers are presented with a check, which further supports the subtextual notion of the lucrative future of Ghana's alliance with this international NGO, perhaps a trickle-down effect. Thus the chain-quoting in this story emphasizes consensus and coordination of foreign and local development initiatives under the authority of the state.

Big English

Since who-leads and chain-quoting are prominent features of house style at *Graphic*, journalists are highly skilled in the reconstruction and attribution of public rhetoric. These are relatively easy tasks when the printed speeches of principle speakers are distributed to journalists at the end of the assignment. Such speeches are frequently written in an erudite rhetorical language, popularly called "Big English," that lends itself particularly well to who-leads. Examples of who-leads cited earlier reflect the Big English in the public speeches of state officials. Another front-page article from August 8, 1996, provides a further example:

> Mr John Atta-Quayson, National Co-ordinator of Free, Compulsory and Universal Basic Education (FCUBE), yesterday assured that the programme will be pursued gradually to rectify all anomalies that would inhibit its effective implementation.
> He said the aim is to ensure that the programme attains the objective of its implementation.

The cumbersome, officious vocabulary in vague and paternalistic assurances of "effective implementation" mark this mystifying English as truly big. Not only news stories, but editorials, many features, and several regular columns (e.g., those of K. B. Asante and R.B.W. Hesse) adopt this pontificating language. An essential feature of *Graphic* style, Big English is a distinctively postcolonial linguistic strategy, poaching on the symbolic capital of the colonizer's language while simultaneously drawing on African features of authoritative oratory.

A number of Ghanaian linguists (Yankah 1995, 1989; Saah 1986; Nketia 1971) as well as many other Africanist scholars (Furniss and Gunner 1995; Piot 1993; Finnegan 1976) have described the strong emphasis in West African societies on linguistic ability and propriety. Several scholars note that Africans form distinct opinions of one another according to their everyday speaking styles, creativity, and mastery of forms (Barber 1991). According to Ghanaian linguist Kofi Saah, embellished language signifies wisdom whereas "one who indulges in plain speech is considered ordinary" (1986, 368). Most of the literature on African linguistic practices, however, focuses on the role of public oratory in the construction and maintenance of authority. While earlier studies emphasized the rigidity of forms, the subordination of content, and the systemic containment of dissent, more recently scholars have demonstrated how these same linguistic forms open up multiple possibilities for individual creativity and renegotiation of social relationships.

In an Akan chief's court, the authoritative pronouncements of the chief are publicly rendered through his professional orator, the *okyeame* (or "linguist," as early ethnographers translated the term). A chief never addresses the court directly, nor is anyone allowed to address him but through the okyeame. Through this highly trained linguistic professional, the chief's speech is embellished with proverbs, metaphors, and idioms designed to display his mental agility while situating chiefly judgment in historical precedent and popular consensus (Yankah 1995; Casely Hayford 1903). The density of linguistic techniques used by the okyeame renders the chief's pronouncements highly allusive, polysemic, and even obscure. Situated in the pageantry of an Asante court, the baroque quality of courtly language parallels the material wealth displayed in a diverse array of gold regalia, kente cloth, stools, and servants—together symbolizing the wealth and accumulation of the Asante state (Price 1974). Asante historians (especially McCaskie 1995, 1983) have emphasized the importance of these public performances of stately wealth, essential to the legitimacy of an Asante chief.

State officials are certainly not chiefs,[9] but they face a similar need to reinscribe their authority as African leaders through embellished oratory at public ceremonies. Mbembe (1992, 4) has described the penchant of African leadership for continual "dramatizations of its own magnificence," through excessive displays of language and wealth. While English is comparatively poor in such embellishing tools as proverb and metaphor, colonial authority impressed on Ghanaian political culture a rich bureaucratic vocabulary, signifying an ethnically transcendent governmentality and the elite trappings of British education. As the erudite English of nineteenth-century Ghanaian newspapers indicates, English-educated Africans in the colonial period deployed an officious style of language in an effort to position themselves for participation in colonial government, hoping eventually to inherit the authority of the British. Thus early versions of Big English reveal the attempts of this new class of African elites to convert their foreign-acquired intellectual capital into politically effective social capital at home. While Akan courtly language alludes to the "traditional" wisdom of ancestors, Big English appropriates the authority of the British in the construction of the "modern" hegemony of the nation-state. As the density of linguistic embellishment indicates the material wealth and accumulation of the Asante state, the density of bureaucratic language indicates the intellectual accumulation of foreign-educated African elites and their access to crucial flows of foreign trade and development aid. Since the adoption of the Structural Adjustment Program, the World Bank, and the IMF (along with numerous aid and development agencies) have reinforced and expanded this bureaucratic vocabulary among state officials, requiring constant textual and dialogic performances of it as a condition of further support.

In response to the excessive pageantry of the state, Mbembe also describes the popular tactics of parody and irony that "kidnap power and force it, as if by accident, to contemplate its own vulgarity" (1992, 12). If Big English has become a strategy of constructing and mystifying state authority, it has also been appropriated as both a tool of resistant confrontation in the private press (more on this in chapter 5) and a target of popular derision. In his collection of essays, *Woes of a Kwatriot: No Big English* (1996), linguist and popular columnist Kwesi Yankah makes fun of the pompous language of the state and the mystified responses of Ghanaians. Like the rumors and anecdotes described by Mbembe, Yankah's spoof of Big English reveals the suppressed banality of bodily functions beneath the elaborate and euphemistic rhetoric. This parody, spoofing a Secretary of State's visit to the poor district of Kraboa-Coaltar, appeared in Yankah's column for the *Mirror,* the entertainment weekender affiliated with the *Daily Graphic.*

> The gross per capita income of this our national metropolis has satisfactorily progressed unabated; but lest we are blinded by the rapacity of our conceitedness, let me on behalf of the government pontificate that our modest economic growth is bound to pale into nothingness if pomposity clouds our ocular apparatus and kyinkyinga (kebab) overwhelms our national appetite.
>
> The present recovery programme implies a condition of economic malaise and surgical liability, such that measures ought to be instituted to arrest the unimpeded decline of our economic sewerage and political sanitation. (1996, 1)

Sparing no one, Yankah pokes fun at members of the audience who either fall asleep or nod respectfully, pretending to understand.

Missing in Yankah's parody is the figure of the *Graphic* journalist, a well-dressed stranger in the front row, politely asking the Secretary of State to clarify his position on the implementation of the new measures specified in his speech. Following the ceremony, the journalist would wait for his copy of the speech and then make his way back to the office, marking sections of the speech for use in the verbatim who-lead.

Speaking for the Chief

Printed speeches are not always available, however. Ghanaian journalists are often forced to rely on sketchy notes, lacking tape recorders or training in shorthand. Particularly when officials make impromptu comments or respond to questions, a journalist must rely heavily on memory and a sense of the speaker's intended meaning. A further complication, state officials cannot always maintain the authoritative rhetorical style when speaking off-the-cuff and sometimes make grammatical and even factual errors. President Rawlings was particularly renowned for this. When I asked journalists what they would do if a minister or other government official spoke badly or falsely at an assignment, they either denied that such a thing ever occurred or said that they simply would open the story with the occasion-lead instead. What I witnessed, however, is that journalists with the state media (*Graphic* and the Ghana News Agency, in particular) routinely transform the rough, extemporaneous comments of state officials into the authoritative and officious style of Big English.

Thus the experience with Kweku Tetteh, described at the start of the previous chapter, is merely a variation of a general practice. While journalists everywhere are forced to reconstruct events and comments from memory, *Graphic* journalists rely on a specific kind of language with a particular set of themes to imagine what an authoritative speaker said or intended to say.

Writing another story with a senior state journalist, we discovered that neither of us had taken notes on the speech of a deputy minister, the third or fourth speaker at this particular event. Since his comments were necessary to complete the sequence in a chain of quotes, my partner on the story composed an official-sounding comment that fit quite well into the cooperative dialogue portrayed in the story. Through some subtle facial expression, I must have inadvertently conveyed some hesitation about this rather loose but nicely worded quote. The senior journalist told me not to worry, that the official would never complain that he was misquoted. Again, the point here is not that we "made something up" but rather that our best guess at what the deputy minister had actually said followed a common set of expectations for official speech, consensual public dialogue, and interpretive practice.

Official sources not only tolerate such constructive quoting practices, many have come to rely on *Graphic* journalists to transform their statements into official rhetoric. On assignment to the Department of Wildlife, Sebastian Kwesi Mensah and I were covering the launching of a study on the feasibility of cultivating Ghanaian pythons for export to Europe and the United States (at $175 per snake!). Arriving at the department, journalists with *Graphic,* the Ghana News Agency, and the Ghana Broadcasting Corporation met with some confusion as no one seemed prepared to give us an official briefing, even though we had been invited. Clearly embarrassed about the mistake, the assistant to the director assured us that he would give us an impromptu briefing on the project so that we would not go away empty-handed. We waited for an hour while he obtained permission from his boss to speak with us. Returning at last, he delivered quite a detailed lesson on the business of pythons. Since Ghana was no longer allowed to export bred animals to Europe, the Department of Wildlife was forced to come up with an alternative method of cultivation: capturing the eggs of wild snakes. As a junior official, he was reluctant to give us any sort of sensitive information, such as how much the project would cost and why exactly the European Union had rejected animals bred in Ghana. When questioned explicitly on this latter issue, the assistant seemed pressed between his obligation to give us a good story and his fear of circumventing his boss's authority. After vaguely and haltingly equivocating on the "doubts" expressed by the EU, the assistant seemed to sense the awkwardness of his comments. "But you can put it in your Big English," he instructed the group of state journalists.

And so we did. In the fifth paragraph of the story, appearing in the center spread of the January 16, 1997, edition of *Graphic,* our treatment of the sensitive issue read: "He said the report of the study will help clear the doubts in the minds of Europeans and other buyers which necessitated a ban on Royal Pythons from Ghana last year."

This example illustrates that the bigness of Big English is not so much in the vocabulary, which is not very remarkable in this case. Big English is not just big words. Rather, language is big when it meets the standards of official pronouncement, matching cultural and political expectations for what a bigman in the ministry should say. While the assistant was not a bigman in the Department of Wildlife, he was speaking on behalf of his boss and certainly wanted to observe the correct discursive procedures and represent the department well. When he felt that his speech was falling short of official standards, he requested that we complete the task of constructing the official language in "our" Big English. What is big about the language in our story, then, is the suppression of an apparently contentious issue in smooth, rhetorical assurances that the government will clear away all "doubts" standing in the way of prosperity, in this case the lucrative trade in pythons.

So Big English, who-leads, and speech-driven stories not only structure the news narrative around well-spoken authority figures, but also position *Graphic* in a specific interpretive role between that authority and the national audience. Interposed between the state and its audience, rendering the rough speech of state officials into the elaborate rhetoric of Big English, *Graphic* assumes a mediating role quite similar to that of the okyeame.

In societies throughout West Africa the formal oratory of chiefs and elders is rarely delivered directly to a public audience but rather is routed through a professional mediator who "smooths the rough edges" and "completes" the speech with linguistic embellishments (Yankah 1995, 19, 107). In Ghana, among the Akan and most other ethnic groups, professional mediation of public discourse is institutionalized in the role of the okyeame (Casely Hayford 1903, 68–75). In his excellent study of okyeame, Yankah shows how chiefly speech is rendered public through a combination of verbatim quoting and embellished "analysis," paraphrasing and improving without undermining the essential logic of the chief's commentary. Even in a society emphasizing oratic prowess, royal speech is often hurried and stuttering, requiring the professional linguistic treatment of the okyeame to make it eloquent and official. Often the okyeame is considered more politically sophisticated than the chief himself.

Similarly Maxwell Appenteng, the *Graphic* correspondent to the Castle Osu, the seat of the Ghanaian executive (equivalent to the American White House), described the politically complex guesswork of crafting the extemporaneous comments of President Rawlings into official discourse.

> We quote him verbatim; but we have been there a long time and we know what he wants to say. At times, he talks in quotes and then it can be a bit confusing. He has a certain kind of philosophical talk so if he starts something then you know what he is going to talk about. At times, to someone new, he may not be making much sense; but immediately we know what he is driving at. Mostly when he has a prepared speech, he doesn't read all, he puts aside and talks extemporaneously. We have to know what he wants reported and what he doesn't want reported. We can do the gatekeeping ourselves.

Trained in a "modern" discursive profession, *Graphic* journalists are certainly not in any literal sense the okyeame of the state in general or the president in particular. As Ghanaians, however, their sense of discursive propriety is shaped by the formal authoritative performances of elders and chiefs at frequent ceremonial occasions (durbars, naming ceremonies, weddings, funerals, etc.) as well as everyday forms of discursive address (visits, requests). Both ceremonial and everyday discursive situations are often mediated through a third party who perfects both authoritative and appellant speech while softening and managing public controversy. The discursive situations at invited assignments to state ceremonies invoke these pervasive notions of discursive propriety and authority for both state officials who deliver authoritative oratory and state journalists who relay and interpret it for the public audience.

Yankah describes how okyeame are employed to manage the critical dangers of face-to-face interaction by "softening" immanent controversy through discursive techniques of indirection and politeness. Similarly positioned to manage official discourse, *Graphic* journalists are likewise motivated to emphasize authoritative consensus and elide controversy, as the above example with the Department of Wildlife illustrates.[10] The aversion to controversy is so strong that when confronted with contradictory accounts by rivaling state officials, Appenteng said he would simply avoid the story altogether.[11] Appenteng recalled the notorious incident in late December 1995 when a cabinet meeting reportedly erupted in violence when the president allegedly attacked his own vice president, punching him and throwing him to the floor. Appenteng heard reports of the violent attack along with the president's own outright denial of the incident. Appenteng wrote nothing, and *Graphic* published a story that quoted five members of the cabinet denying that Arkaah was beaten.[12]

This suppression of conflict combines with the discursive presentation of consensus, both among state officials and between the state and the state media. In both royal and state contexts the reiteration of authoritative pronouncements through a professional mediator presents those comments as the product of public consensus (albeit a performed consensus), lending "a measure of objectivity to the opinion expressed, implying that the speaker's viewpoint is not a subjective one, but one based on shared experience" (Yankah 1995, 20). When linked in a chain of supportive quotes by lesser state officials, authoritative comments become even more compelling and persuasive.

Presidential Contempt and *Graphic* Redemption

In moments of royal wrath, an agent is needed to contain the destabilizing forces capable of being activated. Thus boisterous or undignified remarks indiscreetly made by the chief are instantly softened and passed on without retroactive damage; for, since the royal speech act is not complete until relayed by the chief's okyeame, it does not take effect until that point either. (Yankah 1995, 19)

As Appenteng has indicated, reporters on presidential assignments are particularly pressed to represent the Head of State as a well-spoken authority, even when he digresses from his written speech to make embarrassing and often shocking comments. In 1998, the president gave a speech at the National Theater for the "official opening" of Emancipation Day celebrations, organized to commemorate the day in 1834 when Great Britain abolished slavery in the British colonies. Capitalizing on the holiday, the Ghana Tourist Board had organized week-long celebrations, attracting Africans from the Caribbean (where Emancipation Day is celebrated every year), as well as African American visitors and expatriate residents in Ghana

5. In the midst of a cabinet meeting, President Rawlings reportedly attacked Vice President Kow Nkensen Arkaah from behind with a powerful punch on the shoulder that sent the vice president sprawling on the floor. The accompanying photo shows Rawlings in dark glasses, pointing angrily in the direction of the reader (an insulting gesture). Below, the usually dapper Arkaah looks frightened and affronted in his bow tie and torn suit coat. Moreover, readers may be drawn to consider the president's choice of expletives—Rawlings' own Scottish father and Ewe mother were never married. *Courtesy of the* Ghanaian Chronicle, *January 7, 1996.*

(Hasty 2003, 2004). After a sing-along of Bob Marley's "Redemption Song" and a depiction of the horrors of slavery by the Ghana Dance Ensemble, several speakers from the diaspora gave speeches calling for a new spirit of Pan-Africanism, involving concrete policy changes like relaxed visa requirements and cultural and economic exchanges between Africans, African Americans, and Afro-Caribbeans.

As a reporter for the Ghana News Agency at the time, I sat in a section with the rest of the press corps, mostly journalists with the state press. My partner on the story, George Yeboah, pointed out a few familiar faces in the press corps, among them Maxwell Appenteng, *Graphic* correspondent to the Castle.

Then President Rawlings took the podium to address the international audience at this distinctively Pan-Africanist event. The president began his presentation by reading out a speech in typical Big English, welcoming the guests from the diaspora and calling vaguely for a new era of economic emancipation in Africa. After about ten minutes of this rhetoric, it appeared that most of the press corps were restless and bored. Then the president paused and looked up from his speech, appraising his audience. "You know," he said, "I don't even know what cocaine looks like."

Slumped over with boredom, we sat up with a start at this provocative non sequitur. I took the cap off my pen and began taking notes. I was the only journalist to do so, I noticed.

"And my wife doesn't know what cocaine looks like," he went on, describing how the private press had accused him of international drug dealing in outrageous front-page stories four years ago. "We took them to court," he said, "and the journalists were jailed for contempt. I asked if I could release them after a week, just to teach them a lesson; but I was told no, that I had no jurisdiction over the courts."

The context to this seemingly off-the-wall reference was that the editor of the paper that first ran the story, Kofi Coomson of the *Ghanaian Chronicle*, was currently in court facing criminal charges of seditious libel based on that story. Furthermore, two other private press editors, Harruna Attah of the *Statesman* and Kweku Baako of the *Guide*, were then in prison for contempt of court in the proceedings of a civil libel case for allegedly misquoting the First Lady. In this context, the president was obliquely responding to popular outrage over the prison sentences and widespread criticism of the conciliatory relationship between Rawlings and the judiciary—many were saying that Rawlings himself had ordered the imprisonment of the journalists. Inappropriate as the venue might have been, at least Rawlings was finally addressing the controversy in public. Out of the murk of Emancipation rhetoric, I thought, at least we might get a relevant comment on something in this speech.

But before completing that thought, Rawlings moved on to another argument, launching a diatribe against an international businessman named Aggrey. Born in Ghana, Aggrey currently resides in the United States, skipping continents in his spurious business dealings and somehow swindling the Ghanaian government out of some money. After explaining his troubles with Aggrey at length, Rawlings finally concluded with a reference to the policy changes proposed by previous speakers. "So you see," he said with deliberate gentility, "you must understand us if we are reluctant to relax our visa requirements. You must understand."

As his audience was still piecing together the logic of this connection, Rawlings delivered the ultimate blow. "Forgive me," he said smiling, "but I was thinking to myself that the slave trade could have been a blessing in disguise."

Someone in the audience shrieked. People were shifting in their seats uncomfortably, and whispers rippled through the crowd. I stopped scribbling and looked around the press section, but, unlike everyone else, the journalists did not seem too surprised at this shocking statement. Envisioning the impossible headline and the who-lead that might be based on this comment, I realized why I was the only one taking notes.

The slave trade was very unfortunate, Rawlings continued, but some good had come out of it. In the same way that the atomic bomb had sparked the ecology movement, he reasoned, the slave trade had "helped to build an army of disciples around the world."

Throughout this performance I noticed George sighing and looking slightly aggrieved (but not particularly surprised). As we left the ceremony I searched for some way to elicit his honest opinion without entirely revealing my own (my political leanings were by then pretty obvious but I still wanted to avoid leading questions, especially with my immediate supervisor).

"That was some speech," I said tentatively.

"It was very unfortunate that the President used this forum to go on like that. This is not the forum for that kind of talk," George said, agitated. "He is just confusing these people from the Caribbean who don't need to hear about it."

"You mean the Aggrey part?" I pressed.

"As for that story, I would like to hear Aggrey's side because I bet Aggrey could be someone who got a contract and the government wanted him to work for the party and he refused," George explained. "So Rawlings is now smearing his name in public. It wouldn't be the first time Rawlings did that."

"I was wondering if the whole speech fit together logically," I ventured, an admittedly leading comment but I really wanted to know what George thought.

"Sometimes you really wonder about this man," he said, disgusted. "That speech was so inappropriate, such an anticlimax to the ceremony."

Certainly inappropriate, I thought, but also provocative. A journalist could pursue these issues for several great stories: maybe an investigative story on Aggrey, a feature on how Ghanaians reason historically about slavery, a front-page story on Rawlings' fighting words against the private press.

On the way back to the office I was silently speculating what kind of story we would actually write for GNA on Rawlings' speech. As if confirming my suspicion about the only kind of story we could write, George concluded, "Rawlings said nothing relevant today at all."

> Accra, July 30, GNA—President Jerry John Rawlings today called for a strong bond between Africans on the continent and those in the Diaspora to ensure unity and progress of the black race.
>
> "If the nations and peoples of Africa and of the Diaspora can come together with determination to build a strong economic base, our people can live in peace and dignity," he said.
>
> President Rawlings was speaking at the official opening ceremony of the First Emancipation Day celebration to be hosted by Ghana in Accra. . . .

Rawlings' musings on slavery were rendered thus:

> President Rawlings recounted the atrocities of slavery and said the sacrifices made by Africans should spur them on to a greater sense of unity and well-being.

Two stories were written by GNA on the Emancipation Day celebrations, one for the speech and another for "color," meaning the pageantry: drumming, dancing, costumes, themes, and so forth. No story was ever pursued by GNA on the troublesome Aggrey. Likewise, Rawlings' defensive condemnation of the private press was simply ignored.

The next morning I checked the *Daily Graphic* to see how Appenteng had covered the story. Emancipation Day filled the front page, with two stories and a large photograph. A smaller story captured the "color" of the event, while the lead story presented Rawlings' speech.

AFRICA NEEDS ECONOMIC FREEDOM
BY MAXWELL APPENTENG

> President Jerry John Rawlings said yesterday that economic emancipation of Africa is the greatest task confronting the present generation of African people.

6. Front-page coverage of the opening ceremony of Emancipation Day in the premiere state newspaper, the *Daily Graphic.* Note the article on ceremonial "color" in the upper right and the "who-lead" article on Rawlings' speech in the lower left. In the photo Rawlings, in funeral cloth, ambiguously gestures (to the past? to the diaspora? thumbs-up?) under a banner for the Ministry of Tourism. *Courtesy of the* Daily Graphic, *July 31, 1998.*

He said the emancipation which has come about because of a passing of a law which changed the status of a man from a piece of property to a free man is merely giving back what was already his basic human right.

President Rawlings, who was speaking at the official opening of the First Emancipation Day celebration in Africa, noted that the next step in the process of emancipation cannot be handed to the African by some external entity.

"It can only be achieved through our own efforts, our own soul-searching, our struggles to achieve discipline, justice and orderly development," he said. . . .

As journalists with the state media, we uniformly depicted the event as a rhetorical tribute to economic pan-Africanism and development rather than the national embarrassment that I actually witnessed. Yet no collaboration between the *Graphic* and GNA was ever necessary to suppress Rawlings' scandalous and inappropriate comments. In my thirteenth month of field-work on the press in Ghana, I knew that Appenteng, George, and I were just doing our job.

3

Practice and Privilege
in the State Media

On Graphic Road, the offices of the *Daily Graphic* sprawl for half a city block in an industrial area shared by the state-owned Accra Brewing Company (makers of Club beer) and the Mitsubishi auto parts plant. As a state newspaper, *Graphic* is housed in a large, walled compound with separate buildings for reception, newsrooms, typesetting, and printing presses. Going to work, journalists pass the guard station at the outer door of the compound, through a parking lot filled with the cars of the editorial staff and the vans used to transport journalists and newspapers, proceed past two reception points, and then climb the steps to the air-conditioned offices of the *Daily Graphic* and its sister weekender, the *Mirror*.

Monday through Friday journalists report to the newsroom by 9:00 A.M. and leave work at 5:00 P.M. During the day journalists usually cover an assignment in the morning and then return to the office to write and submit their stories before the editorial conference at 2:00 P.M. Journalists must explain any unusual delay in returning from an assignment. On Saturday journalists go directly to their assignments and then report to the office in the afternoon, leaving work a bit earlier than on weekdays. Some *Graphic* journalists have Sunday off; but many work some part of that day as well. Journalists are jokingly criticized for going to church instead of coming to work on Sundays. With so much time invested in their jobs, *Graphic* journalists have little time left over to participate in civil or political society outside their professional role as state journalists. This might seem to confirm Ayeboafoh's vision of the professional journalist lifted free from the politically charged social system and performing the neutral task of information transfer between institutions and groups. In reality, of course, the state media occupies a structurally partisan position within the system, making the job of the state journalist deeply political. The monopoly that the job exercises over the lives of state journalists crowds out opportunities for alternative social or political activities. In place of alternative civil and political ties, journalists come to rely primarily on relationships formed on the job to provide them with opportunities for advancement and accumulation.

This control over a journalist's time is matched by a control over the professional spaces of state journalism. Unlike the bustling public offices of the private *Ghanaian Chronicle* or the *Independent,* the *Graphic* newsroom is housed on the second floor of an internal building in the compound, removed from public access and mostly restricted to *Graphic* journalists. Visitors must sign in with one receptionist and then explain their purpose to another, who will telephone the appropriate *Graphic* office for permission for the visitor to enter. Visitors must wear tags to identify them as visitors. On-site interviews are conducted in an office next to the reception area and not in the newsroom.

One afternoon Charlie Benson, the advertising editor of the *Independent,* dropped by to visit his girlfriend, a junior reporter for *Graphic.* I knew Charlie from my internship at *Independent* and, when I saw him in the hallway, I waved him into the newsroom. He hesitated and then backed away from the threshold, preferring to wait in the hall. Remembering his sociability with friends and visitors in his own offices, I was surprised at his reticence. When I saw him sometime later, he explained to me, grimacing, that he never liked to come to *Graphic* because they don't like visitors. The wisdom of this observation became more obvious when a young journalist on practical attachment to a private newspaper came to visit his GIJ friends on attachment at *Graphic.* Scrutinizing this suspicious stranger, the news editor suddenly spoke up, addressing the intruder for the audience of *Graphic* journalists. "Who are you? Are you with us?" Her manner was joking, but her message was clear, and the young man, explaining himself, retreated from the newsroom.

While the popular notion of the roving reporter, like Ayeboafoh's professional vision, emphasizes the freedom and mobility of the journalist, in reality the sequestered territory of state journalism is merely extended as journalists go out on their routine assignments to state functions and interviews in state offices. Each morning, reporters assemble in the newsroom and then go down to the parking lot to board the two *Graphic* mini-vans that deliver them to their assignments. Most of these invited assignments are located at government ministries, the courts, and embassies. Arriving at an assignment, journalists identify themselves as members of the state press (very rarely the receptionist will demand to see a press card) and then ask for directions to the appropriate office. At this point, any journalist for the private press would be turned away from an invited assignment at a state office.

On such assignments the state journalist is essentially a representative witness to some beneficent or particularly remarkable (or not) act of the state such as commissioning a development project, formally accepting a donation of international aid, or launching a state-supported trade fair. As a witness to the actions of the state, the journalist is expected to faithfully record the events, asking questions only for clarification. In months of participant-observation as a journalist, I never heard a state journalist pose a critical question while on assignment. One journalist explained to me that state journalists on assignment to the Castle only ask friendly questions because they would never want to embarrass the president. Such an explanation illustrates how the controlled spaces of state assignments are shaped by an underlying sense of social propriety that obliges state journalists (as subordinate guests in the state hierarchy) to politely participate in the construction and reinforcement of state authority. Since private journalists are excluded from nearly all state assignments, especially those at the Castle, these state functions proceed routinely and smoothly, sequestered from the disturbances of inquiry and dissent.

The Cultural Context of Invited Assignments

By formally inviting journalists into its own domain, the state places the processes of information exchange and journalistic representation into a particular socio-cultural context, using the situation to frame the roles and relationships of journalists and state officials. On assignment, state journalists observe widely held notions of appropriate behavior as invited guests in the house of patron or benefactor. Generally speaking, an invited visit to anyone's house is a somewhat formal occasion in Ghana (Yankah 1995). An invited guest in the home of a status superior is escorted to a relatively public place in the house to wait for the patron. The visitor is more or less confined to his assigned space, expected to wait patiently for the patron's arrival—the wait can be long and sometimes intentionally so. But it would be terribly rude for an invited guest to go snooping around, introducing himself to other members of the house. When the patron arrives, the guest will greet him appropriately and then wait for the patron to state the purpose of the invitation. As a subordinate, the guest is responsive to the address of his host, avoiding any direct verbal challenges or off-the-topic distractions from the purpose at hand. The host always offers some kind of refreshment, ice water or preferably a "mineral" (soft drink) and perhaps cake or biscuits. When requesting a service or errand, the host often gives a small cash gift to the guest to seal the arrangement. This format is, of course, highly variable, but the existence of a strong cultural frame is evident in the formality of invited visits, the recognition of a social and cultural code of conduct, and the humiliating consequences of any breach of that code. While on invited assignment to a state office, state journalists generally behave according to the logic of that cultural frame: waiting patiently, never straying from their assigned spaces, following the conversational lead of the host, and avoiding direct verbal confrontation. To some extent, all Ghanaian journalism is influenced by this model; but the tendency to deference and assent is more pronounced in the domain and presence of state authority.

One key to the way this model structures the substance of invited assignments as well the underlying relationships between journalists and state officials is the provision of refreshment and cash by the host to the guest. On nearly every assignment I covered as a *Graphic* reporter, the assignment ended with "Item 13," sometimes even printed on the program. When the official business of the assignment was completed, we remained in our seats to be served a selected mineral and cake or meat pie. The urge to provide us with something to eat was so strong that we were occasionally escorted to an office to wait while someone went out to fetch something from a street vendor. I never saw any journalist leave at this point to go back to the office and write the story, even when we were running late. Always, we stayed to eat the cake and drink the Fanta.

The ritual of Item 13 was predictably followed by the distribution of envelopes to each journalist. As a state journalist on invited assignments, we nearly always received a cash gift of 5,000 cedis ($2.50) each. A variation of the "dash" so common in other bureaucratic contexts (Price 1975), this cash gift from source to journalist is specifically referred to as "soli" (short for "solidarity") and is ostensibly intended to cover the journalist's taxi fare back to the office. The amount is easily twice the fare back to the offices of *Graphic* or *Times* and several journalists nearly always share a single taxi, splitting the fare. Soli is a widespread practice in West African journalism, and hardly confined to the state press. The difference in state journalism is that state officials often arrange for transportation back to the offices of the state media in addition to providing soli for journalists. Second, whereas soli is an occasional treat for journalists in the private press, state journalists on invited assignments receive it nearly every day. When I went to work for *Graphic* after several months of working for the *Independent,* one of my colleagues remarked, "Ei, now you are becoming very rich with soli every day!"

Castle Reporting

Clearly the invited assignment takes on a cultural meaning far beyond news gathering. The consequences of this model for the kind of journalism practiced by the state media are most striking at Osu Castle. Correspondents from the state media report each day to their assigned office there. They are met by an official with Castle Information Services/Public Affairs Secretariat who briefs them on the media assignments of the day and escorts them to the place where the president will receive them (usually the president's office or the Castle gardens). Journalists are expected to cover the intended angle of the assignment in their news stories. Their questions must be friendly and stick to the topic at hand. If a journalist finds the assignment itself irrelevant and chooses to write a story about some other interesting aspect or comment, he will have to face the wrath of the president the next morning. Maxwell Appenteng, the *Graphic* correspondent to the Castle, told me how he once covered the launching of an oil rig. During the ceremony the president, as he often does, strayed off the topic with some interesting commentary about prisons. In his story Appenteng emphasized the prison angle. The next morning Rawlings lashed out at him. "What is more important is why you came there, not what you find interesting!" the president fumed. "Why you came there" evidently means "why I summoned you there," defined by the representational strategies of the president and not by the journalistic standards (not to mention objectivity) of the correspondent.[1] When Appenteng recently visited the United States to participate in a media program, he was surprised to discover that correspondents to the White House have so much freedom to roam around and pursue their own stories, choosing where, when, and how to cover the president. Appenteng sees the central office of the state media at the Castle, combined with the coordination of Castle Information Services and the expectations of editors, as strong constraints on the freedom of Castle correspondents.

Surveillance, Identity, and Intimacy

Framing news coverage as an invited visit into the domain of a powerful patron carries a number of troubling contradictions and ironies, involving not only time and space but the control of social and professional identity as well. Professionally speaking, the job of the journalist on assignment is to cover the story and interview the newsmakers, suspending the constraints and biases of her own social identity. In this sense journalism is a fundamentally voyeuristic profession, a private institution of modern public surveillance. The state journalist, however, is not only an agent of surveillance, but is also the object of that surveillance. While all journalists in Ghana are required to obtain formal accreditation from the Ministry of Information, state journalists more often apply for special accreditation to attend especially formal state ceremonies and events involving interaction with the president. Agents with the Bureau of National Investigations (BNI) frequently pose as journalists at assignments, using press cards identifying them with the Ghana News Agency. This technique is used not only to spy on newsmakers, but to spy on journalists as well. Some journalists even believe that the BNI has student operatives at the Ghana Institute of Journalism. In the *Graphic* office state journalists say that they are regularly disciplined with the reminder, "Your name is at the Castle!" Castle Information Services monitors the performance of the state press, noting any critical content and reprimanding any journalist who repeatedly steps out of line. David Oakley, the former features editor at *Graphic,* described Castle Information Services as something "like a Spying and Investigations Bureau, spying on the work of journalists, reading the materials to see which of them are offensive to the government."

This spying extends beyond the printed text and into the personal lives of journalists with important postings, especially at the Castle. Maxwell Appenteng, the current Castle correspondent, told me that he first began to suspect that the Castle was keeping a file on him when the president addressed him by a personal name used only at home and known only by family and close friends. Through other such subtle indications, Appenteng has come to realize that people follow him around on the weekends to see where he goes and who he "moves with," his relationships with important businesspeople and politicians. If the tenets of objective reporting demand the formal suspension of social identity, the state subtly and informally reinscribes it, using surveillance to insinuate subordination and social intimacy (Herzfeld 1997) in the personalized hierarchy of the state.

Thus, while the tenets of their profession empower journalists to gather information about the president and deliver it to the Ghanaian public, that formal power is preemptively overwhelmed by the informal power of the state to gather information on journalists through its monitoring and surveillance mechanisms. The intimacy constructed through this informal knowledge, combined with a solidarity sealed through money, detaches state journalists from their professionally ambivalent position at the intersection of divided loyalties to sources and the public. Through the daily routine of invited assignments, heavy with insinuated power, journalists are repositioned as subordinate guests in the domain of their benevolent but disciplinary patron who claims for himself the right to dictate their journalistic responsibility to the public interest.

Relationships with State Sources

This intimacy forged through invitation, surveillance, and prestation provides a foundation for informal relationships between journalists and state officials, relationships of mutual need, obligation, and secrecy. As official witnesses to the daily rituals of state authority, state journalists are also privileged witnesses to the actual workings of the state, the constant "behind-the-scenes" controversies plaguing state institutions and "off-the-record" commentary by state officials. For example, watching the stiff behavior of two state officials together and chatting with secretaries in their offices (during the long wait to see a minister), a journalist may come to know of the factional antagonisms disabling a particular ministry. In the midst of such bickering, rumors circulate about the financial and personal indiscretions of rivaling bigmen. During Item 13 state officials may chat informally with one another, including certain trusted state journalists in confidential conversations about current affairs and office politics.

> One hears that there is infighting within a ministry. Or that a minister has used state funds to buy so-and-so [*sic!*] for his personal use. One hears that a minister is having an affair with so-and-so. You hear all kinds of information. I wouldn't say it's not meant for the public but then it borders on privacy. (Franklin Botsio)

Rarely, state journalists use this form of information as an anonymous tip, and then pursue the story through official channels. State journalists learn through frustrating experiences, however, that provocative stories aimed at state officials are not well received by *Graphic* editors. Presented with such a story, editors will label it "unbalanced" and demand that the journalist get the response of the accused official and then frame the story around the official's defense. As Isaac Opoku explained:

> Like you would hear this minister is having three cars or riding in a Pajero but if I should, I would go for the story, if there's anybody I can go to for the information and then present it to the news editor and see what to do. They would not have the courage . . . all that they would do is go back to the minister and get his side of the story. . . . The moment you go to get their side, that means cooling off and diluting the whole story.

Through this process state journalists learn that pursuing such stories is essentially a waste of time and not worth the risk. Journalists at the *Ghanaian Chronicle,* the leading investigative paper, claim that state journalists regularly leak their privileged information to the private press, hoping to see it in print even if they cannot pursue the stories themselves. One *Chronicle* journalist even named several state journalists that channel tips to him. Actually, I witnessed such a leak while accompanying the editor of a private newspaper around on his Sunday visits to friends and family. We stopped off to visit with the private editor's friend, a regional correspondent from the state media on home for holiday. The correspondent told my editor about a recent ruling-party rally in his region in which the president declared that too many members of opposition parties were defecting to the NDC just to obtain government contracts and privileges. After we left, the editor commented that this would make a great story for his own paper, showing how these defections to the ruling party are motivated by greed instead of loyalty.[2]

Every single *Graphic* journalist I interviewed strenuously denied leaking information to the private press, calling that practice a breach of professional ethics. In this case, the professional ethics that state journalists are so concerned to maintain seem less a matter of objective truth or social responsibility to the national interest and more a matter of their professional fidelity and commitment to the positional interests of their newspaper.

Most of the time journalists simply ignore the newsworthiness of their privileged information, passing it along in their informal discussions with other state journalists, as well as friends and family, but avoiding the official realm altogether. While many journalists (like Isaac Opoku) complain about external obstacles to using their inside information, they also explain their strategic silences as a kind of responsible self-restraint, stressing their concerns for "state security" and "the public interest."

This self-censorship is not driven by anything so simple as fear, repression, or any such violation of the right to free speech; rather, it is the product of an implicit contract between journalists and state officials. In 1995 journalists with the private press began pursuing the ubiquitous rumors of state corruption and abuse of office, coming out with a series of unprecedented stories exposing several cabinet ministers. In the midst of the multiplying exposés, state officials became especially nervous about the confidentiality of their informal talk—but not so nervous that they felt the need to stop talking informally with state journalists. During Item 13 of an invited assignment, one state official observed that the Deputy Minister of the Environment was building a chain of stores and a beautiful building even though he surely could not afford it on his official salary. With a *Graphic* journalist standing near him, the official went on to say that a number of ministers could be exposed by the private press if journalists should pursue these issues. Realizing the sensitivity of this remark, he then quoted a slogan of the ruling party, a Ga phrase meaning "plenty." In that context, according to James (the *Graphic* journalist who witnessed the incident), the slogan conveyed the message that, "Oh, all of us there, we were members of the party and there was no cause for alarm. You could say anything and nothing would come out. . . . *Graphic* understands." While the use of an NDC slogan certainly alluded to the common assumption that all *Graphic* reporters were with the ruling party, the use of this particular slogan in a conversation about corruption further reveals the basis of the solidarity between journalists and the state: their inclusion in the "plenty" supplied by the party, both officially and unofficially.

For state journalists, this "plenty" refers to the money, perks, and opportunities that journalists enjoy through their attachment to the state. But, more fundamentally, the "plenty" distributed by the state also includes the steady and reliable supply of official stories, the "daily bread" of a journalist working for a daily newspaper. Aside from the cakes and Fanta at invited assignments, state officials regularly feed exclusive stories to state journalists, under explicit guarantee of anonymity. Protection of anonymity is a primary way that journalists establish relationships of trust with important sources. Such a relationship can become a dependable supply of exclusive stories, enhancing a journalist's reputation. Geoffrey Yakubu demonstrates how these relationships are initially established:

> I used one police source then when the story appealed to them, the man said, "Ooh, you didn't use my name." So now if he has something, he will call and ask of Yakubu. He said, "There are some of you who call yourselves journalists, you will come and you will put us into trouble." But I've never come across that—where the people will call the office to find out who wrote the story. I've never had that happen.

While these relationships, based on tips and anonymity, seem straightforwardly strategic, *Graphic* journalists sometimes characterize the issue of anonymity in terms of their professional obligation to the protection of privacy. As Franklin Botsio explained, "Sometimes someone wants to maintain his own privacy so he may tell you, 'Though my name is Mr. Amuako or Mr. Afrifa, don't go and mention my name. Say a source close to the Ministry of So-and-So or the company of So-and-So.'"

So while state officials trust *Graphic* journalists not to reveal their unofficial commentary in print, they often have reason to publicize such stories anonymously. Important officials may want to advertise their own accomplishments or the failures of their rivals while disguising their political or factional motivations through anonymity. Subordinate workers in state offices are frequently afraid to speak to the press without getting permission from the boss and so demand anonymity.

In addition to feeding anonymous stories, state sources often share confidential information with journalists "maybe as a friend or for your personal knowledge—'oh, Charlie, we intend on doing this but it is not at the stage where we should come public with it, we are just preparing'" (Franklin Botsio). In another example the police may tell a *Graphic* journalist about a certain crime but demand that he refrain from writing the story while a sensitive investigation is under way. In such situations, sources often say, "As for you, *koraa* (Twi word for emphasis), you are from *Graphic* so I know you are not going to make use of it" (Isaac Opoku). Journalists who exercise restraint and protect the anonymity of state sources are rewarded in the long run with exclusive stories.

Thus the trust between state sources and journalists is a strategic alliance designed to preserve the basic livelihood of each. As Geoffrey Yakubu observed, they will give you the story because you are from *Graphic* and they can be sure you will not threaten their "daily bread." In other words, a *Graphic* journalist understands the differences between off-the-record commentary, an anonymous tip, and an official statement—without ever having to ask.

Occasionally, however, state sources press the limits of that contract with extraordinary demands for secrecy and control over publication. Journalists are usually responsive to requests for anonymity and recommendations to emphasize one particular angle of a story (as they often do at the Castle). But when excessive demands inhibit productivity and interfere with deadlines, journalists become resistant to sources, asserting the primacy of their own professional obligations. Geoffrey Yakubu tells how a source in the Ministry of Mines gave him information for a story and then instructed him to fax the story to her for approval before publication. He wrote the story but refused to fax it to her. Noticing some problems in the story, the news editor sent Yakubu back to the source for clarification. He rewrote the story and it was published, still without her prior approval of the text. The consequence of such subtle resistance is usually a complaining phone call from the source after the story is published. As Franklin Botsio reports, they often say, "'Oh, but I didn't tell you to put this in (the story)!'" Surprisingly, though, in this case, Yakubu received no such complaint, and his relationship with this particular source was not compromised. "Since then, the woman has been very helpful and anytime I want a story, she will give it to me," Yakubu says.

While state sources have come to rely on the anonymity of unofficial leaks and comments, journalists have come to rely on their right to publish official statements. *Graphic* journalists become particularly annoyed when state sources attempt to renegotiate the established boundary between the two. Franklin Botsio recalls a particular incident:

> On one occasion, someone said, "When you write, don't use this [particular information]." But I thought that it was the journalist's duty to perform. So there is no need telling me not to carry it—he didn't say it in confidence. It was part of the speech. If he said it in confidence, this is off-the-record, not meant to be reported. But it is in the speech. So I carried that part and he phoned and said

that this is not the time for it to come out. And I had to explain to him and he didn't take it kindly. If I'm damaging your reputation, that is a different story but I'm trying to say what he said without malice.

Both incidents reveal how resistant state journalists can be when sources become too demanding and manipulative.

As this struggle over representational control indicates, the strategic alliance between state sources and state journalists is deeply ambivalent. So long as journalists assume a passive role, crafting stories around official statements and intentional leaks, the trust remains secure. But those kinds of stories, while cementing relationships with state sources, actually do very little to further a journalist's popularity and professional reputation. As Sebastian Kwesi Mensah explained, "Anyone can write *'he said, he said . . .'* but if you are doing the analytical aspect, that one will make you a journalist." In the state press, analytical writing is done in features and editorials, although a certain critical analytical knack is also essential to writing investigative stories. While invited assignments are a necessary skill at the state press houses, it is through features and other self-initiated stories that stringers and students on attachment slowly build their reputations and eventually secure permanent jobs in the state press houses. As further motivation, features carry a great deal of prestige and earn 10,000 cedis per published article (twice the average soli). As journalists move up the professional hierarchy from junior to senior reporter, the pressure to produce self-initiated and exclusive stories increases. These stories may take the form of features, but more often result in a moderated version of the exposé, based on rumors of inner turmoil in the opposition parties or mass opposition defection to the ruling party, parallel "investigations" in response to private press exposés, and public statements of denial by officials accused of improprieties by the private press. If rumors of the eventual privatization of *Graphic* are true, state journalists may face an intensified imperative to produce the kind of political exposé and provocative analysis that boost circulation of any newspaper.

The imperative to generate their own stories (and not just wait around for assignments and leaks) forces state journalists to use the same techniques of information gathering employed by the private press, techniques developed in an environment of exclusion and state secrecy. Often high-ranking state officials simply refuse to talk to the press or, when they grant an interview, refuse to address the journalist's questions. The most common method journalists employ for eliciting direct response from a minister on a controversial issue is to indicate that they already have access to sensitive and potentially incriminating information. This information is gathered anonymously from lower-level employees in the ministry. Isaac Opoku explains:

> Every journalist worth his salt needs sources. Both high and low. Before you can get somebody at the top, you know, they always worry about you being a journalist so you have to go down low, then go up and seek clarification. It is only when they realize you have the information already that they begin to open up. But you can't just go straight to somebody, no matter how close the person is to you. The person is trying to protect his job.

Only then will a minister recognize his vital interest in a story and speak directly and strategically in an effort to control the means of representation.

Thus the professional agendas of a journalist and her newspaper are potentially at odds with the conservative interests of state sources. The trend has not gone unnoticed among high-ranking officials. Already somewhat resentful of any public query for information (ask any researcher), government ministers have become increasingly suspicious of the press in general in the wake of recent exposés in the private press. In his humorous feature, "No More Nice Guys . . .?" (March 18, 1997), renowned *Graphic* journalist George Sydney Abugri observes the consequences of this deepening suspicion in his transformed relationships with ministers. During his stint as a *Graphic* correspondent in the Upper West Region, Abugri recalls how the Upper West Regional Secretary, Edward Saliah, used to complain that Abugri was avoiding him, a complaint which seems to indicate that Saliah was seeking a closer and more productive relationship with local journalists. However, times have changed. Abugri describes his recent interview with Mr Saliah, now Minister of Roads and Transport.

> He sounded so cold I had to ask whether he had gotten my name right. Sure he had, he said in a tone quite uncharacteristic of him. He told me he was fed up with being a nice guy where the press is concerned. The man had been at the center of press and public criticisms over the sale of Ghana Telecom to a Malaysian business firm. Some sections of the press have suggested impropriety on his part in the sale of the company.
>
> Saliah repeated, "I am no more a nice guy." He told me he had appeared on radio and television, granted interviews with the press and appeared before Parliament to explain elaborately the sale of Telecom at U.S.$38 million "but the press seems bent on destroying my image." He said bad press had cast him in a new light among some friends and acquaintances and so and so on.[3]

In another recent interview Abugri described an even more adversarial response to press inquiries, albeit provoked by Abugri's unconventional, confrontational questions.

Quite recently, Lands and Forestry Minister Dr Kwabena Adjei made an un-
enthusiastic promise to answer some questions I have on the timber industry.
He did not hide the fact that he was not particularly enamoured to the press
these days and was only being civil and polite.

**I asked him bluntly if it was true that he is a self-proclaimed enemy of the
press. He replied that he appreciated the role of the press in society and
would normally not refer to the press as an enemy but added without seeming to contradict himself, that come to think of it, the press was his enemy al-
right.** (bold in original text)[4]

Again, the logic of this ambivalent and implicit contract was especially
striking in the relationships President Rawlings cultivated with his Castle
correspondents from the state media. In addition to their daily encounters
with Rawlings at formal invited assignments, members of the Castle Press
Corps often met informally with the president to discuss politics and current
events. Most Saturdays Rawlings invited journalists to his home for these
meetings. Occasionally he took them for a cruise at Akosombo or other such
privileged excursion. The president even telephoned certain trusted journalists at home or at work to ask for an opinion on an issue or to discuss the implications of a certain story.

These informal conversations and meetings followed a different dynamic than formal, invited assignments. While the preordained agenda and
formal etiquette of state meetings constrain journalists into passivity, these
informal meetings were orchestrated to open up a more lively dialogue between the president and the Castle Press Corps. Here, journalists were encouraged to take more initiative in the discussion and ask the president
about his position on a wide variety of issues (unlike an actual press conference, however, all this was strictly off-the-record). In turn, the president
used these occasions to quiz journalists about public opinion as well as the
latest political rumors and gossip circulating in town. According to Appenteng, "He asks the press corps, 'What is the latest in town?' and 'This is what
I hear; what is your opinion?' And then we discuss."

The combination of formal and informal meetings with state sources
sets up a two-way dynamic of formal and informal flows of information
with the state press crucially situated at the nexus of social representation.
Through the state media Rawlings aimed at controlling the means of formal
representation by organizing the flow of official information through the sequestered spaces of the state. However, hemmed in himself by that sequestered space, Rawlings also recognized the need to access unofficial forms of
public discourse, especially those that might counter and undermine the official realm. So, while the state press is charged with the official task of representing the formal activities of the state to the public audience, it is also

called upon to represent popular news and commentary to the private audience of the president. Rawlings also had access to such popular accounts by reading the private press (which specializes in this kind of news because it lacks access to official state news). But the one-way access of the reader is insufficient to establish the kind of informal and personalized control of information flow desired by the state. Denied access to the spaces, sources, and official activities of the state, the private press also escapes its primary means of representational control. This may explain why Rawlings so frequently and extemporaneously lambasted the private press in the midst of his most formal speeches and for his largest public audiences.

Cannily Rawlings used his informal meetings with the Castle Press Corps to consolidate his relationships with state journalists, differentiating them from their colleagues in the private press while simultaneously attempting to establish some kind of personalized (albeit indirect) link through state journalists to the private press. In these meetings he often picked out a provocative, oppositional story from the private papers and argued that it could not possibly be true. For instance, he took issue with a particular article in the *Guide* that accused the Deputy Director of Public Affairs of embezzling $50,000. Rawlings argued that the Public Affairs Secretariat does not even have access to that amount of money so how could any official there embezzle that much? By showing his exasperation with these alleged breaches of truth and public responsibility, Rawlings appealed to the professional commitments of journalists, even urging state journalists to confront their colleagues in the private press and enforce more rigorous standards in the profession.

Many journalists in the state press recognize that private journalists so often trade in rumors and speculation simply because they do not have access to official news. Most of the state journalists I interviewed argued that the private press would be less adversarial and more accurate if they were granted access to the Castle and other primary state assignments. Maxwell Appenteng and other Castle correspondents have appealed to the Public Affairs Secretariat (also called Castle Information Services or Castle Public Affairs) to include the major private papers in the Castle Press Corps. State journalists are ambivalent about their privileged access to state assignments in general and tend to resist efforts to divide them from their colleagues in the private press. Rather, they stress their common professional identity and urge the Ghana Journalists Association to lobby for the inclusion of the private press at state assignments, especially at the Castle.

When I spoke with the director of Castle Information Services, Mrs. Valerie Sackey,[5] she stressed that the exclusion of the private press from the Castle is purely a matter of logistics and has nothing at all to do with politics.

According to Sackey, the official rooms at the Castle used for press briefings are simply too small to accommodate a larger group of journalists. Setting aside the sheer unlikelihood of this logistical excuse, Castle correspondents report that many Castle assignments are actually held outside, in the Castle gardens, where space is not a problem. Sackey insists, however, that private journalists can only be invited to the Castle if the government builds a more spacious facility, a press center just outside the Castle grounds where all journalists could come for briefings. She indicated a specific site near the Castle gates where such a center could be built, but could not say if actual plans were under way to build it.

Under increasing pressure from professional groups and journals, the Castle took a surprising step in January 1998 by admitting a group of twelve private journalists, escorted by soldiers, to a press briefing held by the Minister of Communications, the Minister of Mines and Energy, the Cabinet Secretary, and the Director of Castle Public Affairs (the aforementioned Mrs. Sackey). So far this experimental briefing of the private press at the Castle remains an isolated incident.[6]

While journalists argue that the inclusion of private journalists at state assignments would improve the quality of political reporting in the private press, such a move would fundamentally transform the workings of the state information apparatus as well. Mrs. Sackey's disingenuous arguments to the contrary, this issue is not merely a matter of numbers and space but, more crucially, a matter of transforming the strategic nature of formal and informal relationships between journalists and state sources. With a history of mutual suspicion and outright antagonism between the state and the private press, private journalists could not possibly conceptualize invited assignments as formal visits in the domain of a powerful patron. Throughout the 1990s the editorial policies of some private papers were wholly dedicated to depicting Rawlings as the enemy, while most other private papers viewed the state with suspicion and resentment. Whereas state journalists are positioned within the state apparatus through practices of control and privilege, private journalists are positioned outside and in opposition to the state through practices of exclusion, detainment, legal harassment, and Rawlings' own frequent diatribes against them. Private journalists may be intimidated by the university degrees and other status advantages of state officials, but they are not obliged to observe the same implicit rules of politeness and passivity in the presence of the state. If private journalists are invited, the smooth routine of state functions could be disrupted by certain journalists who are less concerned about embarrassing the president and more concerned about boosting the circulation of their newspapers by confronting state officials and provoking controversy.

Although some argue that the inclusion of private journalists would improve their reporting and make them more accountable to the truth, a reciprocal influence on the state media may also result. If state journalists are joined by their private colleagues at state assignments, their common professional identity as journalists may be foregrounded, interfering with their subordination in the representational apparatus and perhaps making them more accountable for their routine passivity and deference to the state. If private journalists are asking direct questions, demanding information, and resisting state control over their stories, the implicit rules of appropriate behavior at state assignments may be rewritten. State journalists would most certainly take advantage of the new opportunities for news gathering.

Along with formal assignments, the informal relationships between state journalists and state officials would also be transformed by the inclusion of the private press in the domain of the state. Since private journalists are under very little obligation to observe the implicit distinctions between official statements, anonymous tips, and off-the-record commentary, state sources would have to censor their informal chat in the presence of the press or else read about it in the next day's headlines. Rather, the president and other state officials would most likely arrange to meet privately with certain individual state journalists for exchanges of anonymous and off-the-record information. At the Castle, it is doubtful that the president would feel comfortable inviting both state and private journalists into his home every Saturday for extended palavers (not to mention the Akosombo cruises). By proposing a site for the Castle press center just outside the Castle grounds, the Public Affairs Secretariat symbolized the renegotiation of boundaries that would follow from the inclusion of private journalists at the Castle. Faced with oppositional private journalists along with political allies in the state press, the Castle would further formalize and institutionally externalize journalism from the Castle.

Thus, while democratic reforms have done away with overt control and censorship of news at the state newspapers, the subtle game of interpolation and complicity among state officials and state journalists is played out in the same strategically structured field under the same strategically designed set of rules, a discursive regime naturalized as purely professional practice in the state media. While state journalists access the professional rhetoric of objectivity and public responsibility, their daily practices incorporate them, both professionally and personally, as subordinates in the operation and representation of the state. In the following chapters on the private press, I describe the very different set of textual and professional practices of news media that have been mobilized against the discursive regime of state news.

While democratic reforms have done little to change the nature of official reality in the state press, they have allowed for the emergence of new forms of journalism practiced outside the domain of the state, opening up new channels of creative expression and popular resistance to the conservative versions of reality promulgated in the pages of the *Daily Graphic.*

PART II THE PRIVATE PRESS

4

The Private Press and
Professional Solidarity

In the summer of 1999 private newspaper editors Harruna Attah and Kweku Baako were found guilty of contempt of court, each fined the equivalent of $5,000, and thrown in prison for thirty days.

The case against the two editors was this: the previous year their newspapers, the *Statesman* and the *Guide,* respectively, reported that the First Lady was complaining that her own sister had betrayed the family and the ruling party by marrying Harruna Attah, editor of the *Statesman.* Denying the story, First Lady Nana Konadu Agyeman Rawlings launched a libel case against the editors and filed an injunction against their newspapers, prohibiting the publication of any further libelous material while the case was still in court. For reasons that are not entirely clear, stories about the case continued to appear in both newspapers, condemning both the litigious hysteria of the First Lady and the government bias of the Supreme Court. Those stories led to contempt of court charges and, consequently, fines and prison sentences for Attah and Baako.

When the verdict was handed down on Friday, July 25, journalists for the private press mobilized immediately for an emergency meeting and formed an activist group, "Friends of Free Expression." The following Monday they marched through the streets of Accra, singing ("All We Are Saying Is Press Freedom Now!") and waving placards with slogans reading "Some Judges Are Jokers," "Prison or No Prison, We Will Write," and "Behind Every Dictator Is a Monstrous 1st Lady." The rally culminated at the Supreme Court Building where the journalists presented a petition to the Chief Justice, protesting the verdict and the stiff sentences.

At that time I was working as a journalist with the state-owned Ghana News Agency and was assigned to cover the rally along with two other GNA journalists. The premier state newspaper, the *Daily Graphic,* did not send a reporter to cover the story. Unlike many of the private journalists there, who were simultaneously participating in the demonstration and reporting on it, as state journalists we remained at the sidelines and quietly took notes. When we returned to the office, our editor, Mr. Ameyibor, took over the story and wrote the first half of it, portraying the rally as a colorful but peaceful event. Names of participants were listed but the particular substance of their protest was left out entirely, except to say that the group was protesting "what it called 'growing threats to press freedom.'" While the specific reason for the event seemed relatively unimportant to Ameyibor, his story did point out that the police were present but did not interfere. After Ameyibor finished, we took over the rest of the story and elaborated a bit, including some of the slogans (edited out) and mention of the Baako-Attah case. When our story was carried over the air later that day on Radio GAR and at the bottom of page 3 of the *Daily Graphic* the next morning (both state press institutions), all references to Baako and Attah had been cut, as well as any mention of the First Lady and the allegations of judicial bias. No doubt these were considered the "background details" of the story, simply cut for lack of space and air time. But the placement of the specific reason for an event in the final paragraphs of a news story is a curious journalistic practice—especially when other seemingly extraneous details (the loitering police) were foregrounded in the story.

The private press, as one might expect, covered the demonstration with big, dramatic front-page stories and outraged editorials. The front-page stories described in detail the ongoing struggle between the editors and Nana Konadu, and quoted grievances from the petition to the Chief Justice, alleging that the courts were using the law to cripple the media—in this case and many others. Editorials condemned the exorbitant fines and prison terms as excessive and disproportionate to the offense, lamenting that such punishment constitutes a threat to the very existence of the beleaguered private press. Coverage in the private press situated this incident in the larger struggle between an overbearing state and oppositional newspapers, a struggle waged in hundreds of libel cases filed by state officials against the private press.

Over the next few weeks the Friends of Free Expression held numerous vigils with impassioned speeches and rousing discussions on press freedom. In the idiom of human rights protest, one journalist launched a hunger strike and several others joined in. The president of the West African Journalists Association (WAJA) marshaled his international connections to journalists' groups and human rights organizations, demonstrating international support for the cause of the imprisoned editors. Leaning heavily on the language of human rights and free speech, private newspaper journalists

7. Front page of the private newspaper, the *Independent*, devoted entirely to coverage of the protest against the imprisonment of private press editors, Kweku Baako and Harruna Atta. Photos depict an opposition Minister of Parliament leading the protesters and editor Kabral Blay-Amihere presenting a petition to the judicial secretary. *Courtesy of the* Independent, *July 28, 1998.*

unanimously portrayed themselves as "watchdogs . . . ensuring fair play in all aspects of societal activity," essential to democracy and development.

This narrative of struggle between the post-authoritarian state and the private press in Ghana bears a striking resemblance to the recent scholarly literature celebrating the awakening of civil society throughout sub-Saharan Africa. While journalists themselves invoke the discourse of human rights and democratization, civil society scholars have largely ignored the press, seeming less sure that African newspapers are performing their liberal function as an arena of public debate and popular representation.

Indeed, since its reemergence in the early 1990s, the private press has tended to emphasize personalities over policy, often preferring sensational and ad hominem stories at the expense of balanced reporting and policy analysis. Front-page stories mix fact and opinion, frequently using rumor and anonymous speculation as primary sources. It is difficult to see how the *Statesman*'s recurring front-page exposés on the sex life of Nana Konadu have really furthered the cause of democracy in Ghana. While private press journalists have been instrumental in exposing corruption among state officials, they have also been responsible for a tedious preoccupation with big-men in urban politics, neglecting broader social issues especially in rural areas. Furthermore, while private journalists invoke professional ideals and the rule of law, some deploy unprofessional and illegal tactics such as stealing documents, impersonation, and culling stories from other newspapers with no corroboration whatsoever.

Throughout the 1990s President Rawlings publicly denounced the private press in these terms at any and every opportunity. In a speech a few days after the editors were jailed, he ranted against the "irresponsible sensationalism" of private newspapers and smugly referred to contempt of court charges as "our new weapon" against them. With no mention of his wife's involvement in the Baako/Attah case, Rawlings targeted his personal fury at the *Ghanaian Chronicle* for running stories culled from a foreign newspaper accusing the president of involvement in an international drug ring, smuggling cocaine through his diplomatic corps. In response to this story, Rawlings sued the *Chronicle* for criminal libel, a charge inherited from colonial law intended at the time to repress popular uprising against authoritarian rule. It is ironic that this post-authoritarian president whose very political legitimacy hinged on his revolutionary populism came to rely on repressive colonial statutes to defend himself against popular opposition. For his Western admirers, it is furthermore ironic that this role model of democratic reform resorted to neocolonial laws for legal ammunition in his all-out crusade against the most crucial private institution of liberal democracy.

8. This lead story reports on accusations by the president of the Ghana Bar Association that Rawlings is attempting to manipulate the judiciary. As the opposition party NPP repeatedly emphasized its own commitment to democracy and the rule of law, private newspapers continually depicted Rawlings as an unruly, authoritarian outlaw. *Courtesy of the* Ghanaian Chronicle, *March 20, 1997.*

Thus in print, in court, and in public speeches President Rawlings and the private press were engaged in an angry and highly personalized discursive war against each other throughout the recent decade of democratization in Ghana. If the scholarship on civil society has overlooked the press, it is perhaps primarily because both government and opposition seem so furiously engaged in mutual destruction and character assassination instead of the more genteel policy analysis imagined by the foreign supporters of democratic reform. But if we are to understand the reasons for the intense personal and emotional nature of this discursive contest, we must situate the struggle in the larger context of Ghanaian political culture, particularly since the revolution in 1981. In this context, the ad hominem and sensational attacks against the president, his wife, and his cabinet by the private press were a direct response to the daily front-page construction of Rawlings as a charismatic authority figure in the state press. It is impossible to make sense of the discursive practices of the private press without reference to its dialectical relationship with the state information apparatus, inherited by Rawlings from previous authoritarian regimes and crafted to suit his specific ideological project. Rawlings's singular rage against the private press revealed his recognition that control over national political discourse was essential to political legitimacy, even—and perhaps especially—in the new democratic order.

The Reemergence of the Private Press

Currently about forty private newspapers are produced in Ghana, nearly all of them published in Accra. About half are sports papers, and the other half focus on national politics. During the revolutionary 1980s publishing political newspapers became so dangerous that editors and journalists channeled their talents into weekly sports papers instead. Some ventured into veiled political commentary in pseudonymous columns for these sports papers; but outright political criticism only surfaced again after the repeal of the newspaper licensing law in 1991.

Both production and consumption of private newspapers are concentrated in Accra. Given the expenses of printing and staff salaries, only the proportionately larger readership in the capital can support private papers. Compared to the various regions, both literacy and political opposition are much higher in Accra, along with the concentration of wealth necessary to make newspapers affordable (the relationship between these factors is explored later). Moreover, in the linguistic plurality of the capital, people are more accustomed to transcending linguistic boundaries by discussing politics in the common medium of English, thereby broadening both the discursive field of politics and the potential circulation of English newspapers. Finally, in Accra, local politics is synonymous with national politics. Journalists pursuing local beats and assignments in Accra regularly produce front-page stories of national relevance, while "newsworthy" stories from the regions are more sporadic and generally less sensational. From the standpoint of both production and circulation, it makes more sense to publish a newspaper in Accra.

Despite the limitations, a few private newspapers are published outside the capital. These exceptions include the *Ashanti Pioneer* (Kumasi in the Asante Region) and the *New Ghanaian* (Tamale in the Northern Region, if that experimental paper has not folded by now). Another paper, the *Ashanti Independent* is produced in Kumasi but is typeset and published in Accra by the staff and printer of its sister paper, the *Independent.*

While the major private newspapers are based in Accra, a few follow the example of the state press by maintaining offices and correspondents in the regions. The Ghanaian *Chronicle* has offices in Cape Coast (Central Region), Kumasi (Asante), Takoradi (Western Region), Koforidua (Eastern Region), and Ho (Volta Region). The *Independent* keeps an office in Kumasi, devoted primarily to the *Ashanti Independent.* While the state dailies operate offices in all ten regional capitals, no private Accra-based newspaper has opened an office in the strategically deprived and underrepresented northern part of the country, consisting of the Northern Region, Upper West Region, and Upper East Region.

While virtually ignoring "the North," the two major private newspapers regularly publish stories by correspondents in nearby southern regions, and in the Eastern and Central Regions in particular. Unlike regular salaried staff in Accra, regional correspondents for private papers are usually "stringers," paid for each published news story.

Although the competition for readership is intense, the sense of solidarity among journalists for the oppositional private press is remarkably strong. The major private papers represent distinct ideological perspectives and social groups, but all face similar adverse conditions, including high printing costs, lack of equipment, exclusion from state functions, hostile and fearful sources, and difficult access to timely world news. In the early 1990s, economic conditions were so harsh that private newspapers could only afford to publish weekly, although many now appear biweekly and the *Ghanaian Chronicle* comes out three or four times a week. Unable to break the daily hard news, the weekly private papers turned to political commentary and investigative stories in order to compete with the state dailies. In addition to state competition, the systematic exclusion of private journalists from state sources and assignments, combined with lack of access to wire services, forced private journalists to design an alternative set of journalistic techniques, incorporating anonymous sources and popular rumor, and resulting in a unified discursive challenge to the conservative social imaginary depicted in the state media.

To capitalize on circulation, the major private papers tend to come out on different days of the week (e.g., the *Chronicle* on Monday, the *Statesman* on Tuesday, the *Independent* on Wednesday, etc.). Most of the private political papers use the same printer, LJS Colour Publikaxions [*sic*] Limited in the suburb of Dansoman. The printer can only meet the demands of so many private papers by staggering these major print jobs throughout the week.

While staggered publication is a competitive strategy among private papers, journalists in the private press rather interpret the daily appearance of oppositional newspapers as a common offensive against the state dailies. Strung together throughout the week, the private press amounts to a daily opposition paper, they often say, in an environment that has thus far made such a paper impossible. Although more and more private papers are now appearing two and three times a week, and various plans for private dailies are now in progress, the sense of common purpose among private journalists remains quite strong.

The Revitalization of the Ghana Journalists Association

Aside from common conditions, another reason for solidarity among private journalists is the emergence of the Ghana Journalists Association as a forum for the articulation of professional identity and discussion of common problems, standards, and goals.

Established in 1949, GJA was incorporated into the state apparatus by Nkrumah, who donated a building on the premises of the state-run journalism institute (Blay-Amihere 1996). When Nkrumah was overthrown in 1966, GJA was alienated from the state domain, but continued to publicly demure to state intimidation, remaining silent as each new ruler shuffled and dismissed the editorial staff of the state media and harassed the private media with draconian press laws.

In 1992, just as the new constitution rescinded the press licensing law, Kabral Blay-Amihere was elected president of GJA. Blay-Amihere has revitalized and politicized GJA, reorienting a compromised journalism club to "provide a bulwark for the defense and promotion of democracy and development," as he proclaimed at the 1995 Annual GJA Dinner Awards (Blay-Amihere 1996). Knowing from personal experience how government supervision, support, and intimidation have hampered the professional de-

velopment of both the state and private press, Blay-Amihere has transformed GJA into an organization for professional training and socialization
independent and often adversarial to the state. A magnetic and extroverted
character, Blay-Amihere has forged local and international links to secure
this legal, financial, and professional independence from the state. He has
reached out to forge links with international professional and human rights
organizations such as the Committee to Protect Journalists, Reporters Sans
Frontiers, the Index on Censorship, and Amnesty International. He has established productive relationships with foreign governments and governmental organizations (the United States Information Services [USIS], the
British Council, the European Union [EU], and Friedrich Ebert Stiftung
[FES]). The EU provides support for the International Press Center, housing
GJA staff. FES coordinates with GJA to sponsor frequent professional conferences (at least once or twice a month) on media ethics and press law,
among other topics. The multinational corporations Ashanti Goldfields,
Unilever, and the cable TV company M-NET now provide funding for GJA
events, largely through Blay-Amihere's continued efforts. At the end of his
second term as president he recalled the numerous accomplishments of his
administration:

- Establishment of the Ghana International Press Centre and a modern
  secretariat equipped with computers, vehicles, and staff.
- Membership of the International Federation of Journalists.
- Upliftment [*sic*] of the image of the GJA as a major playmaker on the
  media landscape.
- Publication of relevant literature on media and society.
- Ratification of the *Code of Ethics.*
- Guarantee of independence of GJA.
- Establishment of links with international media organizations—Com-
  monwealth Journalists Association, International Federation of Jour-
  nalists.
- Establishment of collaboration and partnership with international and
  local organizations—UNESCO, International Federation of Journalists
  (IFJ), Thomson Foundation, British Council, USIS, NEC, and M-NET
  —to promote professional standards and press freedom in Ghana.
- Co-ordination and organization of over 60 seminars and workshops on
  fundamental press issues.
- Granting of over 27 scholarships and study tours for journalists.
- Institution of the GJA Annual Awards Dinner Dance.
- Launching of a GJA newsletter.
- Institution of the GJA monthly media encounter.

- Empowerment of female journalists to participate in the mainstream of GJA crowned by the election of a woman to lead the GJA for the first time in 48 years.[1]

Under Blay-Amihere, GJA has played the leading role in the sub-region, establishing professional networks across national boundaries for the protection of human rights and freedom of speech. Blay-Amihere has organized the various journalism organizations in the Economic Community of West African States (ECOWAS) into a regional organization, the West African Journalists Association. Representatives from all states are invited to join GJA representatives at the Annual Conference on the State of the Media in West Africa. FES now publishes a yearly book of essays presented at the conference. In 1998 Blay-Amihere completed his second term as GJA president and began a first term (doubtless there will be a second) as president of WAJA.

As GJA has established a series of annual events and professional "traditions," a sense of professional culture has formed among journalists with the private press and the state media. The Annual Conference on the State of the Media provides one of very few opportunities for state and private journalists to openly discuss such controversial topics as bias in the state press.

At the 1997 conference in Kumasi, in December, GJA representatives from the state and private press held a panel on media coverage of the recent elections. Engaging in heated dialogue over bias and irresponsibility, journalists on all sides nonetheless displayed a mutual respect and commitment to common professional ideals. Some state journalists turned the issue of bias into a general problem, recommending that all journalists should stop "fighting the battles of the politicians." Others, however, admitted state intimidation in their daily practices (something I had never heard before in any context) and even cited specific examples.

Yaw Boadu-Ayeboafoh, the *Graphic* sub-editor, criticized the state television station for airing programs on rural development during the week of the elections. "There are cases where pipes are laid down by one government and then taken away after elections. The people at GBC (television) know what impact those images have on people," he said. Continuing in this vein, *Graphic* journalist Franklin Botsio (recall his insightful comments from the previous chapter) complained that his efforts at objectivity were thwarted as his stories were frequently changed and killed by editors. Incoming GJA president and private editor, Gifty Afenyie-Dadzie, replied that perhaps Franklin would be better suited to a different paper. Irascible and intensely political private editor Kwesi Pratt chimed in, "If you feel so strongly about your stories, Franklin, then come and give them to me—I'll publish them!"

This kind of professional dialogue combines with informal socializing at the dinners and dances that invariably complement the agenda of both the State of the Media Conference and the Annual Awards Night. Smaller conferences and press events at the Press Center nearly always end with refreshments and extended socializing. Although actual friendship between state and private journalists seems relatively rare (many private journalists spurn the very thought), GJA reinforces a common professional identity that challenges the polarized political commitments of both state and private newspapers. As GJA has increasingly politicized itself around the concerns of the private press, the continued involvement of state journalists in GJA events and growing opportunities for professional dialogue and camaraderie with private journalists may eventually strain the unspoken alliance between state journalists and the ruling government.

Through Blay-Amihere's various strategies of political and financial extraversion, GJA has become incorporated into an international network of human rights activism. Through these connections, GJA has come to promulgate a human rights discourse, defending free speech in particular and championing the tenets of liberal democracy in general. Cooperative projects with USIS and the British Council are often aimed at "promoting the institutions of constitutional democracy." As Ghana's pioneer in the global network of professional and political activism, Blay-Amihere is also the pioneering author of this human rights discourse among Ghanaian journalists.

Kabral Blay-Amihere

When I came to Ghana in September 1996 for my fieldwork, I had originally planned to start an internship with the *Ghanaian Chronicle,* the most popular private newspaper. When I arrived to set up the details of my internship, however, the editor of the *Chronicle,* Nana Kofi Coomson, was embroiled in a libel case and had traveled to Britain. So instead I sought out Kabral Blay-Amihere, who welcomed me to his newspaper, the *Independent,* and took me out with him on errands and assignments. As we circulated he told me bits about his past, his professional background, and his worldwide travels.

An Nzima like nationalist and newspaperman Kwame Nkrumah, Peter Amihere was born in 1953 to illiterate parents in the Western Region. He grew up with his mother and stepfather and eventually came to take the stepfather's name, Blay. His brother was a championship boxer. Peter Blay-Amihere went to school at St. Augustine's College in Cape Coast, Central Region. The initial site of the British occupation and the original capital of the

Gold Coast Colony, Cape Coast has long been associated with anglophile nationalism. An anglophone Fante elite established itself there in the late nineteenth century (Sampson 1969), attending mission schools and forging a gentlemanly discourse in English newspapers, a discourse that evolved into the fiery nationalism of the next century (Casely Hayford 1903, 171–81). No newspapers are published in Cape Coast anymore, but a legacy remains in mission schools and anglophile manners.

An outstanding student, Peter Blay-Amihere went to the University of Ghana at Legon for a degree in history and sociology and then took a postgraduate degree in journalism. Involved in student politics at the university, he took the name of Kabral, after Amilcar Cabral, the revolutionary in Guinea-Bissau. He changed the initial "C" to a "K" to make this unusual name seem more like a common Ghanaian name.[2]

After Legon, he took up the practice of journalism in 1976. Since journalism pays so little and involves an element of danger, university students, even those in communications studies, rarely consider journalism as a career. As mentioned earlier, nearly all journalists in Ghana are trained at the Ghana Institute of Journalism, a professional school (most apply to GIJ only because they were denied admission to a university). So impressively educated, Blay-Amihere has been able to command an unusual degree of respect from colleagues and government officials, as well as from diplomats and other international contacts.

In the early 1980s he was writing a popular column for the state weekender the *Weekly Spectator* (Blay-Amihere 1994). He also lectured at the Ghanaian Institute of Journalism and served as director of the Institute from 1982 to 1983. He then went to Paris for the Journalists in Europe Programme.

Around this time he was offered a position at the Castle Information Services. Blay-Amihere described to me his difficulty in making this decision. As a successful professional in the capital, the demands from his extended family in the Western Region were heavy (school fees, medical bills, etc.). This financial pressure forced him to consider a job that would have compromised both his professional ideals and his oppositional political orientation. Putting his professional future at risk, he refused the job. He explains that he was able to shrug off the social pressures because he had always been a loner, able to take political chances. As the biggest gamble yet, this difficult refusal marks a turning point in Blay-Amihere's career.

Turning to the private press, he started working for the cutting-edge oppositional newspaper the *Free Press*. As an editor of this provocative paper, Blay-Amihere witnessed the continual harassment of private journalists by the Rawlings regime. These experiences explicitly politicized his work, turning the practice of journalism into a human rights crusade. He describes the environment at the *Free Press* in his memoirs, *Tears for a Continent.*

> Editing the *Free Press* was living next door to danger. I was the second editor of *Free Press,* a paper established in 1979 to safeguard public interests. This is a mission, which in our parts of the world, makes a journal an enemy of rulers since there is nothing like national or public interest in Africa but only narrow government interest. In 1983, both the editor, John Kugblenu, and the publisher, Tommy Thompson, were arrested and detained without trial for one year. The editor died a few weeks after his release. It was my lot to re-start the *Free Press* in 1985. For the next two years, until we were compelled by circumstances beyond our control, harassment by the government, to close down the paper we walked a daily trail of danger. (Blay-Amihere 1994, 6)

The *Free Press* was closed down again in 1986 when another editor, Kweku Baako, was arrested and detained. Blay-Amihere then left for Britain to continue his education at the London School of Economics, taking a postgraduate degree there in international and comparative politics. Returning to Ghana, he started up a sports paper with a colleague and began writing a political column in another sports paper under the pen name Dan Ladd.

Braving the harsh "culture of silence," Blay-Amihere launched a new political newspaper, "to fill the void of a serious analytical paper in Ghana" (1994, 6). Three weeks after the *Independent* appeared, Rawlings issued a newspaper licensing law requiring all publications to secure a license from the Ministry of Information. Before this law a newspaper was only required to register its name and address with the Post Office. Avoiding any reference to the new political paper, the government relied on a moral justification, claiming that the new licensing law was designed to control an alarming rise of pornography in the private press.

Despite this claim, the government awarded licenses to all the private entertainment and sports weeklies except the sports paper Blay-Amihere founded, the sports paper he wrote for, and the *Independent.*

Forced out of work again, he then went to Harvard as a Nieman Fellow, fulfilling his highest aspirations. Thinking back to the early 1980s, Blay-Amihere reasons that he would never have been awarded the Nieman Fellowship if he had taken a job with the government back then. While his resistance to social pressures has brought him personal and professional trouble at home, his personality as a "loner" resonates with the stubborn American individualism prized by international programs like the Nieman Fellows.

As Rawlings faced increasing demands from the Bretton Woods institutions to liberalize both the economy and the political environment as a condition of further aid, a liberal constitution was adopted in 1991 that nullified the newspaper licensing law. Blay-Amihere returned from Harvard, relaunched the *Independent*, and was elected president of the Ghana Journalists Association.

When the term of his GJA "administration" was nearing an end in 1993, Blay-Amihere took advantage of his incumbent position to subtly campaign for reelection as he managed functions in Accra and traveled in the regions on GJA business. As his own newspaper lambasted Rawlings for similar "abuses" of incumbency in both the 1992 and 1996 presidential campaigns, Blay-Amihere noted the irony to me and concluded that such strategies become necessary in the impoverished circumstances of African politics. As well as it worked for Rawlings, it worked for Blay-Amihere. Reelected in 1993, Blay-Amihere served his second term as GJA president and then used similar incumbency techniques to campaign for the presidency of the West African Journalists Association. In 1996 he was elected president of WAJA and now works closely with both organizations from his office in the Press Center.

Handsome and charismatic, Blay-Amihere is a practiced extrovert. Lunching at Country Kitchen, where the rising Ghanaian elite come for afternoon fufu, numerous successful businessmen and prominent professionals stop by his table for a chat. He is hardly stationary for very long, however, preferring to be on the move, making visits and arrangements around town. His restless energy and elite connections have proved enormously productive for GJA, resulting in a packed calendar of events and new sources of funding.

Channeled into his crusade for a free and independent press, Blay-Amihere's restlessness emerges as a canny ability to court international forces against local antagonists. Annoyed with Rawlings's continued harassment of the private press, Blay-Amihere sought out a sympathetic audience among Western diplomats. "When I first met Kabral, he gave me a snootful about the tribulations of running a private newspaper in Accra," said Bruce Lohof, the USIS press attaché. That conversation between Blay-Amihere and Lohof resulted in a five-page document (1997), which was sent to the United States Information Agency (USIA) in Washington, D.C., the Secretary of State, the ECOWAS collective, and the American Embassy in Accra. Predicting "stormy weather" for the independent press, this unclassified document detailed the problems of "poor circulation, aggressive competition, slipshod journalism, and an intimidating government."[3] Based almost solely on Blay-Amihere's "snootful," the document repeated Blay-Amihere's predictions as to which newspapers would survive in the intensely competitive environment, including his own newspaper, the *Independent,* and leaving out his major competitor, the *Ghanaian Chronicle.* The document suggested that USIA might concentrate its support on these potential successes, rather than support the private press en masse. The benefits to Blay-Amihere of such a policy change are obvious.

Continuing his own analogy of GJA elections with presidential elections, Blay-Amihere's administrative positions with GJA and WAJA can be considered a kind of public office, distinguished from his private position as editor-publisher of the *Independent.* Since his ability to speak on behalf of the private press in general is based on his position with professional organizations, his influence with USIS is based more on his public persona than on his private experiences as an editor of a private newspaper. Using his public position to tilt circumstances in favor of his private ventures, the above example illustrates a kind of "straddling" of public and private spheres in efforts of accumulation.

A more striking example of this strategy of "straddling," Blay-Amihere has worked through his international contacts to arrange the money to purchase printing presses for his newspaper. While attending a conference in Brazil as WAJA representative, Blay-Amihere met a representative from a Dutch community development organization. He invited the Dutch representative to Senegal for the upcoming WAJA conference on the state of the media in West Africa. Some months later he applied to the same community development organization for a grant of seventy thousand dollars to purchase used printing presses for the *Independent.* He obtained the grant and now plans to move the *Independent* to larger offices at Weija, a suburb at the edge of Accra. These printing presses will substantially reduce printing costs, the largest expense of publishing a private newspaper. With printing costs down, Blay-Amihere hopes to turn the *Independent* into a daily paper. Moreover, he plans to use the presses to generate side profit by publishing books, pamphlets, and other outside jobs. Explaining why the community development organization awarded the grant, he emphasized to me that his acquaintance with the Dutch representative through the conferences in Brazil and Senegal certainly turned the odds in his favor.

This "straddling" of public and private realms is common in the accumulating strategies of the African politico-commercial bourgeoisie described by Bayart in his comparative description of African politics, *The State in Africa: The Politics of the Belly* (1993). In that work Bayart discusses the hybridized relationship between the realms of business and public administration:

> There is a relationship of complementarity and hybridization between private
> and public capital, rather than a relationship of exclusion and competition.

> We must therefore conceptualize this straddling class, the "mixed bourgeoisie" in its unity as much as in its plasticity. Some experts on Zaire suggest specifying it as a "politico-commercial class," an appealing expression suggestive of the interdependence of two major sectors of the process of accumulation at the top of the social scale. (98–99)

As Blay-Amihere's example illustrates, such strategies of accumulation through "straddling" public and private realms have persisted into democratic dispensations, not only in newly democratized governments like Rawlings's regime but also in the emergent civil institutions of constitutional democracy. Saturating the very civil associations that challenge the corrupt authoritarian state, such practices call into question the role of civil society as purely redemptive forces in the establishment of rationalized democratic systems.

The point here is not to accuse Kabral Blay-Amihere of the same kleptocratic corruption that his newspaper is bent on exposing in Rawlings's administration (such an allegation would be absurd). Rather, I am arguing that the courageous mavericks who build the emergent institutions of "civil society" constitute a new kind of elite class which is nonetheless shaped by the systemic conditions that supported the rise of other versions of the postcolonial elite. Working in the same system as the state and urban entrepreneurial elites, these civil society bigmen, like Blay-Amihere, learn the strategies of accumulation that work in that system. Thus they deploy their social and symbolic capital, their access to foreign education and contacts, and their ability to command a workforce and organize clients in order to achieve their goals.

As Bayart argues that civil servants use their access to the symbolic and material goods of the state to enrich their private enterprises, so the leaders of civil society may use their access to public resources (in organizations independent and often oppositional to the state) to channel advantage to their private projects.

Corruption from Above, Crusade from Below: The Private Press and the Rhetoric of Resistance

Straddling the realms of political opposition and private accumulation, the editors of private newspapers fuse the two interests in a public rhetoric of private journalism. Appealing to an international discourse of free speech and human rights, Kabral Blay-Amihere has constructed this discourse in his public speeches at GJA events and in the editorials and editor's column of his own newspaper. Not merely a style of professional oratory, this crusading rhetoric articulates an entire dispensation of liberal democracy, describing the nature of political discourse, relations between government and opposition, and the individual as citizen with human rights. In the state structure stipulated by the 1991 Constitution, the state is divided into executive, legislative, and judicial branches, all governed by constitutional law. Within the liberal imaginary detailed in the rhetoric of private journalism, the press is positioned as the "fourth estate," an adversarial instrument integral to the functioning of the state but representing the public interest. In this role the private press is charged to act as a moral "watchdog" over the activities of the state, exposing corruption and inefficiency. Blay-Amihere, asserting that the private press has "set the agenda for society and government" since 1991 (GJA 1994, 5), continually stresses that the private press has succeeded in its functional role.

> The private press not only made public morality an issue of consideration for all and sundry, but also revived the holy war for probity and accountability. They have proved that theory that every democracy needs the 4th estate of the realm to flourish. Their total credibility has not suffered in spite of their lapses. (GJA 1994, 6)

Reviving the same "holy war" that motivated Rawlings's 1981 revolutionary coup in the name of probity and accountability, the press is constructed as the moral conscience of a decadent regime. In the new democratic order the press replaces the popular instruments (local legal and military organizations) designed by the revolutionary state to rout corruption and rigorously enforce a strong moral code (Nugent 1996; Oquaye 1993). With the return to constitutional rule, the private press has discovered the widespread abandonment of revolutionary ideals in Rawlings's regime, his revolutionary instruments, and his party. As Rawlings has turned against the moral agenda behind his coup, he is compelled to lash out at the private press for continuing the moral crusade and revealing the truth of his decline. While the adversarial campaign of the private press has been explicitly political (most private publishers are opposition party members), this rhetoric of private journalism relies on an agonistic discourse of endangered democracy to explain why Rawlings continually harasses the private press. In Blay-Amihere's rhetoric, Rawlings's constant efforts to silence the private press through legal and political harassment reveal the double hypocrisy of a socially regressive revolutionary and an anti-democratic president of a constitutional democracy. Blay-Amihere's comments in his own column, "Still on the Block," on World Press Freedom Day seem to be aimed directly at Rawlings:

> You are killing democracy, you are stopping human progress, whenever you kill the word, whenever you attempt to repress the truth.[4]

As suggested by the abstract nature of Blay-Amihere's assertion above, this discourse of the beleaguered private press calls upon a global pro-democracy discourse that structures a narrative of courageous struggle against authoritarianism. Cast as progressive activists pitted against corrupt and backward regimes, this narrative places the private press at the forefront of a worldwide movement for democracy. In this exposed and dangerous position, journalists are continually martyred to the cause, easy targets by repressive Goliath states.

> There are . . . evil forces of intolerance who have constituted themselves into opponents of a free press. Such evil forces which cannot stand the reporting of the truth have unleashed on the press acts of violence, intimidation and harassment. Everywhere the press is under siege, under pressure. The casualty list is high and expensive in terms of deaths, detentions and broken lives.[5]

While situating the Ghanaian private press in this global pro-democracy discourse, Blay-Amihere defines the specific repressive dynamic unique to the press in sub-Saharan Africa. Referring to the detainment of private journalists and the dismissal of those who work for the state media, Blay-Amihere portrays the situation in many sub-Saharan African countries. He depicts a docile state media that "sings the praises of government" opposed by a daring private media harassed and repressed by the state.

Championing the private press in Africa, Blay-Amihere summons the pro-democracy rhetoric of courageous struggle and situates that narrative historically in the anticolonial campaigns of the private press in the nationalist period of the mid-century.

> Significantly, the African press has not always been docile and domesticated. There was a time the press set the agenda and not slavishly obeyed governments. In the 50's and 60's the media in most African countries were . . . in the frontline of the struggle for independence from colonial rule. (Blay-Amihere 1994, 62)

Speaking on Ghana, the specific reference to the private press is yet more clear.

> Independence in Ghana was facilitated by the crusading journalism of the indigenous private press published and edited by politicians turned journalists like Kwame Nkrumah, the first Prime Minister of Ghana, who edited and published the *Evening News*. . . . While the colonial administration allowed the flourishing of a private press, they created a severe legal regime which was used to throw several journalists of the period into jail. (Blay-Amihere 1994, 59)

Note that Blay-Amihere avoids mentioning how Nkrumah, after relying on his private press to wage his campaign, later abolished the private press and designed the tightly controlled state media as a representational tool in his state apparatus. Overlooking such an obvious point, this narrative is revealed as a rather strategic use of history. While struggling against the illegitimate and repressive colonial state, the private press earned a rightful position in African governance. Similarly struggling against the illegitimate and repressive Rawlings regime, the private press seeks to claim a rightful role in the new constitutional democracy. In both cases, the struggles of the private press were animated by oppositional political campaigns, motivations which are rhetorically subordinated in this narrative in order to highlight professional and democratic ideals that resonate with international discourses (and support).

This historicized narrative of the anti-authoritarian struggles of the private press not only structures a moral claim on pro-democracy discourse, but also establishes a historical precedent for a legitimate role in the activities of the state. Contrarily any reference to the transformation of Nkrumah from journalist-hero to corrupt autocrat would seem to suggest that any role in the activities of the state might ultimately corrupt the crusading journalist. Thus the narrative of Nkrumah's rise to power through the private press has lent support to the professional project of GJA in the period of democratization; while any mention of Nkrumah's slide to venality might imply that the moral and democratic crusades of the private press could be merely circumstantial, motivated not by political and professional ideals but by exclusion from the plenty of the state.

Evident in this historical narrative, Blay-Amihere's depiction of the media in Africa relies on a fundamental distinction between the private press and the state media. While GJA may be working for professional solidarity among state and private journalists, Blay-Amihere's rhetoric summons and reinforces the distinction between them. As the president of an organization that represents state journalists along with private ones, Blay-Amihere's indictment of the state media is nonetheless critical and politically charged. Aware of his representative position, he constructs a kind of professional distance from which to level this strong critique. While the allegations may be fueled by the frustrations of competing with the state apparatus, Blay-Amihere is careful to rhetorically set aside his interests as an editor of a private newspaper. His critique is meant to "represent" popular opinion and not to express concerns about his own newspaper's competitive disadvantages with the state media. In the *State of the Media in Ghana* (GJA 1994, 6) he rehearses the widespread complaints about the state media while avoiding any personal accusations.

> To a section of the public the state-owned media continue to serve as mouthpieces and mirrors for the government. The state-owned media have also been

accused of failing in their constitutional duty of offering equal opportunity to
all interest groups and political parties. Above all, critics of the state-owned
media believe that the state-owned media are not models of excellence in journalism for emerging papers to emulate.

This rhetoric not only points to breaches of political responsibility, but emphasizes constitutional and professional lapses as well. While the international discourses on which Blay-Amihere relies might allow for sheer political conservatism in a liberal and competitive environment, unconstitutional
bias contradicts the liberal imaginary of pro-democracy and human rights
discourses while slack standards offend the professional sensibilities of international journalists' groups.

As we saw in chapter 1, Yao Ayeboafoh's journalistic rhetoric sought to
erase the everyday practices that overdetermine the conservative content of
state journalism. Blay-Amihere, instead, emphasizes the subtle manipulation of the state media through editorial shuffling and other methods of intimidation.

> After all the government continues to appoint chief executives for the state-
> owned media and sends signals to chief executives of the state-owned media
> and their subordinates that it is still the manipulator and executor of their fate
> when it announces that it is sending some chief executives on indefinite leave
> and later recalls them at will. The message is never lost upon journalists. (GJA
> 1994, 5)

So heavily compromised, the state media cannot perform its social and
constitutional functions. Only the private press, independent of the state apparatus, can perform the critical, evaluative, and representational functions
so vital to the political process in a liberal democracy. This distinction is important to Blay-Amihere's rhetoric, valorizing the role of journalism in African political struggles while subordinating the sullied standards of the state
press to the historic mission of the private press.

Foregrounding professional standards, this rhetorical move indicates a
larger attempt to carve out an entirely new position for journalism in the political field, a professionalized position free from the hold of political forces.

Locked in dialectical opposition, the state and oppositional parties have
waged their political battles through the state and private press. As private
journalists have accused the state media of "singing the praises" of the state,
journalists with the state media have likewise lambasted the private press for
its furious and sensational campaign against the president and the ruling
party. For instance, in the pages of the *Free Press* Rawlings is often referred to
as a crazed drug addict. In response, Rawlings unleashes frequent diatribes

against the "irresponsibility" and rumor-mongering of the "opposition" (never "independent") press. With his frequent insistence that "We Got to Be Independent,"[6] Blay-Amihere seems to indicate that the irresponsible practices of both the state and private press are attributed to their narrow political projects.

However, while privately acknowledging the active role of many private newspapers in this political deadlock, Blay-Amihere tends to publicly attribute the professional lapses of the private press not to politics per se, but rather to a lack of experience in the newly liberalized environment combined with a lack of resources. While substantiating the criticism of the state press, he portrays the criticism of the private press as hyperbolic and repressive. Falling back on the pro-democracy rhetoric, Blay-Amihere laments the constant rage vented on the private press as so many unjust "assaults."

> President Rawlings himself, Presidential Advisor P. V. Obeng, Minister of Information Kofi Totobi-Quakyi and some members of the general public have assaulted the private press of sheer sensationalism for the sake of profit, and publication of half-truths and falsehoods as truths. Their patriotism and commitment to national security have been questioned. Their adversary role is in that sense even regarded by the critics as attempts to destabilize the country through irresponsible journalism. (GJA 1994, 6)

Never publicly conceding that some of these allegations may have some merit, Blay-Amihere portrays the more serious threat to professional journalism in the power of the state to use these allegations to justify harassment and repression. His speech on International Press Freedom Day (1996) calls on the state to forsake these repressive strategies in order to allow the free development of the profession.

> Let governments and society not resort to negative and inimical laws to promote a responsible press. Excellence in the press, press responsibility comes with time and unfettered exercise of freedom of expression.[7]

Inherent to international pro-democracy and human rights discourses lurking in Blay-Amihere's rhetoric, the liberal imaginary foregrounds the ultimate wisdom of the market, an upward pressure on quality and freedom. Not surprisingly Blay-Amihere's solution to the unprofessional practices of both the state and private press focuses on a liberalized economy, revealing an abiding faith in the selectivity of market competition.

> Both the state and private media, now compelled to operate under the weight of market forces more than under the standing orders of government, are working towards a qualitative growth of the industry. (GJA 1994, 6)

Rather than using the lapses of journalists to justify repression, a liberal environment allows the market to discipline the profession as a whole, forcing improvements of professional standards as a matter of economic survival while granting the widest margin of freedom yet known for the media in Ghana. Blay-Amihere's celebration of the market reveals the indebtedness of this discourse to the metaphors of liberal democracy articulated in the West.

> So we say let a thousand flowers, let a thousand ideas blossom in the media superhighway. We are equally saying that by the very laws that govern growth, the bad [newspapers] will fall by the roadside, choked out of print by their own irresponsibility while the good ones will survive and flourish.[8]

In this narrative authoritarian repression is replaced by the benevolent market, and those newspapers performing their prescribed "watchdog" function in the new democratic dispensation will inevitably edge out those shoddy papers captured by purely political interests. While relying on the market, GJA steps in to train journalists to perform their assigned function, highlighting issues of ethics and press law, regulatory measures beyond the executive discipline of the state.

So, this public rhetoric of journalism constructs a heroic and highly politicized narrative for the private press situated in Ghanaian history while transmuting the very political nature of private journalism into the neutral professionalism of ethics and economic liberalism. Straddling the realms of political opposition and private accumulation, this public rhetoric of private journalism fuses the two interests.

Politics and Professional Ideals in Private Journalism

While the president of GJA and some leading private editors might be motivated to appeal to these international discourses of democracy and human rights, journalists at private newspapers are more constrained by their practical positions in the highly polarized political field. Facing the hostility of state sources combined with the sympathy of opposition parties and the support of an opposition audience, private journalists have had much less to gain from professional neutrality and much more to gain from personal and political alliances.

In the 1990s, most journalists who worked for private newspapers were politically oppositional and viewed their work as part of an overall project to expose and finally depose their enemy, President Rawlings. For these journalists, international standards of objectivity and observance of a strict ethical code have proven to be professionally impractical and politically unwise.

While GJA may be mapping out a professionally neutral and objective space for the practice of private journalism, the professional positionality of these journalists suggests that such a neutral space in Ghana may be uninhabitable.

As the most extreme example of politically driven private journalism, the *Free Press* led an oppositional crusade (if sporadic and frequently dangerous) against the ruling government throughout Rawlings's nineteen years in power. Editor Eben Quarcoo describes the paper as a crusade "against deceit and falsehood, against the murder of innocent victims . . . against widespread human rights abuses, arrest and detention." Appearing in 1980, as Rawlings was gearing up for his second coup, the *Free Press* was a critical but fundamentally analytical newspaper, full of articles evaluating policy, development projects, and foreign affairs. Following the coup of December 31, 1980, Rawlings defined the newspaper as an enemy of the revolution, unleashing a host of repressive measures to silence the independent voice. *Free Press* editors were imprisoned without trial, offices were raided, equipment destroyed. Rawlings even sent a truck to dump a load of human excrement on the *Free Press* compound.

Suffering such abuses, the publisher and editorial staff of the paper have been critical of the call for journalistic independence and strict professional standards. Their crusade against Rawlings turned angry and vindictive, justifying a kind of "guerrilla journalism" based on rumors and provocative accusations. In the 1990s, the paper was explicitly partisan and full of personal attacks against Rawlings and the First Lady. "We are accused of failing to see any good in this government," Quarcoo explains, "but the devil is the devil. Nothing from the devil can be good. No good can come from the blood of innocent people, nothing can compensate." For Quarcoo and the *Free Press*, the professional rhetoric of balance and objectivity is morally vacant, antithetical to the crusade of the newspaper. The recent surge of international interest in the courageous struggles of the African press came too little and too late. Rejecting international professional ideals, Quarcoo laments that so many nations and international organizations claim to be committed to democracy and development while virtually ignoring the real needs of the private press—"We have to fight our own fight." While younger publisher-editors like Kabral Blay-Amihere and Kofi Coomson have been able to forge strategic alliances with foreign support, Quarcoo is suspicious of the political restraints that come with such professional collaboration.

Oppositional passion in the practice of private journalism extends beyond the *Free Press* as a widespread vocation among journalists at many private newspapers. While I worked for the *Independent* during the 1996 presidential and parliamentary campaigns, the political commitments of

9. The front page of the irascible *Free Press* blames Rawlings for price hikes in school fees, beer, cooking oil, rice, flour, and other "consumables." Note the thumbnail picture of an inscrutable Rawlings in mirrored sunglasses beside the accusing headline—in contrast to the direct, open, and "jolly good" countenance of the "Face of Victory," opposition candidate J. A. Kufour. *Courtesy of the Free Press, October 15, 1996.*

journalists were particularly obvious. Around the office, journalists at the *Independent* were constantly narrating the atrocities of the Rawlings regime and celebrating the slogans and personalities of opposition parties. Their personal politics surfaced in blatantly partisan coverage of opposition candidates and problems in the ruling party, especially in stories by the young acting editor William Duncan. Although not as angry as Quarcoo, *Independent* journalists tend to reject the demands of journalistic objectivity in such a polarized political field. In an interview, Emmanuel Boateng and Victoria Frimpong foreground their personal judgment in the structure and slant of stories, summoning notions of relativism to dismantle the very idea of journalistic objectivity.

> Emmanuel: I don't think there is any objectivity. There isn't one rule for objectivity. I listen to a story and I filter it. Victoria listens to a story and she filters it. The best I can do is to put myself out of the story. It's not proper to make comments—I have to separate my comments from what the person said. Some people mix them up. I am solely responsible for my comments. Objectivity is relative.
>
> Victoria: You can't rule out the possibility of your own ideas in the story. As a journalist, you have the tendency to give more room to the position that shows your own ideas than the people you think are saying nonsense. Like this man who says that people who are selling dog chains in the street are all gainfully employed. Maybe I might use what he said because I want to expose it. If people make a proper genuine comment then I would want to use it. Then I would put it in a way to convince people to accept it . . . use portions to make an impact. Maybe not consciously, but subconsciously.

Identifying themselves as active participants in political discourse, private journalists believe that the very skills required to discern truth from falsehood have been developed through their opposition to the "lies" of the government and the state press. Opposition is then essential to critical analysis. Recognizing that all stories are inevitably shaped by preconceived opinions, the goal of the journalist is to avoid direct editorializing in news stories while nonetheless convincing the reader of the "proper genuine" position.

This critique of objectivity directly contradicts the professional ideals in the journalistic rhetoric of GJA. This contradiction between GJA rhetoric and the political orientation of private journalists is manifested in an ongoing struggle over the editorial policies of the *Independent*, the GJA president's own newspaper at the time. Every Tuesday, before sending the front page to the printer, Blay-Amihere convened a meeting with the staff of the *Independent* to discuss the content of the front page. When I came to work for the *Independent*, I participated in these brainstorming sessions. The first indication that the political orientation of the paper was a matter of some controversy was the young journalists' frequent and blatantly partisan suggestions for the headlines of lead stories, while Blay-Amihere pressed them for more descriptive, balanced headlines. When someone suggested an openly celebratory headline for a story covering a rally for the opposition New Patriotic Party (NPP), Blay-Amihere responded with a confrontational jibe, "Are you NPP?" Embarrassed, the journalist only smiled. Throughout the course of the 1996 campaign, this situation was repeated several times, with Blay-Amihere turning and pointing to one journalist after another, joking, "Are you NPP? Are you? And you? Are you *all* NPP?"

This same conflict surfaced again and again. Writing a story on the corruption probe of the Commission for Human Rights and Administrative Justice, Victoria Frimpong consulted acting editor William Duncan, who suggested that she take a slant supportive of the probe. When the story was finished, she showed it to Blay-Amihere who criticized the slant and asked her to rewrite the story objectively, without the slant. "Write it 'straight,'" he told her. Personally agreeing with Duncan's advice, she followed Blay-Amihere's orders.

With her critique of objectivity, Frimpong disagrees with Blay-Amihere's nonpartisan strategy for the *Independent,* complaining to me several times that such a policy is bad for circulation. "You have to give the people what they want if you have a private paper," she told me, "and people want critical stories, opposition stories, and exposés." Referring to rumors of falling circulation, Victoria explained that Blay-Amihere is reluctant to run such critical stories because he has so many friends throughout the social and political spectrum. Not wanting to offend his friends and risk his productive connections, Blay-Amihere summons professional ideals of balance and journalistic independence to justify his editorial policies.

Despite his articulated preference for objectivity, journalists at the *Independent* insist that Blay-Amihere himself is hardly an icon of professional detachment, often using his newspaper to give publicity to friends and allies. In yet another tactic of straddling private and public realms, Blay-Amihere provides free advertising to his favorite high-life star, Amakye Dede, a favor returned by Dede with free performances at GJA events such as the Annual Dinner Dance. In a similar move, Blay-Amihere sent his environmental journalist out on assignment to do a favorable environmental story on the controversial Ghana National Petroleum Corporation (GNPC). Caught between Blay-Amihere's commitments and her own conscience, Victoria Frimpong went on the assignment and then wrote a critical story instead.

I hate that company, may God forgive me, I hate them and I don't want to publish their activities. It's a waste of resources. GJA wanted something from them,
Kabral wanted something. So when I came back—they took us to Ada—I didn't
want to write anything. But I wrote something and it wasn't used and I didn't
bother. I didn't want to write anything positive. They wanted something on environmental issues and of course it wasn't going to be in their favor. I knew
Kabral wasn't going to be too cool because GJA was making for some assistance,
so we were giving them publicity, carrying their press releases, and meanwhile
we weren't on good terms with them. There was a report that they've overdrawn
their accounts and made the last Finance Minister resign.

Journalists at the *Independent* argue that Blay-Amihere's biases are not
only aimed at promoting his professional interests but that they also reflect
his political convictions. His partisan editorial policy follows the Nkrumahist tradition of his family and region. Blay-Amihere's cousin, Freddie Blay,
is PCP MP (People's Convention Party Minister of Parliament) for a constituency in the Central Region. Chiding his journalists about their NPP
sympathies, Blay-Amihere is not only reminding them to be more balanced,
but is also indicating that he himself is committed to the ideals of the other
opposition party, the Nkrumahist PCP.

> Kabral is trying to represent both sides; but he is leaning towards PCP, the
> Nkrumahists. That determines Kabral's political ideology. He's Nkrumahist. He
> makes sure he balances it; but he has an Nkrumahist bias.
> Sometimes he says, "Ei, there are a lot of NPPs here at the *Independent*. The
> number of NPPs outnumber the Nkrumahists!" You see, most private papers
> reflect the Nkrumahist agenda. (Emmanuel Boateng)

As a mass medium, the press has long been associated with the popular
"veranda boy" politics of the African socialist tradition founded in Ghana by
Kwame Nkrumah. Breaking away from the more conservative and conciliatory UGCC (United Gold Coast Convention) Party, the young Nkrumah
began to demand "Self-Government Now!" through his own newspaper,
shifting the heart of the nationalist movement from professional bigmen to
the "school leavers" and "veranda boys." As a method of courting younger
and more revolutionary energies, newspapers are particularly suited to such
a populist turn. The view of the press as essentially Nkrumahist is shared by
private journalists and party functionaries of the main Nkrumahist party,
the PCP. As private journalists, we were always warmly welcomed at PCP
headquarters and quickly ushered to the general-secretary who eagerly an-
swered our questions and filled us in on party news. A particularly helpful
source of party information, PCP activist (and newspaper editor) Kwesi

Pratt was most attentive to Victoria Frimpong, columnist for the *Independent* (indeed, he had a long-standing crush). During my first few months in Accra, I lived in the same neighborhood as the PCP headquarters. One evening a party worker tracked me down at home to tell me to return to PCP headquarters to collect some documents I had been asking about. Such personal incidents are not merely trivial gossip but an indication of the warm relationship of mutual admiration and political imbrication between the PCP party and the private press.

In addition to the populist connection between the private press and the PCP, ethnic and regional commonalities bind them together as well. As mentioned above, Blay-Amihere is from the same ethnic group and region as Nkrumah. Acting editor of the *Independent* William Duncan refers to Blay-Amihere as "a tribalistic Nkrumahist through and through." Schooling at Cape Coast in Central Region, Blay-Amihere is further linked to a region historically associated with Ghanaian journalism. When I worked there his office was predominantly staffed by Fantes from the Central Region (most notedly Duncan). Fante was the primary language spoken in the office. Similarly the editor of the *Crusading Guide*, Kweku Baako, is a Fante from the Central Region whose father was a minister in Nkrumah's government. Since so many prominent editors of the private press are Fantes (Kofi Coomson of the *Ghanaian Chronicle* is another), the oppositional private press are commonly referred to as part of a "Fante conspiracy."

This sympathy between the Nkrumahists and the private press signals an ideological split between the two most active professional organizations in the political field. While most of the private media are pro-PCP, journalists told me that most of the lawyers are pro-NPP. This is not surprising. Inheriting the conservative Busia-Danquah UP tradition, the NPP is a liberal-democratic party emphasizing constitutionality and the rule of law. In contrast to Nkrumahist "veranda boy" politics, the NPP is associated with wealthy Asante cocoa farmers and businessmen and is often accused of ethnocentric elitism. NPP party officers seem to rely on an unspoken entitlement to rule, rather than active campaigns of ideological persuasion. Thus the NPP tends to spurn the press as an instrument of populism, interfering with the party's ability to conduct important party business.

In the early years of the Fourth Republic, some private newspapers supported the NPP. That support has largely fallen away, however, as the party has reinforced its reputation for elitism and high-handedness. NPP leaders tended to bully and intimidate other (Nkrumahist) opposition parties in the political maneuverings aimed at overturning the massive incumbent machinery of the Rawlings regime. The NPP has twice formed a "Great Alliance" with the PCP; but such alliances are always riddled with difficulties and break up just after the elections. While conceding the presidential candidate to the NPP, the PCP struggled to place their MP candidates on the alliance ticket. Owing to a mutual reluctance to compromise, both parties were running candidates in several constituencies throughout the campaign.

In the midst of the stalemate between the parties, Kwesi Pratt's newspaper, the *Weekly Insight,* ran a preliminary list of MP candidates in its center spread, featuring PCP candidates in the contested slots. At a small fund-raising party, I met NPP Public Relations Officer Jake Obetsebi-Lamptey in the heat of the crisis in the Alliance. He ranted against the PCP "politician-journalists" like Kwesi Pratt for confusing their political and business interests. "As journalists, they want to print off-the-record comments and proceedings in order to sell their newspapers—even if it hurts the Great Alliance," he fumed. Obetsebi-Lamptey was further annoyed with the private press for publicizing certain ethnic slurs made against Muslims by NPP General-Secretary Agyenim-Boateng.

In contrast to the warm reception at PCP headquarters, private journalists visiting the NPP are coldly scrutinized and made to wait for an interview with the general-secretary. Admitted into Agyenim-Boateng's office, journalists sit quietly (often against the wall) as he conducts other business and takes phone calls at his desk. With any luck, a lull in office activity may provide the opportunity for a hurried interview. Even with such luck, the general-secretary is usually evasive and easily annoyed with probing questions. "They have very unprofessional press relations because the top hierarchy is ignorant of the role we play in politics," *Chronicle* journalist Arthur Adjei explained. "We have to go and harass them for information."

Reginald Clottey told me how he was sent over to NPP during the elections and that Agyenim-Boateng had disconnected the phones and fax because they had been flooded with calls. Complaining that, "you people are worrying me!" the NPP general-secretary sent Clottey out of the office empty-handed. Suspicious of the PCP sympathies of the press, Agyenim-Boateng is known for lashing out at inquiring journalists. After the *Independent* started covering the internal struggles of the Great Alliance, the general-secretary became particularly hostile. "You at the *Independent,* you are always trying to destroy us with your negative stories on the Alliance," he grumbled to Duncan.

Ethnically and professionally positioned in the political field, many private journalists find the rhetoric of objectivity professionally counterproductive as well as politically irresponsible. Facing the hostility of state sources in the Rawlings regime, private journalists found themselves in need of some reliable line of information into the political field. With or without enthusiasm, the opposition parties have provided that crucial access to political news, allowing interviews and issuing invitations to press conferences, rallies, and other party events. Moreover, strong urban opposition is a fundamental condition of possibility of the private press. Popular discontent with the state and dissatisfaction with the state press have provided the primary audience for private newspapers. Government and ruling party supporters read the cheaper and more attractive state dailies. Writing for an oppositional audience based on oppositional sources, the private press is always already political, whether striving for balance or championing a partisan cause. Reinforcing the local historical relationship of the private press with political opposition, the practical bond of mutual need between the parties and the private press preempts the abstract discourses of international professional standards. While Blay-Amihere's rhetoric attempts to transmute politics into liberal professionalism, the local demands of the media market combine with historical and cultural factors to continually reinscribe the political oppositionality of the private press.

Crusade from Below, Critique from Undercover: Manipulating Professional and Political Positionality

Beginning in 1993 journalists at the *Ghanaian Chronicle* and the *Independent* launched a series of provocative stories exposing the luxurious lifestyles and corrupt practices of government ministers. Based on investigation as well as popular rumor, these stories prompted Rawlings to initiate a probe against five of his cabinet ministers, resulting in a damning report from the Commission for Human Rights and Administrative Justice. Vindicated and popularized by the CHRAJ probe, journalists at the *Ghanaian Chronicle* began to specialize in investigative reporting, focusing on government scandals like election-rigging and improper divestiture. As competition among private newspapers intensifies, private journalists are pressured to develop the investigative skills and contacts to break such scandalous stories regularly. Scouting for tips and leaks from sources in government and the opposition, *Chronicle* journalists often veil their political allegiances as well as their actual identities in the course of their investigations. While capitalizing on an oppositional audience, journalists at the *Ghanaian Chronicle* recognize the advantages of courting state sources and cooperating with state agencies in the pursuit of their investigations. Negotiating the fields of business and politics, cultivating alliances in all parties in addition to the government, *Chronicle* journalists circumvent the explicit political positionality of private journalists in the Nkrumahist tradition.

Some of them [in the government] are our friends. A journalist should not be seen as an enemy. A good journalist should be a friend to everybody. I am an example—I have friends in all political parties. Anytime I want to write a story, I get their reaction. They say, the president is bothered by this story. Because those people too, they are also Ghanaians. (Reginald Clottey)

Relying on such transgressive networks, Reginald Clottey and other *Chronicle* journalists summon the concept of objectivity to describe how they gather and cross-check information.

JH: Do you practice objectivity?

RC: Yes! Speaking for myself, I don't write a story without cross-checking from another source. By telephone, by letter, or driving to the office. If you sack me, fine. A paper should not be seen as prejudging issues. It should be an independent package. The reader is allowed to form his own judgment.

This strategic use of the concept of objectivity works at de-politicizing the essentially oppositional content of the *Ghanaian Chronicle* while channeling oppositional interests into the discourse of human rights. Journalists at the *Ghanaian Chronicle* reference concepts of objectivity and neutrality to professionally validate their own methods of straddling party, state, and private domains. Drawing from the international rhetoric of GJA, *Chronicle* journalists deploy notions of objectivity and human rights to justify their controversial methods, manipulating political identities and capitalizing on any and all controversy.

As a journalist I see myself as a human rights activist. In a case of the abuse of the rights of the people to fair trial, damn the consequences, I'll go undercover and bring up the story and open up the debate. (Richard Gyasi)

While relying on concepts of objectivity and human rights, the fundamental thrust of the *Chronicle's* investigative journalism throughout the 1990s was antigovernment. While negotiating contradictory positions in the polarized political field, investigative journalists took up a position in the discursive crusade against Rawlings by writing oppositional stories aimed at an oppositional readership. So like most private journalists, *Chronicle* journalists unanimously professed oppositional political commitments so long as Rawlings was in power. After all, the discourse of human rights emerged as an oppositional vocabulary in the Ghanaian context, specifically resonating with the liberal-democratic tradition of the NPP. Journalists at both the *Independent* and the *Ghanaian Chronicle* have been quick to recognize the implication of their own interests in the forces of liberal democracy. But unlike journalists at the *Independent,* journalists at the *Chronicle* were apt to disarticulate their criticality from political oppositionality in the course of their investigations, rearticulating the link just in time to write oppositional stories.

Unlike the publisher of the *Independent,* the editor-publisher of the *Ghanaian Chronicle,* Nana Kofi Coomson, openly professed his political commitments during the 1996 presidential and parliamentary campaigns, using his newspaper to delegitimate Rawlings and the ruling party while promoting opposition candidates in his own stories on the front page. It would seem that the explicitly politicized orientation of *Independent* journalists coincides with Coomson's editorial policy, while the detached professionalism and dedication to human rights of *Chronicle* journalists more nearly resembles Blay-Amihere's GJA rhetoric.

Beyond this rhetorical cross-match, however, the practices of journalism at both newspapers contradict the professional standards that go along with the international discourses of liberal democracy.

The global rhetoric of crusading watchdogs against authoritarian oppression has provided the very conditions of possibility for the remarkable comeback of the private press in Ghana in the 1990s, summoning the support of foreign governments, aid agencies, and transnational NGOs for the cause of democratization, civil society, and free expression. Such global articulations have also supported the rise of a new class of civil society elites, straddling realms of public and private, global and local, in their projects of galvanization and accumulation. For such elites as private newspaper editor Kabral Blay-Amihere, the watchdog rhetoric of private journalism is part of a larger developmental vision that relies on free markets to discipline the field of Ghanaian journalism in the interests of integrity, neutrality, and objectivity.

In the everyday world of private journalism, however, objective fact is one thing; but social fact is quite another. Positioning private journalists politically, regionally, ethnically, historically, and educationally, Ghanaian political culture defines the kinds of stories private journalists are able and motivated to write as well as the kinds of stories their newspapers can and must publish. What can objectivity possibly mean when sources, colleagues, and readers all recognize journalism as an essentially political practice? Some dismiss the pretense of objectivity altogether, articulating alternative models of journalistic relativism, self-reflexivity, and public responsibility. Others seize on the notion of neutrality to justify the cultivation of sources across the political spectrum, frequently disguising their prescribed identities in the course of investigations and then reinscribing their politics in the fashioning of oppositional exposés. Like the global liberal ideals embraced by their bosses, the alternative models of journalism articulated by private journalists are the product of an ongoing dialectic of the pragmatics and professional commitments of journalism. This dialectical interplay of professional ideals, practical conditions, and social relations has generated a distinctive set of strategies for the production of private journalism.

5

Corruption, Investigation, and Extraversion

While state journalism is practiced in a tightly regulated space largely within the domain of the state, private journalism is excluded from this domain and defined in opposition to the plenty and privilege of state support. Excluded from state patronage, private journalists also escape the subtle mechanisms of state control and surveillance over their daily work while negotiating the different political and professional agendas of their editors who are more politically and professionally insulated.

Sociality and the Constraints of Freedom

When I came to work for the *Independent,* the newspaper occupied four sparse rooms in a dilapidated office building just opposite the Mitsubishi auto parts plant and down the road from the impressive compound of the *Daily Graphic.* Since the editor-publisher Blay-Amihere is more often at the International Press Center, the paper is essentially run by his young acting-editor William Duncan along with a staff of around fifteen, most of them in their twenties. Blay-Amihere's absence leaves a somewhat unsupervised feel to the daily work of journalism there, in sharp contrast to the patrimonial surveillance of the work place at *Graphic.*

Journalists come and go with much more freedom at the *Independent,* milling from room to room for consultations and taking breaks for conversation and refreshment. In the three rooms downstairs the two older copy editors work at their desks, more stationary than the young journalists but constantly listening to radio news and talking politics. Both copy editors are oppositional figures who lost their jobs in the revolutionary tumult, one from Ghana Publishing Company and the other a former editor with the now politically compromised *Ashanti Pioneer.* Their animated conversation on local and national politics is indignant and often bitterly oppositional.

Journalists from other newspapers frequently come to visit their friends at the *Independent,* sitting on the couch in the copy editors' room and joining in the conversation.

The upstairs room is primarily devoted to typesetting. The young editors often hang out upstairs to supervise page layouts and cool off in the air conditioning. Since the air conditioning is specifically for the computers, the rest of the staff is discouraged from lingering too long in this small sanctuary of cool relief. In this room three secretaries type in stories and arrange page layouts on the newspaper's two computers. The performance of the secretaries has been a source of some controversy at the *Independent.* One journalist complains that Blay-Amihere hires the girlfriends and nieces of his friends, young women who cannot type and "just pick out the keys with one finger." Since these secretaries lack training, the *Independent* has suffered from rather sloppy layouts and stories riddled with typos. Blay-Amihere has recently supplemented his editorial staff with a "supervising editor" and another sub-editor, instructing them to go through the copy more carefully. When I visited the upstairs office in 1999, I was surprised to find a dictionary on the sub-editor's desk. In fact, the grammar and spelling of news stories has improved remarkably over past years.

The lack of restrictive controls at the *Independent* is accompanied by a lack of resources that poses a different set of restrictions on the practices of private journalism. While state journalists are delivered every day to invited assignments in state minivans, journalists at the *Independent* depend on one car that only seems to be available about half the time. With fewer invited assignments (mainly to press conferences and cultural events), private journalists are more pressed to initiate their own stories through tips and interviews. This imperative is complicated, however, by limited access to the telephone. The only telephone at the *Independent,* located upstairs in the typists' office, is guarded by a secretary and requires a key. The phone line is very fuzzy, and often the phone simply does not work. When it does, outgoing calls are limited and often judged "unnecessary" by the jury of typesetters. Messages to journalists are frequently lost, forgotten, or haphazardly conveyed at the discretion of the secretary. With communications so severely constrained, journalists are forced to make numerous visits around town just to find one source willing and available to speak on a particular issue. With limited access to a car, they resort to time-consuming public transport in "tro-tro" buses or the more expensive shared taxis. In a pinch, a journalist may take a taxi straight to an assignment (called "dropping"). Never sure of reimbursement for dropping, *Independent* journalists do a considerable amount of walking and waiting for tro-tros and shared taxis.

While this lack of resources makes the practice of private journalism difficult, the lack of restrictions over time and space encourages more dialogic and improvisational forms of social engagement between the public and the private press. Excluded from the domain of the state, the private press is alternatively situated at the boundaries of political and popular culture. Rather than reinforced by walls and checkpoints, these boundaries defining the social positionality of the private press are fluid, permeable, and continually transgressed. Journalists at the *Ghanaian Chronicle* are constantly on the move around town, visiting important friends, checking on key sources, and chasing documents. Journalists are rarely asked to account for their absence from the office but rather are encouraged to keep up the active pursuit of their investigations.

As journalists themselves are free to engage with the public, so the public is free to engage with them. The work places of private journalism are public spaces with frequent visitors and liberal socializing. At the offices of the *Ghanaian Chronicle,* visitors are constantly arriving with tips and stories, bringing documents and other evidence to initiate investigations. A victim of ruling party intimidation or other political wrongdoing may despair at the conservative bias of the courts and come to plead his case to the editor of the *Chronicle* instead, hoping for vindication through investigation and publication. Given the expense and delay of court cases, the private press has become a common resort for oppositional grievances. Where the state has monopolized the construction of social reality for more than a decade, popular challenges to state authority, validated in print and widely circulated, provide a form of social justice for those rendered silent in the previous regime.

Just off the central Ring Road in Accra, the offices of the *Ghanaian Chronicle* are located among the old two-story homes in Kokomlemle, once the neighborhood of politicians and important businessmen, and now more humbly known for the Accra Technical Training College and the many guest houses and small businesses that have sprung up in recent years. As reminders of the historical importance of the neighborhood, as well as its centrality, both the ruling party, NDC, and the largest opposition party, NPP, are located in Kokomlemle (although at opposite ends of the neighborhood). The *Ghanaian Chronicle* is situated in a converted two-story house, with newsrooms and secretarial offices downstairs and page layouts and editorial offices upstairs.

More prosperous than the *Independent,* the *Ghanaian Chronicle* owns around ten computers, and journalists use them to type in their own stories. This gives them much more control over the copy and makes for fewer typos in the final text, since journalists receive English language training at GIJ while secretaries often learn on the job. Since *Chronicle* offices are more centrally located, transportation poses less of a problem. Most press conferences are held at party headquarters or the International Press Center, all within walking distance of the *Chronicle* office. Journalists traveling across town on assignment regularly take share-taxi and dropping, assured of reimbursement from the newspaper.

Communications equipment at the *Chronicle* is more plentiful and reliable than at the *Independent*. Telephones in almost every room and several clear phone lines provide much better access to sources and appointments. A few prominent investigative journalists at the *Chronicle* (Richard Gyasi, Reginald Clottey) even carry Mobitel, a cellular phone, requiring an investment of at least a million cedis (U.S.$500). Several *Chronicle* journalists carry tape recorders for recording interviews, a very useful practice in a discursive context so preoccupied with the pronouncements of important figures. Such a luxury is simply out of reach for most other private journalists.

As the best-selling private newspaper in Ghana, the *Chronicle* is an exception to the general circumstances of material privation of the private press. Journalists at most private newspapers share the same difficulties with telephones and transportation as journalists at the *Independent*. The material environment at the *Ghanaian Chronicle* may more nearly resemble that of a state newspaper, with such production equipment and communications infrastructure, but the similarity ends in the abstract. The social positionality of the *Chronicle* is predicated on an exclusion from the state and an alternative engagement with oppositional energies, a strategy common to the private press. The daily practices of private journalism continually reinscribe a common cause for the private press as journalists at all private newspapers struggle for access to information and sources of national news.

Sources and Tactics of Private Journalism

Well-placed and reliable sources are vital to journalism; yet, with revolutionary violence in recent memory, most Ghanaians are reluctant to give their names for publication or supply information to journalists. Workers in businesses and state offices refuse to comment on the record and defer all inquiries to their bosses who are seldom available. This situation has forced private journalists to repeatedly attribute stories to the few oppositional sources willing to tolerate publicity (officials in opposition political parties). Complementing these recognized sources, private journalists cultivate a broad network of anonymous sources as well, often using the information from these tips to pry unwilling commentary from uncooperative state sources.

While journalists in the state press participate every day in the elaborate rituals of invited assignments in the domain of the state, journalists in the private press have very limited access to the official channels of state information. As uninvited intruders, private journalists are routinely ignored or harassed by state officials when they phone for comment or arrive at state offices to set up interviews.

> If you have a government official and a reporter from the *Chronicle* goes to interview him on the subject that relates to him, it will be almost impossible for him to grant the interview or he will use whatever means necessary to frustrate his efforts. (Richard Gyasi)

This response from state officials varies slightly from paper to paper. Since the *Chronicle* is an investigative paper, the mention of the name arouses extreme suspicion and fear of exposure among state officials and so *Chronicle* journalists are often turned away. Journalists for the *Independent,* with that newspaper's reputation for greater subtly and balance in reporting, are more often stalled or frustrated rather than simply refused an interview.

On the pretext that the official is in a meeting, journalists are vaguely told to "go and come." After several repetitions of this futile exercise, many journalists simply give up or publish the story without official confirmation or comment. Victoria Frimpong describes a particularly harrowing experience when she went to investigate some complaints against the Environmental Protection Agency (EPA).

> They always have to seek permission. It should be on the record, sometimes you have to sit down and discuss which portions they wish to quote. We don't just want one minister, we must consult many. With the information on the EPA factory in Achimota, a resident wrote a letter to the EPA so I went to find out their position. The Public Relations Officer wanted a letter from my office stating what I wanted, so I typed up the story and brought it and he told me to go home and come back the next morning. The next day, I was five minutes late and I was told the person has just walked out and no one could help me. Later, I met a reporter who gave me an EPA phone number and so I phoned him and he told me to go see someone. He told him I would come. I got there and a man told me he still has to discuss things with the director, he can't just say it of his own will. He asked to excuse himself, he phoned the director while I waited outside. He said they have taken specific actions but if I want to know what actions, I would have to go back to the office and bring another letter specifying the things I would write before they could give it to me. So I decided to abandon it after that.

While the response of government officials to private journalists is generally hostile, this response not only varies somewhat according to the newspaper but also according to the specific branch or ministry of government. During the presidential and parliamentary campaigns of 1996, the Electoral Commission (EC) made an effort to inform both state and private media of its official activities and to include all journalists at its press conferences. Despite these efforts, EC officials remained suspicious of private journalists. In November, when working for the *Independent*, I was sent to the Electoral Commission to interview the Deputy Director, David Kanga, about widespread worries over potential electoral fraud. Meeting Kanga, I introduced myself as a journalist and asked for an appointment for the interview. Sizing me up suspiciously, Kanga asked me for which newspaper was I working. "Because if it is the *Chronicle* or the *Free Press*," he said, "I would have to go and consult the Public Relations Officer—the PRO would have to sit in on any interview and we would have to tape record." I told him that I worked for the *Independent*. "Well. . . .," he paused. "It looks as if they are trying to be more fair than some of the others," he conceded and granted the interview.

In the course of the interview I presented Kanga with the doubts and suspicions over electoral procedures that had surfaced in the private press throughout the campaign: selling of voter ID cards, underage voters, fraudulent tabulations, harassment of opposition witnesses at the polls, and so on. Carefully and deliberately Kanga outlined the procedures and explained that such forms of malpractice were virtually impossible. He invited me to come with him on election day on his rounds and see for myself how the procedures worked. Returning to the newspaper, I wrote a fairly neutral story of Kanga's response to the allegations of bias and fraud at the Electoral Commission. Knowing the struggles over editorial policy at the *Independent*, I was curious to see how journalists would react to a story representing the position of a government official (Blay-Amihere was by this time out of the country). The story was never published. No one at the *Independent* ever asked me to rewrite or revise it—indeed, no one ever commented on the story at all.

Seven months later I was working for the *Ghanaian Chronicle* and was assigned to write a story implicating South Senchi district electoral officials in an NDC plot to oust an opposition assemblyman. Again, I was sent to confront Kanga with allegations of NDC bias. Kanga greeted me warmly and asked me how things were going at the *Independent*. I told him that, in fact, I had moved to the *Chronicle*. Clearly disapproving, he conveyed his "surprise" that I would work for such a "funny" newspaper whose journalists are bent on twisting the truth and outright fabrication. Unleashing a diatribe against the malpractices of the private press, his criticism evolved into a subtle threat of violence. "They seem to be promoting chaos but when chaos comes, people like them will be the first to suffer, the first to be shot."

He noted that, in Sierra Leone, journalists were recently shot dead, and nearby an explanation was scrawled on the wall: "Your pen is mighty but our guns are stronger." Softening a bit, Kanga assured me that he did not blame me for the faults of my newspaper because "you are only learning." He insisted, however, that he had to be very careful in order to "preserve the dignity of the EC." Stalling the interview, Kanga said that he needed to consult the Public Relations Officer and the Electoral Commissioner. When I returned a few days later Kanga stalled again, saying that they were waiting on a report on the incident from EC officials in the Eastern Region.

Each time I returned to the Electoral Commission Kanga continued his bitter critique of the *Ghanaian Chronicle*. Getting to the heart of the matter, he eventually told me how a *Chronicle* journalist had recently stolen a letter that Kanga had written to the attorney general, Obed Asamoah, regarding the disputed election of a ruling party MP in the Ayawaso West constituency. The *Chronicle* journalist had apparently "liberated" the document from Asamoah's desk, publishing it on the front page of the *Chronicle* in the heat of the controversy on May 6, 1997. Based on EC investigations into the matter, Kanga admitted in the letter to the attorney general that certain "administrative errors" in vote counting suggested that the election results were, in fact, tainted and that the opposition candidate should have won instead. Reproduced in full on the front page (next to a rather unflattering picture of Kanga himself), Kanga's letter enumerated the various "anomalies," including wrong entries by vote counters at the polling stations, "wrong information" on vote counts given to regional electoral officers, and the complete loss of results from one polling station. In his preliminary conclusion based on available data, Kanga tabulated that the opposition candidate won 15,401 votes, while the ruling party candidate took only 15,191. Without the lost results added into the total, however, Kanga could not conclusively decide the matter. "A recount of ballots in the Ayawaso West-Wuogon is the better option to clear all doubts about the election results."

By his own account and in his own words, the *Chronicle* story disproved Kanga's earlier assurances of electoral probity and the impossibility of fraud. Consequently the story outraged Kanga. As he continued to rant against the unethical practices of *Chronicle* journalists, I began to understand just why I had been assigned to this story and not another *Chronicle* journalist. At that point in time no other *Chronicle* journalist could have gotten any comment from Kanga or even, perhaps, from any EC official. In a tactic that would be repeated throughout my attachment to the *Chronicle*, editors attempted to circumvent the reputation of *Chronicle* journalists, inserting my alternative identity as a foreign white woman in confrontations with unwilling sources. Senior journalist Reginald Clottey explained to me that government officials would be intimidated by my presence as a sort of foreign observer of Ghanaian politics, essentially scaring them into telling the truth. As Kanga indicated, however, the opposite was more often the case. Kanga was only willing to talk to me because, as an innocent neophyte, I did not pose a threat to his position or to the "dignity" of the EC. Considering my foreign academic training, Kanga may have reasoned that I was unlikely to twist and reshape the truth (or steal documents) merely to suit the political and commercial interests of the *Chronicle.* Further, my presence gave Kanga an audience for his critique of the *Chronicle,* a possible wedge against the allegations of EC bias. If I could be persuaded that *Chronicle* journalists were unethical and unfair, I might perhaps break with *Chronicle* policy and represent the EC in a more favorable light.

Although concerned over the document theft perpetrated by journalists at my own newspaper, I did not break with *Chronicle* policy when it finally came to writing the story on South Senchi. While my alternative identity was essential to getting the interview with the EC (a rather useless exercise anyway), in the end I had to strategically set aside my foreign academic sensibilities and write the kind of story I was expected to write for the *Ghanaian Chronicle.* After all, I was on the payroll (unlike the *Independent,* the *Chronicle* insisted on paying me).

As I sat down at the computer to compose the story, senior reporter Reginald Clottey came to check on my progress and to tell me they needed the story immediately. Clottey had originally assigned the story to me, on the instructions of editor-publisher Kofi Coomson. Quizzing me on my interview with the Electoral Commission, Clottey considered the angle of the story. The real issue in this story, he directed, is the partisan behavior of the EC. So my premiere front-page story, "Electoral Officials Colluding with NDC,"[1] essentially followed that angle, foregrounding allegations that EC officials were conspiring in an NDC plot to unseat the opposition South Senchi assemblyman, Mac Goodness Kumadey. After Clottey read the story and approved, I prepared to go home, leaving Kumadey's letter of allegations on the desk in the newsroom. "You'd better keep that letter," Clottey advised, "in case there's a rejoinder."

After turning in the story, I mulled over the contents on the way home from work. Knowing that we could not be sure the allegations were true, I had attributed them to Kumadey and other (anonymous) witnesses. The structure of the story betrayed a clear commitment to those claims, however, as Kumadey's account constituted the first eight paragraphs of the thirteen paragraph story. I had included the EC's denial of wrongdoing, although tacked onto the end. Worried over the implications of this lack of balance, I lamented to my landlady at dinner, "I will surely be sued for libel." In a final effort to retrieve some small control over my strategic role in the murky maneuverings of the *Chronicle,* I phoned the office and had them replace my (white, foreign, woman's) name on the story with the anonymous byline: "By *Chronicle* Reporter." Annoyed with myself, I wondered over the next several days why I had not written a more balanced and "objective" story, or simply refused to write the story on our scant evidence.

I was, however, luckier than many *Chronicle* journalists assigned to scandalous stories—at least the EC officials finally granted me the interview so their response could be incorporated into the story. Often journalists in the private press, especially those who work for the *Chronicle,* are stalled and dismissed, if not harassed, by official sources, as Victoria's experience illustrates. In the face of such obstacles, journalists either abandon the story altogether, as Victoria did, or else resort to less conventional methods of news gathering involving anonymous sources and undercover research.

Like many private journalists, Richard Gyasi, a prominent investigative reporter at the *Chronicle,* classifies sources into two categories: willing and unwilling.

> Over time, I have cultivated sources to help me out, give me tips. They have ears to the ground, and eyes. I get information from them in two ways—some are willing sources, others are unwilling. Unwilling sources don't know that I'm a journalist. Sometimes I deliberately push people to talk, engage a cab driver in conversation. "You see how things are going, it's getting tough in this country!" "Yes, they are looting the coffers." Then I drop it, "The other day, I heard this or that . . ." That is unwilling sources, those that don't know me. I won't appear on television because I know that probably won't facilitate my work. These sources are cultivated over time. Policemen, soldiers, government people, so I have a network. So that is how a story starts.

Willing sources recognize their role as sources, purposely channeling information to journalists either on the record or anonymously. Unwilling sources typically refuse to give information or to make a comment if they recognize that they are speaking to a journalist with the private press. However, unwilling sources may provide such information if a journalist shields his identity. Unaware of the situation, an unwilling source may "drop" some vital information or relate a controversial incident that triggers a sensational story.

Gaining access to particularly valuable yet unwilling sources is not so easy as picking a taxi but rather requires elaborate undercover schemes and subtle inducements. Eager to make a name for himself as an investigative reporter at the *Chronicle,* Reginald Clottey devised a plan for an exclusive interview with the president's daughter, Ezaneter Rawlings, despite the heavy security surrounding the First Family. Until then, no journalist had ever spoken to the president's children. Although suspicious, editor-publisher Kofi Coomson gave Clottey 50,000 cedis ($30) to go to Cape Coast where the girl was schooling.

> I went to the school prefect and I told him that I was doing some research on education, that I wanted some information. We chatted about ten or twenty minutes. Then I said, "Oh, I was informed that the president's daughter is here." She said, "Oh, do you want to see her? Let me call her for you." (Laughs fondly). I know what schoolkids like so I had used some of the money to buy chocolates and biscuits, and while I was talking I was giving to them. A smart game. The girl answered almost all of the questions I asked her, not knowing that I was a journalist.

When the story came out the president was furious, banning all visitors to his children at school. The information revealed by Ezaneter about her hopes and feelings as a First Daughter was actually rather trivial. What enraged the president was the circumvention of his security apparatus, demonstrating a breakdown in his control over the flow of official information. Like the numerous stories in the private press designed to besmirch Rawlings' wife, this story illustrated his lack of control over his own daughter, co-opted as an unwilling source for his arch-enemy, the private press. While Clottey speaks very warmly of Ezanater, his sincere affection makes his cunning intrusion into Rawlings' family sphere even more threatening: "I even told her that I love her and she said, if I can visit her at home, that is fine."

While Ezaneter was clearly a one-shot source for the *Chronicle,* most key figures in the *Chronicle*'s broad network of willing and reliable sources of inside information were originally courted in similar undercover situations. *Chronicle* reporter Arthur Adjei explains how such relationships are forged.

> You take someone out to dinner and become friends and the person doesn't realize where you are working. Then you tell the person, "it's ok but if you can help me." You pick a person who is educated enough to realize it's just a job we are doing and they're just being helpful. In official circles people get punished even for doing their duty so you pick a person, go out to befriend people, cultivate them as sources.

For my first assignment at the *Chronicle* I worked with Arthur on a story exposing internal dissent and reconfiguration in the main opposition party, the NPP. Continually frustrated in our attempts at getting any information or comment from party officials, Arthur had been pursuing an alternative "back-door" strategy with an NPP office secretary. Although this secretary was "too big" and "not really his type," Arthur took her out to dinner several times and she chatted at length about office matters, never realizing that she was channeling important information into Arthur's investigation (I'm not sure exactly when she discovered that Arthur was actually a journalist).

In an attempt to justify this technique, investigative journalists with the private press refer to the climate of fear that forces most sources into the unwilling category. At some point in the course of undercover investigations, a journalist may deliberately shed or accidentally lose his cover, striking sudden fear into unwilling sources. Such dread of public exposure in the private press is widespread, owing to periods of revolutionary violence and repression in recent memory.

> Even when people can talk to you, when managers have given the go-ahead, they would still not want to talk to you. There is a phobia—they just don't want to see their names in the paper, their names mentioned. Some people don't want to appear on television. They don't feel their position requires them to give assistance to the public. I don't know whether they are ignorant or just refusing to be responsible. You can't blame them much because of what has happened in the past. (Victoria Frimpong)

As journalists see it, withholding valuable information from the public is irresponsible cowardice. In the process of courting such sources, journalists must "educate" them to perform their public duty to cooperate with the press.

The goal of much investigative reporting is not merely to gain information (which would be useless without attribution and evidence) but, more important, it is to turn unwilling sources into willing ones. As demonstrated, most government officials, when approached by a journalist with the private press, are frequently unwilling to give information or official comment on the record. However, lower-level employees at government offices may be quite willing to leak tips and evidence anonymously, if given the proper incentive, even when well aware that they are providing information to the private press. In the right context, even key officials may share provocative rumors and important information on government activities, if assured of anonymity.

When confronted with rejection by an official source, journalists may resort to these reliable anonymous sources instead. Some journalists are even able to capitalize on initial rejection to forge new relationships with sources. Reginald Clottey describes such a maneuver with a highly placed source in the Ministry of Finance.

> Once your byline starts appearing, people are shocked and some get excited to see you. Some, too, get scared. If I am doing a story about the Minister of Finance, I go directly there as a reporter. I go to the director of the budget and,

when I go there, they say they cannot give me the information I need. But I will not give in or be disappointed—rather, I will court his friendship. I will not write the story because I did not get what I wanted. The man becomes my friend and I will be visiting him, saying, "Oh, how are you getting on, how is the family?" So now he will say, "This one . . . don't mention my name." That is how I establish my network. I don't terrorize my informants (laughs).

Guaranteed anonymity, such sources can channel a steady supply of tips and leaks to the patient and persistently friendly journalist. When a journalist is searching for official confirmation to meet an impending deadline, however, such demands for anonymity and social intimacy can pose an annoying constraint.

Chocolates and informal visits may woo the exceptional source; but lower-level employees in government offices often require less subtle inducements to solicit their cooperation in the investigations of private journalists. Arthur Adjei describes how the *Chronicle* mobilizes its network of informants in government offices, motivating government employees to search out and supply information for *Chronicle* investigations.

> If we suspect corruption in an organization, we have established relations with certain key people, a rapport. At the police services, at the army, at the ministries. We tell them what to do. Sometimes they have to draw files or copy documents—go and do this or that. Sometimes we have to pay for information, for research. When the information comes, it becomes meaningful to us when they may see it as harmless. So we use people in certain organizations.

Journalists with the *Chronicle* openly admit that they pay for the cooperation of sources in obtaining information and documents. Echoing the ambivalent descriptions of "soli," some journalists hasten to distinguish this financial inducement from the unethical and unprofessional act of "bribery," describing it instead as an appreciative gift or compensation for risk.

> People realize what they are doing is risky so we go out, say "Oh, take this for running around or taxi fare." It's too big even for taxi fare for the whole month but they realize that we are giving it because we are grateful for the account they are giving us. Mutually this is a gift and not payment for what they did for us but, because of the embarrassment, we say, "Oh, I know you have incurred some things here and there, running around, gathering these things for us. Or, "Well, you run a risk so take this for your trouble." So that is how we do it. Sometimes it's embarrassing, but we do it often. (Arthur Adjei)

> See, it's not as though we pay for information. What we do is, we appreciate people who volunteer information for us. Because some information is very sensitive and someone risks his life to say, "Charlie, some corruption is going on here, try and investigate it." We try to give a token amount of money for having the nation's interest at heart. It's not bribery. We are not buying a story. I'll in-

vestigate the story and write it. We appreciate our sources, but we are not buying stories. (Reginald Clottey)

These nuanced accounts of prestation by the two *Chronicle* journalists are
openly contradicted by the more forthright interpretation of their colleague
Richard Gyasi. For Gyasi, the exchange of information for money is a simple
business transaction, supported by the editor. In Gyasi's account, paying for
tips and inside information is not unlike purchasing public documents.

> We buy information. Most people come to realize that you are selling a newspa-
> per, selling information to the public so we have to buy information from them.
> So we buy it! My editor gives me a special allowance for it. Sometimes I have to
> buy documents.

While government ministries regularly dole out soli to journalists with
the state media, lower-level employees in those same ministries regularly accept similar cash gifts from journalists in the private press. Through money,
the state secures the cooperation of state journalists in the construction of
state hegemony. Simultaneously money secures the cooperation of state employees in the deconstruction of state hegemony through the scandals and
exposés of private journalists. Like journalists with the state press, lower-
level state employees occupy an ambivalent social position. While enjoying a
coveted position in the material and informational "plenty" of the state,
lower-level employees may resent their underpaid subordination, susceptible to the whims of officious bigmen. Like the soli given so often to state
journalists, cash gifts to state employees combine with informal socializing
among journalists and sources (visits, dating, friendships), forging social
and material bonds aimed at compelling obligation and fidelity.

Thus, while state journalists are invited everyday to participate in state
rituals, providing them with regular access to official sources of information,
private journalists are excluded from these sources, compelled to come up
with alternative tactics to generate news. From dinner dates and cash gifts to
document theft and impersonation, private journalists have crafted a cunning repertoire of devices designed to elicit information from alternative
sources when official sources refuse to grant interviews. "Going through the
back door" for access to inside information, journalists piece together the
narratives for regular news stories as well as the more provocative scandals and exposés. While sometimes supplemented with documentation, the
anonymous tips of informants are often based on rumor and speculation.
Such stories are incomplete without some sort of official verification. When
sources continually shrink from publicity, private journalists are faced with
two possibilities. Honoring the anonymity of their sources, journalists fre-

quently go ahead and publish stories without official attribution, stories seemingly based on rumor and speculation. Recognizing the contradiction of this practice with the professional standards espoused by GJA and other journalist organizations, private journalists nonetheless justify these rumor-based stories with their own integrity and conviction that the story is, in fact, true.

> We still have to protect our sources. According to the Constitution, you cannot force anybody to disclose a source unless a judge orders it through the court. We still have to produce newspapers. We still have to look for information. So once what we have written is true, we don't care whether you believe that just because we haven't quoted a direct source it is a lie or . . . we don't mind that. (Victoria Frimpong)

While no one but a judge can force a journalist to reveal his or her anonymous sources, sometimes journalists expose their sources deliberately out of frustration with the unreasonable demands for anonymity. Emmanuel and Victoria discussed how they are sometimes forced to "out" their reluctant sources, compromising their vital links to government information.

> Emmanuel Boateng: Whoever the source is, whoever the authorities are, they should try to come out of their shell. Sometimes you can even talk to a deputy minister—he talks to you freely but because the minister is there, he will also tell you that you can't quote him.
> Victoria Frimpong: Remember when we were doing that human rights story? The deputy did not want to talk but I put her name down and she didn't say anything.
> EB: What happens next time is that if Victoria needs to contact this woman, she wouldn't say anything at all—just that the minister isn't there, wait for him. Conditions are created such that, even if it is a rumor, we are forced to publish it.

The decision to protect or reveal the identity of sources is primarily determined by the nature of the story. For straight news stories, a deputy may hint at government actions but then refuse to be quoted, deferring to her elusive and dismissive boss, the minister. Since publication of facts does not seriously endanger the safety or livelihood of such sources, journalists sometimes quote them anyway. For reports on scandals, however, private journalists rigorously protect their anonymous sources. Sources for such stories undertake considerable personal and professional risk to provide tips and evidence to document corruption and other dishonorable activity.

Keeping these valuable and reliable sources anonymous, investigative journalists use their hard-won information to pressure state officials to respond. Winding up an investigation into corruption, a private journalist will then confront the bigman with the incriminating evidence, threatening to publish with or without his comment. Journalists may embellish their allegations with speculations or deliberate exaggerations in order to force a corrective response from the official. Richard Gyasi describes a combination of these tactics:

> If I have information that you [a government official] have embezzled 500 million cedis, if somebody tells me that, I would not come to you directly and say, "Please, I understand that . . ." I would try to dig deeper. Maybe last month you took 100 million, the month before you took 100 million, you went here and you went there. I should have the facts, that is my ammunition. Only after the investigation, then I can come to you with the ammunition. I begin with harmless questions. Sometimes I come out directly. Sometimes I get it on paper.
> "Could you please disabuse my mind on how 500 million cedis sprinted away from the account books?"
> "Well, I don't know about that."
> "I know last month you took 100 million, so you know I have the facts . . ."

If an official refuses to succumb to this sort of intimidation, journalists feel justified in publishing the story anyway, despite the lack of official corroboration or denial.

Discursive Style and the Genre of Scandal

When the newspaper licensing law was lifted in 1991, the private press entered a discursive field dominated by the conservative state-owned media. Including two daily newspapers, two entertainment weekenders, regional and national radio stations, and two television channels, the institutions of the state-owned media cooperated in the articulation of a specific social hegemony unique to the Rawlings regime. With who-leads and chain-quoting, the state media consistently portray Rawlings as an eloquent and charismatic authority figure with strong links to international flows of trade and aid, channeling those flows into rural development and urban accumulation. In the nineteen years that Rawlings presided over the state, the state media collaborated in the refashioning of his revolutionary-populist image as a wiry young junior officer, transforming him into the portrait of political legitimacy and mature respectability as a proper African statesman.

Entering this discursive field, the private press was not merely satisfied to practice journalism as a business but was fundamentally motivated by a political desire to disarticulate the representational hegemony of the state media. Not immune to market forces, the private press positioned itself firmly as an oppositional discourse, capitalizing on popular outrage at the repression and human rights abuses of the revolution along with widespread rumors of corruption among government ministers. Getting behind the well-crafted rhetoric of the state, private journalists began to seize on the reckless public remarks that seemed to reveal the selfishness, irresponsibility, and ethnic biases of state officials. Writing for the *Ghanaian Chronicle* and the *Independent,* journalists know that they are expected to write the kinds of stories that will sell newspapers. When asked to specify exactly what their audiences are looking for, Arthur Adjei gave a common response.

> Political scandals, corruption in official circles. Politicians and their outrageous remarks sell. Here politics is highly polarized, either you are here or there. In the United States . . . they don't take polarization very seriously; but here, if you are here you are not there—the two are enemies. That's how we understand it. So if someone on the other side says something outrageous, everyone would want to read it. Scandals, corruption, excesses in official circles.

While corruption scandal is a global genre of commercial journalism, the textual construction of this genre of journalism in Ghana reflects the political and historical circumstances of its local emergence. As the field of private journalism took shape in the early 1990s, corruption scandals came to constitute the primary form of front-page critique leveled by the private press, aimed at illustrating the hypocrisy and illegitimacy of Rawlings' postrevolutionary regime. This genre began with allegations of mismanagement at state organizations, particularly the Ghana National Petroleum Company and the Cocoa Marketing Board (Agyeman-Duah 1996). As noted in the previous chapter, these corruption exposés reached a peak of popularity with a slew of stories, appearing in the *Independent,* the *Ghanaian Chronicle* and the *Free Press,* indirectly linking this mismanagement to the stunning wealth and luxurious lifestyles of government ministers. Focusing on houses as symbols of accumulation and "bigman status" (Price 1974), several stories were generated by the "discovery" of conspicuously large houses under construction for certain ministers of state. Among those targeted by the private press were four of Rawlings' valuable allies: Ibrahim Adam, Minister of Food and Agriculture; P. V. Obeng, Special Adviser on Governmental Affairs; Colonel E. M. Osei-Owusu, Minister of the Interior; and Dr Isaac Adjei-Maafo, Presidential Staffer on Cocoa Affairs. The front-page exposé on Osei-Owusu exemplifies the discursive features of this genre. Under the masthead, two photographs displayed an apparently large two-story building surrounded by several smaller structures, all obscured by a high brick wall. The headline identified this compound as "Osei-Wusu's 600m (cedi) Gold House."

Somewhere along the road to Ghana's Atomic Energy Commission at Kwabenya, near the national capital is situated a housing complex called Kwabia Lodge, part of which is shown above. It is yet to be listed by a house number.

The complex consists of a storey building and four outer houses, which valuers estimate cost as much as 600 million cedis.

The house, sources say, belongs to Colonel Osei-Wusu, the Minister of Interior of the Republic of Ghana whose salary is just around 4 million cedis a year.

How he built this house in a record time of about one year on his salary as a Regional Secretary for Ashanti Region and Minister of Interior is a puzzle that Colonel Osei-Wusu would have had to answer if this era was June 4, 1979, when the AFRC [Armed Forces Revolutionary Council] insisted on probity and accountability.

And in the wake of the June 4 rally at Mankessim where President Rawlings once again has raised the big issue of probity and accountability, accusing other regimes of corruption, Colonel Osei-Wusu's ownership of the house re-opens the issue once again for his own regime.[2]

Although argued with the material evidence of photographs, the story is actually based on the accounts of anonymous sources who identify the minister as the owner of the house, along with anonymous "valuers" who estimate its cost. Shielding these useful informants, the story obscures the path of rumor and circumstance that led to the reporter's discovery of the house. While the essential elements of the narrative are based on rumor, the very relevance of the story hinges on an implied speculation that the house was improperly financed. Leaving the link between salary and house as a provocative "puzzle," the story points out that the road in front of the house has been tarred, unusual in this part of town. The grandeur of the house arouses suspicion; but the smooth road suggests government connections and access to public funds—a more direct insinuation that a minister is involved, abusing his public office for his own private comfort.

Turning to the broader historical and political context, the article is not content to incriminate one minister. The government corruption suggested in the story is literally juxtaposed with Rawlings' continual celebration of his June 4, 1979, revolutionary assault on corruption. Mentioned in the fifth paragraph of the story, Rawlings' anti-corruption rhetoric at Mankessim is further detailed in a story placed just next to the Osei-Wusu story on the front page. Thus this example of corruption is used to illustrate the failure of Rawlings' revolution and the hypocrisy of his regime. Calling into question

Rawlings' revolutionary claim to political legitimacy, the *Independent* demonstrates that the Rawlings regime has abdicated the crusade for probity and accountability. This article, along with the numerous others in this genre, takes up that crusade and positions the private press as the moral conscience of a decadent and hypocritical regime. The article not only aims at exposing corruption but, more important, works to establish a legitimate role for the private press in the affairs of state.

As illustrated in chapter 2, many *Daily Graphic* stories structure a kind of polished rhetorical dialogue among the several government officials at an event, a staged conversation aimed at consensus over the legitimacy, effectiveness, and benevolence of the state. Presented as social consensus, these official conversations are predicated on the exclusion of the unofficial voices of popular dissent. In contrast, corruption exposés such as this one tend to submerge the identities and statements of their sources, creating a rather isolated narrative position for the reporter, whose impassioned and scrutinizing voice is foregrounded. Ironically the staged dialogue of *Graphic* stories attempts to compensate for the suppression of popular commentary while the lone cry of corruption in the *Independent* actually emerges from popular discourses, drawing from a heavy traffic of rumor and social commentary on the daily affairs of the state and behavior of government officials.

Moreover, as weekly newspapers specializing in political commentary, private papers tend to pick up and engage with the top stories of the week (in both state and private papers), adding results from their own investigations as well as posing questions and speculations. As these corruption exposés multiplied, the *Independent* and the *Ghanaian Chronicle*, along with the *Free Press*, the *Guide*, and *Public Agenda*, were all participating in the unfolding investigations against the ministers, commenting on one another's coverage and the broader historical and political implications. While the *Graphic* typically ignores other newspapers (along with any other voice outside the state information apparatus), the intertextuality of the private press constitutes an ongoing dialogue across the spectrum of the news media, engaged with popular discourses and linking those anonymous voices to the official political field.

Under increasing pressure to respond to the multiplying allegations of corruption among his cabinet ministers, Rawlings finally turned the matter over to the Commission for Human Rights and Administrative Justice, instructing Commissioner Emile Short to investigate the allegations. The ministers were required to declare their assets and document their sources of income. The editors of the private press were called in to testify to the truth of the stories they had published. In the case of Osei-Owusu (as CHRAJ spells his name), the Commission discovered that the minister's "gold house" was actually valued at 161 million cedis and not 600 million as alleged by the *Independent* story. However, the official CHRAJ "Report on Investigation into Allegations of Corruption against Col. E. M. Osei-Owusu, Minister of the Interior" found that the minister was unable to account for 33 million cedis of excess income during the time the house was constructed. Although no allegations of corruption were leveled by CHRAJ, the Commission recommended that Osei-Owusu "should be made to refund to the State, the excess income of 33,023,182.48 (cedis)."[3] Following the verdict, Osei-Owusu resigned from his post "to enable him to contest the findings of the Commission," as a publication of the Information Services Department explained.[4]

Although the figures were certainly exaggerated (perhaps intentionally), the allegations of corruption by the private press were essentially vindicated by the findings of CHRAJ against the ministers. The Commission reached more serious conclusions against both Ibrahim Adam and Adjei Maafo.[5] CHRAJ investigations revealed that Adam, as Minister of Agriculture, waived customs duties and taxes on foreign ships, losing billions of cedis of state revenue. CHRAJ found Adjei Maafo, staffer on Cocoa Affairs, guilty of tax evasion. Adjei Maafo was further reprimanded by CHRAJ for purchasing a house in the name of his son and then lying about it. P. V. Obeng was exonerated from allegations that he improperly acquired a luxurious "gilded" house along with a string of other valuable properties.

In these allegations of corruption the private press has gone further than moral critique of postrevolutionary hypocrisy, challenging Rawlings' more recent claims to political legitimacy based on state accumulation and distribution. The postrevolutionary Rawlings has attempted a transformation into a respectable African statesman, portraying himself as an effective economic commander and benevolent patron. These stories of corruption within Rawlings' own cabinet are meant to overturn these charismatic constructions, circulated in the state press. Vindicated by CHRAJ, a state organization, the charges of mismanagement and misappropriation call into question Rawlings' command over his own staff as well as the ability of the state to channel its resources into development projects both in the capital and throughout the regions.

As both unofficial and official investigations into the dubious wealth of state officials petered out, the private press has ventured into new categories of corruption, focusing on divestiture kickbacks, electoral fraud, and other political scandals. In January 1996 both the *Free Press* and the *Ghanaian Chronicle* culled a story from the New York–based *African Observer*, reporting on the arrest of Ghanaian diplomat Frank Benneh in Switzerland for drug trafficking. The story further alleged that Rawlings was interfering in

10. This article in the *Ghanaian Chronicle* alleges widespread corruption in the NDC government, based on the public comments of Rawlings' "right-hand man," the former chairman of the Divestiture Implementation Committee. In the photo an unkempt Rawlings, with bushy beard and dark glasses, appears defiant in the face of the accusations. The unrelated story in the lower left refers to Rawlings as a "half-caste" and a "mullato" [*sic*], and therefore not a "full-blooded Ghanaian."*Courtesy of the* Ghanaian Chronicle, *September 16, 1996.*

11. The classic oppositional exposé: this front-page story in the private newspaper the *Independent* alleges disorganization, administrative lapses, and corruption at the Ghana Immigration Service. Such an exposé on illicit flows of goods, people, and money carries the implication that President Rawlings is neither in control of the national borders nor of his own government ministry, a charge that calls into question Rawlings' own authority and political legitimacy. *Courtesy of the* Independent, *May 22, 1997.*

the prosecution of Benneh in order to cover up his own involvement in international drug smuggling.[6] Using his own diplomatic corps to smuggle drugs, the story charged that Rawlings funneled profits from the drug trade to purchase weapons for his "paramilitary forces," scattered throughout the countryside.

> In preparations for possible violence in 1996 because of the crucial general elections, Rawlings last year bought several millions of dollars worth of weapons from the black market for his para-military forces. Sources suspect the money had come from drug dealing.[7]

This story resonated with widespread rumors, surfacing in other *Free Press* stories, that Rawlings himself abuses drugs, particularly cocaine.

Enraged by the Benneh story, Rawlings sued the editors of the *Free Press* and the *Ghanaian Chronicle* for criminal libel under Section 185 of the Criminal Code, a remnant of colonial law continually revived by authoritarian regimes in Ghana to suppress dissent. Section 185 specifies the crime of "injuring the credit or reputation of Ghana or the government by false reports" (Mensa-Bonsu 1997, 43). Four years later the case continues to drag on in the courts. If found guilty, the editors of the *Free Press* and the *Chronicle* face up to ten years in prison. In March 1997 the director of USIS in Accra, Nick Robertson, was expelled from Ghana for speaking out against Section 185 and Rawlings' prosecution of the case.[8]

Rawlings' litigious response to allegations of corruption in the private press is only a more serious instance of the common strategy adopted by targets of the private press. Ministers and other politicians exposed in scandal stories frequently respond by suing for civil libel. Since 1991 hundreds of libel cases have been brought against the private press, particularly the *Free Press* and the *Ghanaian Chronicle*. Such libel cases are designed to steer the controversy out of public scrutiny and into the realm of the courts, where politicians exert considerably more influence than journalists. Once the case has gone to court, newspapers are prohibited from pursuing a story in print or else face further charges of contempt of court.

> People are rushing to court to file libel cases because then you must stop writing. A private paper is ready to expose everything. The story comes out and he realizes that the story has more to talk about. The person will rush to court and file a libel suit and you can't go and write anything more. So it stops it there. So that's the trick. And you know, our court system, these things can run for months and years. So when you have a libel suit, the story stops there and the society divides into two—those who believe the paper and those who believe

THE INDEPENDENT

Vol. 4 No. 92 Wednesday, September 11th - 17th Sept., 1996   US $1.00 UK £.50 ¢400

Dispute Over Sale of Ghanair Office

by Kwame Amoateng & Isabella Gyau

Ghana Airways top officials are allegedly considering selling the airline's London based office at 3 Princess Street and move to a less expensive location.

But London based members of staff of the airline have issued a protest claiming the sale will rather incur more debts than profits. They have outlined grave implications over the sale in a memo to Ghanair management and have advised

that the airline maintain its present office.

The memo referred to a meeting held in the Ghanair conference room on Monday, August 19, during which Speedwing representative Mr. Peter Jones informed members of staff about the proposed sale. Speedwing is a British consultancy which currently manages Ghanair. Mr. Jones told employees that the proposed sale had been necessitated by the high cost of running the 3 Princes Street office. Princess Street is a busy commer-

cial area in the United Kingdom of Great Britain, making it a strategic point for trade. But like all commercial districts, operating an office in that area is relatively expensive than less commercial areas.

The monthly interest paid on the building, explained the Speedwing official, was £40,000.

London employees, however, disagree with the Speedwing official. The memo explained that the interest payable on the office building is below £12,000.00 which places the office within reasonable operational limits.

London staff explained that

Cont. on back page

From the NDC Congress

Many memorable things happened at the NDC congress. Our reporters and cameraman were there to capture this scene and others for our readers. See page 3 and centre spread for news and pictures on the NDC Congress as well as a report from the PNC congress.

Corruption At Graphic

• M.D. Cited

[Exclusive]

A time bomb is ticking at the Graphic Corporation.

Nobody knows when it will explode but for the nine-member board of directors of the state-owned corporation, headed by the Okuapehene, Nana Addo Dankwah, they are confronted with their biggest headache since they were inaugurated about a year ago.

The Managing Director of the Graphic Corporation-Kofi Badu is locked in a bitter struggle with the Chief Accountant-James Frimpong. It is not a battle for power but a conflict about financial impropriety.

At the heart of the matter is an allegation that the Graphic Corpo-

ration, publishers of the oldest national daily -Daily Graphic-is being buried again by a wave of massive corruption.

Paradoxically, the man at the centre of the gathering storm is the current Managing Director of the Corporation-veteran journalist-Kofi Badu- who himself at the beginning of his tenure of office brought to light a one-billion fraud at the Graphic Corporation. Today the stone of corruption is being cast at him.

A 13-page document before the board of directors is alleging that Mr. Badu, a former managing Director of Graphic who was re-apppointed the MD in 1992, is involved in a number of malpractices that will make saints out of the accounts people on trial in the one-billion fraud case.

The report talks of fraud perpetrated by the Chief Executive through purchasing and other malpractices.

The crisis at Graphic is no secret to many workers who typically of Ghanaians murmur about it rather than speak openly about it.

One allegation is that a junior worker of Daily Graphic who lives with the MD and has brought forth his child, Agnes Acquaye, has for the last one-year been on an unu-

sual maternity leave.

What workers at Graphic find unusual is the fact that the MD's girlfriend for this long period on maternity leave is still being paid by the Corporation. Another allegation is that Graphic Corporation spends almost two million cedis a month on the M.D.'s residential telephone.

The current crisis at Graphic is supposed to have started when the MD in a surprise move unilaterally without reference to the Board, ordered the Chief Accountant-James Frimpong- to swap office with the Chief Internal Auditor.

The notice of the transferment, on back page

Kofi Badu, Graphic MD

Latest on Arkaah

A press conference is to be held today at the Ghana International Pres Centre. According to our sources, the press conference by Attah Koh, the PCP activist who is supposed to have filed a writ against Veep Nkensen

Cont. on back page

Kumasi Crisis Not Over

by Daniel Batidam

The crises that have bedeviled Ghana's second largest city Kumasi in recent times do not seem to be over yet.

A letter written by all "Drivers Union" and addressed to GBC FM Kumasi last week (Wednesday September 4, 1996) indicated that from September 10 notably yesterday, a

series of "non-stop" demonstrations will begin.

The letter warned that any attempt by the security agents to stop them will mark the beginning of civil war in Ghana.

Among other things, the drivers requested that the Ashanti Regional Chairman of GPRTU Nana John Konadu be removed. They also wanted immediate ceasure of a practice known as "priority loading"

Cont. on back page

12. A front-page story in the *Independent* exposing allegations of fraud and malpractice against the managing director of the *Daily Graphic*. Among the charges: Badu arranged for an "unusual" one-year maternity leave for a "junior worker" at *Graphic* who has recently given birth to the M.D.'s baby. *Graphic* is funded by the state; therefore, this amounts to a kind of state-subsidized extramarital procreation. *Courtesy of the* Independent, *September 11, 1996.*

the person filing the suit. And the libel suit keeps dragging and dragging. So I think it is the style now. (Emmanuel Boateng)

In an environment where documents are difficult to obtain and official sources are reluctant to comment, the private press is particularly vulnerable to the more exacting standards of testimony and evidence applied in the courts. Boateng describes how journalists are manipulated in these flows of power and information.

> If people would talk to you, then they would need to run to court to file a libel suit. Why didn't you just meet with the reporter to give your own version? Because a reporter would contact you and say, "This is the story I have, what do you say?" If you avoid this person, they will go ahead and publish. They are not even writing rejoinders, just going to court. So it is fishy. We have a young democracy. It is the responsibility of journalists and authorities to help one another survive. You should not run to court; you should grant interviews and clear yourself. Because you know you can take some advantages in court. Some cases run for years and no one can comment.

Thus the state information apparatus, excluding private journalists from official sources of fact and truth, intersects with the judiciary which then applies official standards to further disqualify and criminalize private journalism. Even so, Kofi Coomson, editor of the *Ghanaian Chronicle,* maintains that most libel plaintiffs are well aware that they are unable to make a solid case against the newspaper. Coomson refers to most libel suits as exaggerated forms of public denial merely brought to save face. Most plaintiffs, in Coomson's vast experience, stall the case with legal delays for several weeks or months and then attempt to settle out of court.

As the number of libel cases indicates, the controversial issue at stake in the front-page scandals of the private press is not just the matter of corruption but, more pointedly, the reputation of prominent public figures. As the references to guns and impending military action in the *Free Press* story indicate, the private press challenges the benevolent patron figure constructed in the state media by portraying Rawlings as a vulgar and violent revolutionary, opposed to reasoned dialogue, democracy, and the rule of law. When Rawlings beat up his own vice president in a cabinet meeting, rumors of the incident swarmed through the city, capitalized in the front-page stories of the private press even as the state press remained silent. Coverage of such erratic and violent behavior is meant to illustrate Rawlings' smallboy immaturity and cultural degeneracy, essentially his inappropriateness as an African statesman.

Like these allegations of political corruption that resonate with common notions of maturity and morality, sensational stories on the president's wife aim at exposing not only corruption but sexual deviancy. In July 1993 the *Free Press* reported that Nana Konadu had acquired a jacuzzi bathtub at a price of more than 40 million cedis.[9] Subsequent stories alleged "Jacuzzi Can Be Used for Sex," adding, "It Can Induce Orgasm, It Can Excite Libido" (cited in Agyeman-Duah 1996). During the elections in November 1996 the *Statesman* ran a front-page story, "Nana Konadu's Secret Sexual Problems Out," reporting on the "sexual starvation" of the First Lady while her husband was on the campaign trail.[10] The story was based on the well-meant public comments of Cecilia Johnson, a friend and colleague of Nana Konadu in the 31st December Women's Movement. At a public function Johnson earnestly lamented the unfortunate plight of Rawlings and Konadu, "unable to satisfy their sexual desires." The story depicted Konadu, present at the function, hiding her face in embarrassment. Drawing on the usual portrayal of the president's wife as proud and pushy, the article quoted someone in the crowd whispering, "Look at Nana Konadu, the vice president of Ghana behaving like a college girl, has she ever been shy in her life?"[11] While indicting and humiliating Nana Konadu, herself a powerful figure in the ruling party, these front-page exposés on the sexual deviancy and desperation of the First Lady further imply that her husband, President Rawlings, is not quite man enough to satisfy or control her.

Bigmen, Small Boys: Authority and Resistance in the Postcolony

The oppositional discourse of the private press is dedicated to portraying Rawlings and other state officials as vulgar, violent, immature, addicted to drugs and sex, and thoroughly contaminated by corruption. Thus oppositional attempts to disarticulate the constructions of charismatic authority in the state media have generally not attacked the preoccupation with bigmen and their official pronouncements so redundantly reproduced in *Graphic* stories. Rather, the private press seems to take the political centrality of bigmen for granted, committing themselves to exposing the political illegitimacy of these figures as part of a project of deposing and replacing them. In this struggle private journalists are informed by cultural understandings of the role of young men in precolonial and colonial politics in what is now southern Ghana.

In chapter 2, I traced the interpretive position of *Graphic* reporters to the role of okyeame, mediating and improving official discourse for the public audience. Journalists for the private press, however, are differently positioned in the discursive field of Ghanaian politics, systematically excluded from the realm of official discourse and precariously positioned at the

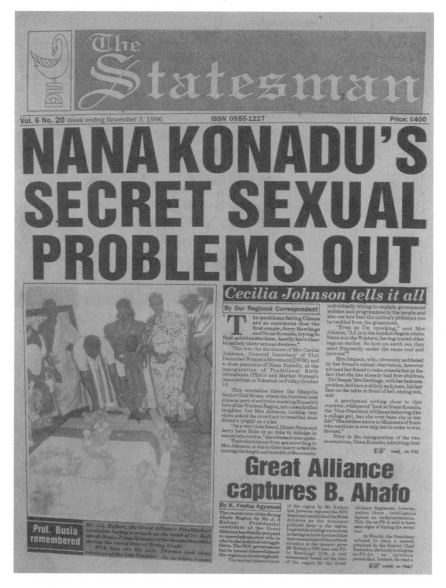

13. In the midst of the 1996 presidential campaign, the November 3 issue of the oppositional newspaper, the *Statesman* declares that First Lady Nana Konadu is complaining of sexual starvation. This story continues an ongoing theme in the private press alleging the sexual voraciousness and deviancy of Nana Konadu. Such an immature lack of self-control, unconcern for national interest, and lapse in discursive propriety are quite out of keeping with popular expectations for a woman of public authority. *Courtesy of the* Statesman, *November 3, 1996.*

boundaries of the political and the popular. Placed here, their discursive role parallels the role of young men in Akan society and Ghanaian political history (Allman 1993).

In Ghana, private journalism is dominated by young men. While the profession as a whole tends to attract more young men than young women, the discursive orientation of the private press seems to appeal particularly to young men. The Ghana Institute of Journalism has recently begun to admit an equal number of men and women for training in journalism and public relations; but a disproportionate number of young men continue to gravitate toward the oppositional private press. As journalists, their practices of news gathering and textual construction are informed by historicized cultural notions about the role of young men in politics and political discourse.

In Akan societies political organization and military organization are intertwined (Nukunya 1992). The hierarchical pyramid of chiefs also defines the functional organization of the army as well as its chain of command. As subordinates in the official realm of chiefs and elders, young men are organized in groups for military defense against intruders (Price 1974; Rattray 1929).[12] However, these groups ("asafo" in Fante or "nkwankaa" in Asante) also function as representatives of all untitled "commoners" in society, and thus as an instrument of popular opinion (Owusu 1989; Busia 1951). If a chief became corrupt, degenerate, drunken, obsessed by women, or otherwise unfit to rule, young men would lead the campaign against the illegitimate chief, requesting punitive and corrective action by the elders. If such action failed, young men could then arrest the chief, remove his sandals, and touch his feet to the ground, thereby defiling him. Then a shotgun would be fired and the chief would officially be declared "destooled."[13] As Kimble (1963, 471) notes on asafo, "This outlet for popular dissatisfaction had formed an essential part of the traditional checks and balances upon the authority of the chief."

British colonial administration in West Africa functioned through a system of indirect rule, incorporating African chiefs into the colonial apparatus by using them to collect fines and taxes and coordinate the implementation of colonial policies at the local level. Implicated in colonial domination, both the political legitimacy and local authority of many chiefs were thrown into jeopardy. In the early twentieth century groups of young men in southern Ghana (in Akim-Abuakwa and Kwahu) mobilized against unpopular chiefs with allegations of corruption and excessive fines (Owusu 1989, 383; Kimble 1963, 469–473). According to Kimble, these asafo protests represented a challenge by the "individualistic, wealth-conscious younger members of the community" (471) against the political-economic monopoly fused together in colonial and chiefly authority. Owusu stresses the redemptive power of these asafo uprisings, animated by popular demands for social justice and representation. "The members of Asafo had a sacred duty to safeguard the interests of the wider local community against rulers or leaders who misused or abused their power" (383).

Described by Owusu, the colonial role of asafo in protests against corrupt chiefs bears a remarkable resemblance to the contemporary role of the private press in campaigns against corrupt and illegitimate state authority. Time and again private journalists describe themselves as the "watchdogs" of the public interest, exposing corruption and abuses of power. Both asafo protests and the private press are fundamentally motivated by campaigns to denounce the corruption and political illegitimacy of bigmen. As rising elites in the private sector, private editors like Blay-Amihere similarly challenge the political-economic monopoly of the ruling-party state with an "individualistic" rhetoric of human rights and free enterprise.

One intriguing key to the cultural and political positioning of private journalists is found in the contradictory treatment of violence and military themes. As noted above, the private press is bent on depicting Rawlings as an irascible smallboy, an unreconstructed military ruler with a history of human rights abuses and violent outbursts against his enemies. While the private press appropriates the international discourses of democracy and human rights against this militaristic violence, they simultaneously invoke the oppositional voice of asafo, a primarily military organization of young men.

The weekly political columns so popular in the private press provide several examples of this contradiction. One weekly column for the *Independent,* entitled "Observation Post," is illustrated by a shadowy silhouette of a young man in a helmet hoisting a monstrous machine gun (although the column is actually written by T. H. Ewusi-Brookman, himself a very gentle, elderly man). The column is primarily devoted to denouncing the violence and authoritarianism of the Rawlings regime. During the 1996 presidential campaign the themes of the column were reinforced by the editorial strategy of the newspaper to publicize Rawlings' continual celebration of the executions and widespread violence of the revolutionary period.[14] Another column, written by *Chronicle* editor Kofi Coomson, depicts a hooded and masked figure, "Politicus," armed with bow and arrow, further emphasizing the fusion of political and militaristic symbols in the shadowy figure of the young man. Appropriate to the *Chronicle,* the masked Politicus resonates with the figure of the investigative journalist, masking his identity in undercover operations aimed at protecting the popular interest. Like "Observation Post," "Politicus" is an anti-authoritarian column often dealing with issues of human rights and violence. Another *Chronicle* column is devoted to weekly analyses of the press, entitled "Watching the Watchman." Yet another, "Baywatch," is written by *Chronicle* journalists under the pseudonym Asebu Amenfi, a military figure in Akan history. Drawing from complex circuits of popular discourse around Accra, this column publicizes the latest rumors of "lies" and corruption (and other varieties of misbehavior) among government officials and other prominent bigmen. An enormously popular column, "Baywatch," displays a rather stunning anonymous reach into the circles of power as well as the circuits of popular commentary in the streets and chop bars of Accra, reinforcing the role of the *Chronicle* as a voice of popular political representation.

Thus the "watchdog" role of the private press is shaped by the historic role of young men's military organizations in campaigns against corruption and abuse of office. However, identification with the forces of state security and defense compels some investigative journalists into strategic collusion with the state, compounding the contradictions of oppositional journalism.

Corruption, Collusion, and Extraversion

In the spring of 1997, as Albanians were rioting over the collapse of the disastrous pyramid financial scheme, *Chronicle* reporter Richard Gyasi set out to investigate a similar financial fad in Accra. Acting on a letter of complaint to the *Chronicle*, Gyasi staked out the building in a suburb of Accra where Friends Business Promotions Limited (FBP) was operating. Posing as a client, Gyasi called the managing director of the "bank," Ben Mat, to inquire about a loan. Satisfied that FBP's practices were illegal, Gyasi then notified the police who came to arrest Mat. With Mat in prison, Gyasi went to interview him. Identifying himself as a reporter for the *Ghanaian Chronicle*, Gyasi neglected to mention that he had been responsible for Mat's arrest. Eager to tell his side of the story, Mat admitted that he did not have a license from the Bank of Ghana but insisted that his company was registered as a business with the Registrar General and financially backed by American and Swiss banks. Unable to verify Mat's claims, the *Chronicle* came out with the lead story, "Watch Out! Another 'Pyram' Opens for Business," reporting on Mat's arrest and warning Ghanaians of his exploitative practices.[15]

As an investigative journalist, Gyasi argues that such strategies of collaboration with state agencies are necessary in undercover investigations. In a lecture entitled "Investigative Journalism—The Reality," given to students at the Ghana Institute of Journalism, Gyasi explained the importance of state sources and allies:

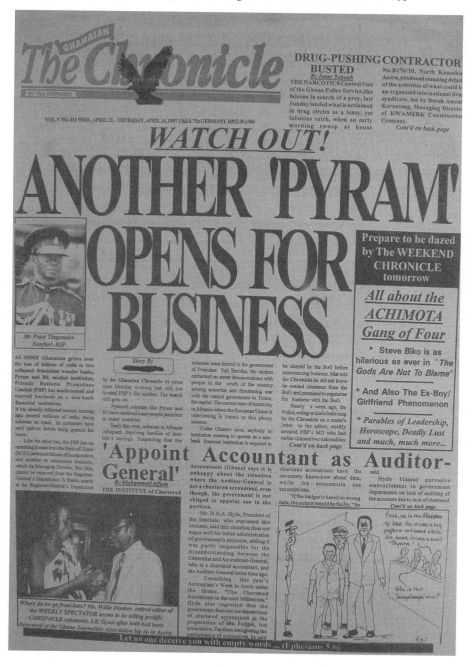

14. Straddle and scoop: Richard Gyasi's front-page "Pyram" exposé. *Courtesy of the* Ghanaian Chronicle, *April 23, 1997.*

The security agencies: Be friends with security agents—the Police, Commandos, Soldiers and even the personnel of the Bureau of National Investigations [BNI] etc.—using your discretion to pick out those who could facilitate your work and others likely to disclose deep-cover information which could provide the sniff of a major story. One of your roles is to help create a sane society and collaborating with these agencies including exposing their wrongdoings is one of them.[16]

Although here attempting to reinscribe an adversarial "watchdog" position despite collaboration with the state, Gyasi argues elsewhere that a journalist should work with the state "in the national interest," echoing the rhetoric of the state press. This revelation came as such a surprise to me, coming from a prominent journalist with the most hard-hitting oppositional paper in the country, that I pressed Gyasi to clarify.

> JH: Are there journalists who supply information to BNI?
> Richard Gyasi: Yes. We are all doing the same work. We all want one thing: information. There are journalists who supply information to BNI and BNI officials who supply information to journalists.
> JH: How do you feel about that practice of giving and taking information from BNI?
> RG: It depends. If it is in the national interest then I would do it. About 30 percent of my information is not printed, it is circulated in a certain community. If I have a hunch that there is a coup, somebody is plotting, then I dig and be sure of the facts. I would do two things—go straight to the top, the boss of the BNI, tell him and they will go and round the person up. Then I'll blow it or publish it.
> JH: Which one? [Note: I misunderstood this as a choice.]
> RG: That depends on the situation, how sure I am then I blow it before the coup is staged. Like Pyram. I supplied information to the police—why? I have a responsibility to the public to help create a safe society.

Through such collaboration, Gyasi has established a network of informants who supply him with tips and leaks (while no doubt providing Gyasi with a measure of personal security).

Gyasi's ambivalent collaboration with the state echoes the commitment to a certain form of objectivity articulated by other *Chronicle* journalists. However, as the textual analysis in this chapter demonstrates, the scandals and exposés on the front pages of the *Chronicle* firmly situate that newspaper in passionate opposition to the state. Poaching on the power of the state, *Chronicle* journalists then direct that power into essentially oppositional discourse.

While the private press is discursively positioned as oppositional, the cooperation of investigative journalists with official sources seems to indicate a more complicated negotiation of social and political commitments. Channeling information and privilege back and forth along the conduit of investigative journalism, *Chronicle* journalists straddle the boundaries dividing the state from the forces of political and popular opposition. While straddling practices constitute a strategy of material accumulation for the African bourgeoisie (including editor-publishers of the private press), the investigative straddling of *Chronicle* journalists instead indicates a strategy of social and symbolic accumulation. Simultaneous implication in projects of state hegemony and resistance not only generates information for top stories but also creates a diverse network of powerful allies.

Unlike journalists at the *Chronicle,* journalists at the *Independent* reject such undercover involvement in the machinations of state organizations, preferring to remain thoroughly and unequivocally oppositional. Rather than poach on the power of the state, the *Independent* summons a different source of social and symbolic power in its extraverted orientation to human rights and professional organizations. Recognizing the power of global positioning and appropriation, the *Independent* often publicizes the critical commentary of nongovernmental organizations and international human rights groups. Alongside Blay-Amihere's columns and editorials on press freedom and the struggles of the GJA, the *Independent* gave extensive coverage of the U.S. government's "Human Rights Report on Ghana, 1996," a report criticizing the judiciary of executive domination and ruling-party bias. In a lead story, "Government Influences Judges—U.S. Report," the paper summoned the "Human Rights Report" as evidence of the unfair treatment of the private press in the judicial process.[17] In another tactic of extraversion, the *Independent* publicizes the world travels of Blay-Amihere and other *Independent* journalists. With help from foreign sponsorship, the private press sends its best journalists abroad for cross-cultural exposure and professional training. Assisted by Blay-Amihere's efforts, several *Independent* journalists have traveled to Great Britain, Germany, Egypt, and the United States for study and travel. Whenever they go abroad, the *Independent* announces their departure and return to Ghana. Frequently they write about their experiences for the paper in features and columns. Blay-Amihere has also been active in recruiting foreign journalists to work at the *Independent.* Through his contacts as president of the West African Journalists Association, he has hired journalists from other ECOWAS countries, other African journalists fleeing harassment and repression. Blay-Amihere is especially quick to incorporate Americans into his staff. Before I arrived, another American researcher, conducting interviews on Ghanaian business practices for a Fulbright project, had been writing an entertaining column for the *Independent* comparing American and Ghanaian ways of doing business. When I came to work for the *Independent,* Blay-Amihere publicized my arrival at the newspaper with a short announcement at the bottom right corner of the front page (along with my passport photo). Assigning me a column to write, Blay-Amihere encouraged me to write about my experiences as an American studying Ghanaian culture and politics.

Finally, the *Independent* has embraced the Internet as yet another strategy of oppositional extraversion. The web came to Ghana in 1996. Two of the private weeklies, along with the *Daily Graphic,* are now available on the Internet via Africa Online. The *Independent* often publishes a full page of the enthusiastic e-mail responses of Ghanaian readers residing in Britain and the United States. The e-mail contribution in "Views from Abroad" are exemplary:

> You are doing a very wonderful work out there my brothers and sisters. You make me proud that I could rely on you for home (Ghana) news. Your job on the election '96 is superb. Please keep it up.
>
> Seidu.
> S.S. Salifa@uclan.ac.uk

> I started reading your papers recently on the internet and I must say your paper is the most fairest and unbiased in Ghana.
> I also love your opinion on the reconciliation of the parties. If they will heed your advice and act on it, I hope it's going to be a good and positive thing for the people and the nation as a whole.
> Thank you and keep up the good work.
>
> K. Baffour-Awuah
> kawuah@yesic.com (Awuah,Kingsley)[18]

The support of Ghanaians abroad for the private press constructs an oppositional diaspora, reinforcing the legitimacy and international support of oppositional discourse.

These multiple strategies of extraversion distinguish the oppositional journalism of the *Independent* from the introverted straddling of the *Chronicle*'s investigative journalism. While participating in the same crusade against the Rawlings regime, the *Chronicle* and the *Independent* have designed structurally unique positions in the social order, accessing different flows of information and support while relying on essentially the same oppositional audience.

Conclusion

In this book I have examined the rhetoric, texts, and practices of Ghanaian journalism in the state and private press. Through the public writings of Yaw Boadu-Ayeboafoh and Kabral Blay-Amihere, I have shown how state journalism draws on development discourse while private journalism accesses the international rhetoric of democracy and human rights. As journalists themselves summon these globalized discursive forms, their local experiences and everyday practices pose an uneasy set of professional contradictions with their fundamentally political positionalities. In practice, state and private journalists have designed distinctive local strategies to negotiate a complex and polarized political field shaped by cultural notions of authority, deference, and resistance. In the who-leads and chain-quoting of state journalism, the narrative authority of the journalist is subordinated to a consensus of state officials while the corruption exposés of the private press construct an isolated narrative position anonymously supported by popular resistance.

This dynamic process of appropriation, contradiction, and dialectical negotiation of global and local forces in the realm of journalistic production draws attention to the subjective complexities of democratization and neoliberal globalization. The scholarship on globalization is largely driven by two fundamental concerns: the nature of globalization as a homogenizing or heterogenizing force, and the consequences of globalization, beneficial or detrimental. What we find in the realm of Ghanaian journalism is neither the homogenizing force of neoliberal modernity nor the pure politics of antiglobal resistance and cultural protectionism (what has been termed "globalization from below"); rather, we find the traversing of both contradictory drives in the subjectivities, practices, and social relations of cultural producers.

At first glance it may seem simply that Ghanaian journalists are saying one thing and doing another; that is, they are touting global ideals of development or democracy or both while serving the local interests of political bigmen. Through the lens of Bourdieu, we might see meconnaisance in the contradictory relations of articulated discourse and everyday practice. A more cynical view might suppose that journalists are lying when they characterize themselves as watchdogs in the public interest. But the contradiction between global discourse and local practice is neither naïve nor disingenuous, as attested by the lengthy, earnest discussions of professionalism and political positionality throughout this book. Ghanaian journalists are well aware of the "difference" of Ghanaian political culture in a global sense and are themselves puzzled and vexed by the contradictory nature of their work in this context. Indeed, a great deal of newsprint is devoted to describing and analyzing what it means to be Ghanaian—politically, professionally, regionally, and continentally. The global engagement of Ghanaian journalists makes their profession distinctively cosmopolitan, particularly so in this neoliberal moment. Through interpolation into global sensibilities, journalists come to recognize and therefore dynamically produce current versions of locality and African political culture. This is to say that the contradiction between articulated discourse (what people say they do) and everyday practice (what they actually do) cannot be understood consequentially—as a contradiction traceable to conscious prevarication or unconscious naïveté—but instead must be recognized productively—as an irreconcilable contradiction of subjectivity which compels the reciprocal production of forces in opposition.

This is why the concept of "alternative modernity" is a misleading way of thinking about cultural difference in this era of neoliberal globalization. Holding modernity as an abstract constant while spinning out an ethnographic array of consequential local "alternatives," the discourse on alternative modernity tends to essentialize cultural difference as a local form of accommodation or resistance to modernity (or both). If Ghanaian journalism is not easily reduced to narratives of globalization or resistance, neither is it easily conceptualized in terms of universal modernity or cultural alterity. Rather than alternative modernity, where the noun is held as a theoretical constant while the modifier shifts to accommodate local circumstances, Ghanaian journalism suggests a kind of pretermodernity in which both modernity and locality are held in a contradictory dialectic, constantly redefining and reproducing each other. Ghanaian journalists are not passive or mystified in this process but are actively engaged in struggles for cultural identity, professional respect, and global participation.

Discursive Style and Political Culture

Throughout this analysis of state and private journalism in Ghana I have detailed the discursive styles distinctive to each, showing how style is embodied in everyday practices that consistently reproduce the style in print. Therefore discursive style is as much a matter of practice as it is of textual representation. As practical elements of everyday life and social relations, the styles described here are not merely journalistic but participate in larger cultural styles of state hegemony and oppositionality in Ghana; that is, they indicate a distinctive style of Ghanaian political culture.

As Benedict Anderson has pointed out, nation-states "are to be distinguished not by their falsity/genuineness, but by the style in which they are imagined" (1983, 6). Lately the African state has haunted the minds of Africanist scholars with visions of chaos, kleptocracy, and criminal menace. In some scholarly nightmares the African state appears as a psychotic freak. Reifying and pathologizing the African state, political science has attempted to explain how the state, as a rational-bureaucratic form of governance, is susceptible in certain tropical conditions to dysfunctions of "softness," "personalism," "patrimonialism," and so on. The effort of many scholars has been to define a conceptual model through which to imagine the African state and explain its deviant maldevelopment in the developmentalist scheme. Scholars may need to imagine the African state in this singular and abstract way, but my research suggests that Africans, at least Ghanaians, do not.

For Ghanaians, the state is not merely an array of bureaucratic institutions for the exercise of rationalized power; it is also a cultural apparatus of legitimate accumulation and distribution. Flows of material and symbolic capital as well as information are channeled into the state and throughout the rhizomatic networks of political economy. Moreover, as Ghanaians access and manipulate these flows through everyday practices and social relationships, they constitute the state as a site of sociality and intimacy, wielded against the alienation and insecurity of rationalized and bureaucratic forms of administration.[1] As imagined in the postcolony, forms of rational-bureaucratic administration are historically associated with colonial domination and exploitation.

Based on the fundamental experience of the state in terms of accumulation and sociality, this analysis of the press and political culture in Ghana points to four thematic elements of style in the imagination and improvisation of Ghanaian political culture: a preoccupation with bigmen, an economy of identity and anonymity, the predicament of corruption, and geo-political extraversion.

Bigmen, Big Language

Political discourse revolves around the activities and pronouncements of prominent politicians and businessmen, usually in Accra. Both state and private newspapers seem to agree on this, at least. As the *Graphic* portrayed Rawlings as a charismatic patron, the *Free Press* portrayed him as a drug dealer. As the *Graphic* linked development projects to the state through the rhetoric of named officials, the *Chronicle* linked corruption scandals to the state through rumors of ministerial involvement. As the *Graphic* and the Ghana News Agency polished and improved the speeches of politicians, the *Chronicle* and the *Free Press* seized on *mis*statements and provocative comments to expose their rudeness and immaturity.

The reason most often given for this fixation is the familiar justification, "That's what people want to read." Judging by the popularity of the *Graphic*, the *Chronicle*, and the *Free Press*, this justification may be true but is also far more complicated. If the state is popularly constituted as a site of accumulation, exchange, and sociality, then the rationalized rules of bureaucracy may be subordinated to more implicit cultural understandings of negotiation and etiquette. Then, the efficacy of leaders depends as much on their mastery of deals and relationships as on the articulation and execution of policy (at least in popular imagination and involvement with the state). The stunning success of Rawlings, ideological metamorph and deal maker extraordinaire, is testimony to the wisdom of this kind of political reasoning. Rawlings reversed himself time and again on policy issues; but he was extremely successful in courting international support while keeping oppositional elites at bay. His success was primarily owing to his executive versatility rather than his expertise. In this context, oppositional criticism that focuses on his erratic and unpredictable behavior, and his tendency to make startling and inappropriate remarks, only makes sense. Such incidents could have easily damaged critical relationships with external sources of support or damaged the delicate consensus behind his legitimacy and the current political and economic stability in the country.

This is not to say that policy expertise counts for nothing in Ghanaian politics. Rawlings' finance minister, Kwesi Botchwey, was extremely popular for his design of the Economic Recovery Program (ERP), Ghana's version of structural adjustment. When Botchwey resigned in 1995, complaining of corruption at the ministry, the private papers chastised Rawlings for letting such a brilliant mind slip away.

Some Ghanaian journalists, though a minority, criticize this fixation on bigmen, suggesting that newspapers should focus more on policy issues. One journalist explained to me that Ghanaians are too dependent on elders and patrons for help and so tend to dwell incessantly on powerful figures. He further opined that Ghanaians need to take individual responsibility for their own ideas and future plans. Again, the situation is complicated. As explained earlier, journalists have degrees from a professional institute while most of their sources of official information (as well as their employers) are educated at the university, establishing a crucial status differential that translates into deference and insecurity among journalists. Furthermore, journalism is a rather poorly paid profession dominated by young men who will later seek a more profitable livelihood in public relations, government, or politics. As young men among their status superiors, journalists feel more comfortable reproducing or exposing the public statements of bigmen than evaluating policy with their own ideas. As young men, in both allied and oppositional relation to the state, journalists are not positioned to make such policy recommendations, and so their requests for specific information on policy evaluation and performance are often ignored. When journalists are prevented from obtaining official statistics and public documents, discussion of policy becomes nearly impossible. Chasing documents is an inefficient use of time when facing a deadline.

One newspaper, *Public Agenda,* is dedicated to overcoming the fixation on bigmen and focusing more on policy, rural issues, and African affairs. *Public Agenda,* moreover, is financially supported by Isodec, an NGO with an emphasis on pan-Africanist cooperation. Through Isodec, the newspaper has access to a wire service on politics and policy issues concerning Africa and the world. Editor-publisher Yao Graham encourages stories that describe the problems of rural people, the urban poor, and women and children. Environmental issues are particularly prominent in the newspaper, an indication of a broader turn from the representation of rural issues in terms of state patronage to a different sort of appeal based on environmental protection. *Public Agenda* also publishes front-page scandal stories; but the circulation imperative for sensational stories is less intense because of external support. Furthermore, *Public Agenda* can afford to pay its journalists much higher salaries than many other private newspapers, perhaps making them less susceptible to the persuasions of "solidarity" and status differentials.

Identity/Anonymity: Intimacy and Flow

While *Public Agenda* is popular among a certain set of young urban professionals in Accra, popular political discourse remains riveted on the reputations of national bigmen. As indicated earlier, the press is not merely engaged in constructing the stylized imaginary of the nation-state; rather, it is committed to performing that imaginary in its everyday practices. State officials and state journalists are mutually committed to an economy of identities through flows of information and money. While "official-says" journalism does little to define a journalist's public reputation, steady supplies of information and money from the state encourage journalists to subordinate their own reputations to the project of constructing the state through the reputations of state officials. Cooperating in this process, journalists are recognized and recognize themselves according to a personal and private reputation that gives them continual access to the spaces and personalities of state news. Moreover, at the highest levels, the state uses surveillance and control to articulate the private identities of Castle journalists, insinuating social intimacy, integration, and obligation to the state.

In contrast, private journalists at investigative newspapers stake their own public, professional reputations on the project of deconstructing (or destroying, some argue) the public reputations of ruling-party bigmen. Disguising their identities to evade recognition, investigative journalists use surveillance and impersonation to invade the intimate spaces of state officials, their lavish homes and vulnerable, trusting daughters (as well as lovers and illegitimate children). Since "nobody will pay you for a destructive story" (Reginald Clottey), investigative journalists seek other forms of remuneration, through the fame and reputation that their sensational stories bring them. In order to gain access to the incriminating information that makes for such a reputation, investigative journalists sometimes use money to establish their own relationships of mutual flow and undiscussed "solidarity" with lower-level employees in businesses and state offices.

Thus the news media is not only an arena of political discourse but is also a complex economy of identity, traded in flows of information and money, negotiated across the manipulated boundaries of public and private.

Sympathetic Corruption and Contagious Corruption

Discussing exchanges of information and money in the practice of Ghanaian journalism, I have referred to the ambiguity of these transactions and the ambivalent feelings and contradictory interpretations revealed as journalists discuss them. Among journalists and sources, money establishes relationships of mutual secrecy and sympathy. A strategic transaction at one level can be used to expose another secret transaction at a different level, higher or lower. Such is the magic of money in this economy of intimacy, identity, and information.[2]

Bribery is strictly prohibited by the Ghana Journalists Association *Code of Ethics,* ratified in 1994. "Article 3: Professional Integrity" specifically states, "Journalist should not accept bribe or any form of inducement to influence the performance of his/her professional duties" (GJA 1994, 2). Recognizing this, journalists often assured me that soli is not a bribe while showing quite a bit of embarrassment about accepting it nonetheless. There is no prohibition on offering bribes, but journalists show ambivalence and uneasiness about the professional implications of that transaction.

In a rare public discussion of these complicated situations, Isaac Fritz Andoh, supervising editor at the Ghana News Agency, delivered a paper at a GJA conference entitled "The GJA *Code of Ethics* and Journalism Practice in Ghana" (1997). To the amusement of the audience of journalists, Andoh indicated the ethical dilemmas in a number of "hypothetical" situations.

> You are a reporter. Your take-home pay is one hundred and twenty thousand cedis a month. You have three children and a wife and a girl friend: Its christmas time, a time to satisfy every member of the family. You were assigned to cover an assignment at "Take-It-Preko" farm, a day before christmas. At the end of your assignment, the farm manager gives you a brown envelope containing fifty thousand cedis and [also gives you] five dressed chicken. He tells you to ensure that the report about the farm appears in your paper by all means. Would you take the gift? How would you share it with your News Editor and your colleagues in the newsroom?
>
> You have just covered a day-long assignment in far away Nsawam. Participants were served delicious lunch and a bottle of beer each but you were left out. Would you complain? If so, on what grounds?
>
> Your father-in-law co-incidentally died at the peak of campaigns in an election year. A party functionary who got wind of your plight asked you to collect ten cartons of beer at an Accra Brewery to assist you. Will you do so? If not, why not?[3]

These "hypothetical" situations, based on familiar experiences, are dramatic illustrations of the intertwining of social and professional obligations, demonstrating the power of money (and beer) to propel specific information into the public realm while keeping other information out of that realm. Through these transactions, the political field (including the state) is constituted as an ambivalent site of sociality, performed in prohibited but compelling prestations.

Geo-politics, Anti-politics, and Extraversion

In local and everyday practice, journalists are deeply implicated in the polarized political field of state and opposition. Their professional extraversions indicate larger political maneuverings. Both state and opposition access global forces (be it the IMF or the IFJ [International Federation of Journalists]) and strategically craft them for deployment in local struggles. Appropriation of Western liberal discourses is less a matter of emulation and more a strategy of extraversion.

Describing the international apparatus of development as an "anti-politics machine," James Ferguson (1990) has shown how the discourses and practices of development simultaneously intensify and "depoliticize" struggles over the distribution of resources in local communities. Similarly, in Ghana, the state press works to publicly "depoliticize" the political legitimacy of the state through the consensual rhetoric of "national development." In its own form of extraversion, the state appropriates a professional scholarship on "development journalism" to structure the training of journalists and construct a certain professional rhetoric of journalism publicized in the *Daily Graphic*. A strong dose of antipolitical "national development" rhetoric was entirely necessary to engineer and justify the ideological turn-around from revolutionary populism to structural adjustment in the early 1980s.

Oddly enough, the private press imports its own form of discursive antipolitics through the rhetoric of professional objectivity. Kabral Blay-Amihere's efforts at extraversion are designed to detach journalists from subordination to political patrons by providing alternative sources of social and financial support. Discourses of human rights and pro-democracy, however, reinscribe the political mission of the private press, inspiring the anti-authoritarian crusade that journalists themselves invoke.

In Ghana emergent democratic institutions such as the private press might appropriate Western rhetoric, but they are, in practice, politically and discursively Ghanaian. Both state and private press are the products of specific historical conditions and are responsive to particular cultural notions of political authority and legitimacy as well as sociality and exchange. This study of the rhetoric, texts, and practices of Ghanaian journalism is aimed at tracing intersections of local and global forces, cultural and historical meanings, informational and material flows. Attention to the sophisticated ways that the African state is imagined and enacted, challenged and disrupted, is necessary to get beyond the empty discourses used to chastise and pathologize the African state. This study contributes to a larger project of scholarly revision of African politics through participation in struggles for hegemony and resistance, accumulation and survival.

Epilogue

This book attempts to capture the passions, practices, and contradictions that distinguish a specific moment in neoliberal democratization in Ghana. Since that moment, a series of professional shifts and political transformations has dramatically altered the context of news media in Ghana.

In 1999 the editor of the *Daily Graphic,* Elvis Aryeh, took a leave of several months. In his absence, Yaw Boadu Ayeboafoh served as acting editor of the newspaper (you will recall Ayeboafoh from chapter 1). Given Ayeboafoh's controversial reputation and his well-known commitment to professionalism over politics, the Board of Directors of *Graphic* refused to allow Ayeboafoh's name to appear in the paper as acting editor; instead, the paper continued to list the absent Aryeh as editor. This, Ayeboafoh told me, was the "last straw." When Elvis Aryeh returned from leave, Yaw Boadu Ayeboafoh left his sinecure position as associate editor at the *Daily Graphic* and assumed a new post as executive secretary of the National Media Commission, a career move with important implications for democracy and press freedom in Ghana.

In December 2000 presidential and parliamentary elections were held in Ghana. In an unprecedented move, the National Media Commission joined forces with the Centre for Democracy and Development to monitor and analyze the content of the media, working to ensure fair and balanced coverage of all political parties. Results of their analytical findings were published in the *Daily Graphic* and the *Ghanaian Chronicle* during the campaign. The NMC also coordinated with the Ghana Journalists Association to hold seminars for political journalists to discuss issues of balance and bias in campaign coverage. The revitalization of the National Media Commission is reminiscent of the resurrection of the Ghana Journalists Association under the leadership of Kabral Blay-Amihere.

In a dramatic runoff election, John Agyekum Kufuor of the New Patriotic Party defeated former vice president John Atta Mills of the NDC, Rawlings' own hand-picked successor. Independent observers reported more balanced coverage of ruling party and opposition candidates in the state media throughout the campaign. Many private newspapers openly rejoiced at Kufuor's victory.

While urging the media to be responsible, President Kufuor has advocated free expression, political pluralism, and an independent media as important elements of liberal democracy—a dramatic shift from Rawlings' furious condemnations of the private press. Shortly after taking office, President Kufuor signaled his commitment to free expression and independent media by repealing the seditious criminal libel law, used as a tool of media repression throughout the 1990s. The repeal was immediately ratified in parliament with bipartisan support.

Another surprise for journalists, President Kufuor also donated a new and larger building to the Ghana Journalists Association, a move that not only demonstrates his extraordinary support of independent media in general but also perhaps his gratitude to the private press in particular. Renovations on the building are currently under way. In a similar gesture of recognition and gratitude, President Kufuor appointed Kabral Blay-Amihere, publisher-editor of the *Independent* and president of the West African Journalists Association, as his new ambassador to Sierra Leone, a precarious but extremely important post in Ghana's foreign service. Ivor Agyeman-Duah, the editor of Blay-Amihere's regional paper, the *Ashanti Independent,* is now the Minister-Counsellor of Information at the Embassy of Ghana in Washington, D.C.

Under President Kufuor, relations between the government and the media have changed dramatically. Shortly after taking office, Kufuor met both state and private journalists in the first press conference held in Ghana in nearly two decades. Private news organizations have been invited to post permanent representatives to the Castle Osu. The president invites both state and private journalists to accompany him on official visits both nationally and internationally.

While the revolutionary transformation in media-government relations has been overwhelmingly positive, the change in government has thrown the media scene into chaos. The private press, hitherto galvanized in a common crusade against their notorious enemy, President Rawlings, is now keen to demonstrate its loyalty to its liberal and magnanimous hero, President Kufuor. However, flattering portrayals of the president and his administration do little to support the circulation of a private newspaper. In competition with the state media apparatus, the key to the survival of the private press has always been oppositionality. Commercially and politically conflicted, the private press as a whole seems to have lost its collective train of thought.

The state press is similarly rife with ambivalence and confusion. In previous regime changes the new head of state would simply dismiss the editors of the state media organizations, considered contaminated by their collusion with the previous government. New editors were appointed from outside or else were promoted up from the junior ranks of the state media. Since the democratic 1991 Constitution prohibits such practices, the Kufuor administration and the editorial staff at *Graphic* are now in an unprecedented circumstance, institutionally collaborative while politically oppositional. Under the new Constitution only the National Media Commission can appoint or dismiss the staff of the state media.

Unable to move *Graphic* editor Elvis Aryeh out of the way, President Kufuor has taken aim at the Castle press corps. Shortly after taking office, Kufuor alerted *Graphic* that he "did not feel comfortable" with Castle correspondent Maxwell Appenteng. *Graphic* journalist Geoffrey Yakubu explained to me that the new NPP government considered Appenteng a possible security threat, given his close association with Rawlings and his training (in Bulgaria) as a propaganda operative for the NDC. Kufuor suggested that *Graphic* editor Elvis Aryeh should draw up a list of possible replacements. First on Aryeh's list was Ebo Hanson, the journalist who had covered Rawlings' vice president John Atta Mills, Kufuor's opponent in the previous elections. Kufuor rejected Hanson in favor of Samuel Sarpong, a younger, more junior journalist with less obvious political baggage. Yakubu noted, "Sarpong had tried to develop an image as neutral while Appenteng was associated with the NDC." Similarly young Sebastian Kwesi Mensah was promoted to cover the new vice president.[1]

Maxwell Appenteng, former Castle correspondent under Rawlings, has been reassigned to a desk job.

In contradiction to his well-known position that the state must rely on the state media as a mouthpiece for its policies, *Graphic* editor Elvis Aryeh announced to me in 2001 that the change in government from Rawlings to Kufuor was no problem for *Graphic* because "the government should not interfere with the news media." Cannily Aryeh revealed his hope that *Graphic* might partially privatize, becoming a Limited Liability Company with shares traded on the Ghana Stock Exchange (Ayeboafoh with the National Media Commission is opposed to such a plan).

Despite so many machinations churning through the state media apparatus, routine practices of state journalism endure in this new period of political and professional flux. After decades of predictably reproducing government rhetoric, *Graphic* now schizophrenically applies the formulaic structure of who-leads and chain-quoting to President Kufuor and his administration while also giving voice to selected critics in oppositional political parties, civil society, and the emerging business elite. Consequently the editorial position of *Graphic* is now entirely unclear; some journalists say that *Graphic* is still in the pocket of the NDC, overly critical of the new NPP government, while others observe that the paper is becoming more balanced and independent. What appears to be the emergence of journalistic neutrality may, in fact, reflect the currently conflicted position of *Graphic* as a commercial enterprise: in the current economic environment *Graphic* cannot survive without state funding. Either the paper cultivates relations of patronage with the new government or else it must privatize and lean on some other political or economic faction in Ghanaian society, as the private press has done. Giving voice to the state and its critics, *Graphic* is hedging bets on its own future.

While the political terrain has undergone such tectonic shifts, some things remain the same. Journalism is still the poorly paid vocation of young people eager to move up or move on. Many journalists I worked with in 1997 have either been promoted to editorial positions or have left journalism for more lucrative work in public relations. They have been replaced by new recruits from the Ghana Institute of Journalism, younger journalists similarly subordinated in age, experience, and educational capital to their sources in government and civil society. Complaining about the lack of pay and public respect, a friend at *Graphic,* veteran of the recent changes, finally confessed to me. "I find it difficult to do journalism here . . . I find it frustrating . . . if there is some change, then I will stay. But if not, then I don't want to continue. I would want to be seen doing something else."

NOTES

Introduction

1. From this perspective, the rhetoric and practices of state journalism, aimed at protecting the national interest and preserving the distinctiveness of local political culture against the Weberian imperatives of "good governance," could be seen as resistance to this global form of ideological domination. Frederic Jameson (1998) describes how the overbearing discourse of postcolonial nationalism may reconfigure as a local stance of resistance against globalization.

2. For Foucault (1972), such a mediated worldview constitutes a modern epistemic regime of social knowledge, a productive and pervasive "positive unconscious" that continually constructs the subjects and entities through which modern power operates. The professional practices of journalism are, then, a set of regulatory practices that discipline the dangerous productivity of discourse by classifying reality, dividing reason and truth from folly and falsity, and steering discourse away from radical or threatening declarations into prescribed modes of commentary and "redundant discovery." Transiting from the archaeological concept of "episteme" (1970) to a more institutionalized, genealogical sense of "apparatus," Foucault's later work (esp. 1978) draws attention to the everyday corporal practices of governmentality and subjectivization through which the disciplinarity of modernity is exercised. From this perspective, the ubiquitous yet hidden optic of news media would appear as an instrument of modern surveillance, a disembodied ritual force that organizes both our epistemic worldview and our corporal sense of being viewed *by* the world.

1. National Discourse and the State Apparatus

1. The identities of all journalists who contributed to this book are disguised with pseudonyms. Editors, however, are referred to by name, with permission.

2. Of the two state-funded newspapers, the *Daily Graphic* has emerged as the more serious and better-selling paper. The *Ghanaian Times* has suffered blows to its respectability, owing to a tendency toward sensationalism, sagging professional quality, and unreliable front-page stories based on unidentified sources. Although both papers are dominated by official rhetoric, *Graphic* is the obvious choice for the sophisticated task of transforming state rhetoric into a cosmopolitan and seemingly neutral version of everyday reality. The bigger and better-maintained offices in the *Graphic* compound are filled with more and newer equipment. Rawlings appointed his own press secretary, Elvis Aryeh, to be the main editor of *Graphic* (some say Aryeh never really quit his old job). As the more heavily utilized favorite of the two state newspapers, *Graphic* is therefore more tightly imbricated in the workings of the state.

For this reason I chose to intern with the *Daily Graphic,* joining the corps of junior reporters routinely sent out on invited assignments to state functions and ceremonies. On most days I covered an assignment with another *Graphic* journalist, and we collaborated on the story. In addition, I frequently typed up stories sent in from regional correspondents. The experiences of my "practical attachment" to the *Daily Graphic* are supplemented by interviews with *Graphic* journalists, conducted several months later. I should note, as well, that several state journalists became friends of mine, and I have continued to correspond and socialize with them throughout my fieldwork and during my visits back to Ghana every summer.

3. Personal interview, July 9, 1997.

4. "Our Constitution and the Media," *Daily Graphic*, January 8, 1998, 5.

5. Ibid.

6. "Reporting Politics," *Daily Graphic*, September 18, 1996, 5.

7. Ibid.

8. In editorials the private press has raised serious doubts about the ability of the National Media Commission to insulate the state press and enforce equal coverage. Some suggest that the NMC itself is politically compromised. On March 30, 1999 the *Independent* ran an editorial complaining that the National Media Commission was allowing the Minister of Information to interfere in the affairs of the Board of Directors of the state media. "We ask each member of the NMC to read the 1992 Constitution in order to realise their obligations. Wake up, National Media Commission."

2. "Who-Leads" and Who Follows

1. Not all news stories at *Graphic* are written in the same style, however. This analysis focuses on a prevailing style of news coverage at *Graphic*.

2. My analysis focuses on the style and practice of journalism in Ghana during a specific period, democratization under President Rawlings in the 1990s. However, archival research on the history of *Graphic* under six previous regimes as well as follow-up fieldwork on *Graphic* under President Kufuor suggests that the style of journalism at *Graphic* is remarkably durable, while the specific ideological project of each regime noticeably shifts the political content of the newspaper, sometimes overnight.

3. "Political Differences Should Not Disrupt Development," *Daily Graphic*, October 10, 1996, 1.

4. "Leadership Is Service," ibid.

5. "Sustain Commitment to NDC—Konadu," ibid., 3.

6. "Workshop on Workers' Safety Opens," ibid.

7. This sort of collusion with the ventriloquist paradox of the state is common to journalism everywhere.

8. "Protection of the Environment Programme Launched." *Daily Graphic*, May 6, 1997, 12.

9. Chiefs are prohibited from participating in party politics.

10. Yankah is both a scholar of okyeame and a critic of the state press. However, he has never explicitly linked his ideas about mediated discourse with the practices of state journalism. In an interview I asked him what he would say to the argument that *Graphic* journalists are the okyeame of the state. "Well, I don't recall having said it," he considered, "but it certainly sounds like something I would say."

In an article for *Media Monitor* Kwasi Kaakyire discusses the tactic of "pre-emptive spin" used by *Graphic* to publicize positive stories about particular government officials just as critical stories break in the private press. Kaakyire identifies the state press and okyeame (plural akyeame) both as practitioners of spin. "Spin generally attempts to restate what is stated by a different source, even when the audience gets to see and hear directly from the original source. Traces of spinning can be found in the performance of akyeame. The *Graphic* story and its like can be categorized among the more negative aspects of spinning" ("Ordinary Talk," *Media Monitor* [January–March 1998]: 22). Lamenting this practice by the state press, Kaakyire suggests that a daily private paper could interfere with the ability of the state press to scoop and pre-empt private revelations.

11. "Perhaps I might save it for a book someday," Appenteng speculated.

12. "Watching the Watchman (column): The Karate Kid." *Ghanaian Chronicle,* January 11, 1996, 4.

3. Practice and Privilege in the State Media

1. "What do you do when he becomes agitated?" I asked Appenteng. "Just keep quiet," he laughed.

2. If a state journalist offends a prominent figure in the ruling party, that journalist may be transferred from Accra to a posting in a distant region. Often these correspondents know little about the region they are transferred to and do not even speak the local language. Because of the practice of "punitive transfer" in the state media, regional correspondents can feel isolated and disgruntled, perhaps more likely to speak freely with a colleague in the private press.

3. "No More Nice Guys . . .?" *Daily Graphic,* April 18, 1997, 5.

4. Ibid., 5.

5. In my interview with Mrs. Sackey, she insisted that she had very little to do with journalists at the Castle and almost nothing to do with the *Daily Graphic.* Despite her own protestations to the contrary, her efforts at controlling information flow have been essential to the project of Rawlings' revolution. In his analysis of law in the revolutionary period, Mike Oquaye notes, "Through the Castle Information Bureau (CIB), headed by Mrs Valerie Sackey, the PNDC [Provisional National Defence Council] was able to maintain a strong hold over the public-owned press and information flow in and out of Ghana generally. Through the CIB, propaganda was subtly pushed through the mass media, editorials were 'ghost' written from the Castle and articles published under pseudonyms or by 'special correspondent'" (Oquaye 1993, 173).

6. "Castle Attempts Opening Up to Private Press," *Media Monitor* (January–March 1998): 18.

4. The Private Press and Professional Solidarity

1. *Independent,* February 19, 1997, 3.

2. Ghanaian "day names," signaling a person's day of birth, are the public names Ghanaians use in everyday circumstances. Most male day names begin with a "K"

(Kwame for Saturday, Kwesi for Sunday, Kojo for Monday, Kobina for Tuesday, etc.).

3. "Stormy Weather ahead for Ghana's Independent Press?" Unclassfied document, USIS, May 6, 1997, 1.

4. *Independent,* May 8, 1996, 3.

5. Ibid.

6. Ibid., February 19, 1997, 3.

7. Ibid., May 8, 1996, 3.

8. Ibid.

5. Corruption, Investigation, and Extraversion

1. *Ghanaian Chronicle,* front page, June 19, 1997.

2. *Independent,* June 7, 1995.

3. Report on Investigation into Allegations of Corruption against Col. E. M. Osei-Owusu, Minister for the Interior, Commission for Human Rights and Administrative Justice, January 7, 1996, 23.

4. "CHRAJ Report." *Home Front,* Information Services Department (October–December 1996): 21.

5. Ibid.

6. This claim is not as far-fetched as it might seem. Throughout West Africa, military regimes are associated with the drug trade. Maliqualim Simone and Pieterse, in "Civil Societies in an Internationalized Africa," refer to the laundering of drug and arms profits as "the sinecure of West Africa's military-merchant class" ((1993, 47). At a recent conference on drugs in Ghana, United Nations Drug Control Programme Officer Franklin Asamoah Mensah reported that, "Ghanaian and Nigerian drug trafficking networks continue to dominate the drug scene" (*Independent,* April 12, 1999). See also Bayart, Ellis, and Hibou 1999.

7. *Free Press,* back page, January 31, 1996.

8. *Independent,* May 29, 1997, 14.

9. *Free Press,* June 22, 1993.

10. *Statesman,* front page, November 3, 1996.

11. Nana Konadu is not the vice president but only the First Lady. She is roundly criticized by the opposition for outstepping her proper wifely role and acting as if she were an elected public officer (with all the powers and protections pertaining to her husband). This criticism is similar to the grumblings over the ambiguous power of Hillary Clinton.

12. See also Ghana Education Service, *Cultural Studies for Junior Secondary Schools, Pupil's Book* 3 (1989): 74.

13. Ibid., 65.

14. For instance, "Executions Cooled Down Tempers—JJ" (*Independent,* front page, November 27, 1996).

15. *Ghanaian Chronicle,* front page, April 23, 1997.

16. Richard Gyasi (pseud.), unpublished copy of lecture. See also Ammuaku-Annan (1998) on investigative reporting in Ghana.

17. *Independent,* front page, February 12, 1997.
18. Ibid., January 8, 1997.

Conclusion

1. When I went with two other journalists to visit editor Kweku Baako in prison, we brought newspapers for Baako to read. The prison administrator pointed to the prison regulations limiting the number of visitors and prohibiting certain gifts such as newspapers. "But these are the rules of our former colonial masters," he explained. "And, after all, we are all human beings. We are all human beings." We were allowed to present our gifts to Baako.

2. When they occur in the bureaucratic realm of the state, these sorts of informal exchanges are analyzed as instances of "corruption," indicating widespread moral decay and explaining the lack of material development and political accountability. See Gyekye 1997; Abotchie 1995; de Graft-Johnson 1976; and Le Vine 1975. However, "soli" or "brown envelope" supplements the salaries of private journalists who either take up the moral crusade against corruption or else publicize the development initiatives of the state (Hasty 2005a, 2005b).

3. "The GJA Code of Ethics and Journalism Practice in Ghana," November 20, 1996, 4–5.

Epilogue

1. Elvis Aryeh, Ebo Hanson, and Samuel Sarpong are the actual names of *Graphic* journalists. Hanson and Sarpong did not participate directly in this study and therefore did not contribute information to warrant the use of a pseudonym. Elvis Aryeh contributed a great deal to this study, through innumerable interviews both formal and informal. However, there is only one editor of *Graphic;* it is impossible to shield his identity. Aware that I was writing a book, Aryeh was eager to represent himself and his newspaper.

Geoffrey Yakubu, Maxwell Appenteng, and Sebastian Kwesi Mensah are pseudonyms throughout the book.

BIBLIOGRAPHY

Abotchie, Chris. 1993. "Finding a Place for Islam: Egyptian Television Serials and the National Interest." *Public Culture* 5 (3): 493–513.

———. 1995. "Political Power and Economic Criminality in Ghana: The Impact of Anomie." *Legon Journal of the Humanities* 8:113–130.

Acquaah, Gaddiel Robert. 1940. *Mfantse-Akan Mbebusem* (Fante-Akan proverbs). Cape Coast: Methodist Book Depot.

Agbaje, Adigun. 1993. "Beyond the State: Civil Society and the Nigerian Press under Military Rule." *Media, Culture & Society* 15:455–472.

Agyeman-Duah, Ivor. 1996. *Watching Over the Flock by Night: Private Press Coverage of Ghana's Fourth Republic.* M.A. thesis, Journalism Studies, University of Wales, Cardiff.

Ainslie, Rosalynde. 1966. *The Press in Africa: Communications Past and Present.* New York: Walker.

Allison, Anne. 1994. *Nightwork: Sexuality, Pleasure, and Corporate Masculinity in a Tokyo Hostess Club.* Chicago: University of Chicago Press.

Allman, Jean. 1993. *The Quills of the Porcupine: Asante Nationalism in an Emergent Ghana.* Madison: University of Wisconsin Press.

Althusser, Louis. 1971. "Ideology and Ideological State Apparatuses: Notes Towards an Investigation." In *Lenin and Philosophy and Other Essays,* trans. B. Brewster, 127–184. New York: New Left Books.

Ammuaku-Annan, Cofie. 1998. "A Glance at Investigative Reporting in Ghana." *Media Monitor* (January–March 1998): 7–8.

Anagnost, Ann. 1993. "The Politicized Body." *Stanford Humanities Review* 2 (1): 86–102.

———. 1997. *National Past-times: Narrative, Representation, and Power in Modern China.* Durham, N.C.: Duke University Press.

Anderson, Benedict. 1983. *Imagined Communities: Reflections on the Origin and Spread of Nationalism.* London: Verso.

Andoh, Isaac Fritz. 1996. "The GJA *Code of Ethics* and Journalism Practice in Ghana." Unpublished lecture, printed copy. Accra: Ghana Journalists Association.

Ansu-Kyeremeh, Kwasi, and Audrey Gadzekpo. 1996. "Who Reads the Newspapers, Why and for What? A Ghanaian Readership Survey." Study conducted for the European Union "Continuing Education for Media Practitioners" Project. Legon: School of Communications Studies.

Appadurai, Arjun. 1996. *Modernity at Large: Cultural Dimensions of Globalization.* Minneapolis: University of Minnesota Press.

———. 2001. "Grassroots Globalization and the Research Imagination." In *Globalization,* ed. Arjun Appadurai, 1–21. Durham: Duck University Press.

———. 2002. "Deep Democracy: Urban Governmentality and the Horizon of Politics." *Public Culture* 14 (1): 21–47.

Appiah, Kwame Anthony. 1992. *In My Father's House: Africa in the Philosophy of Culture.* New York: Oxford University Press.

Apter, Andrew. 1992. *Black Critics and Kings: The Hermeneutics of Power in Yoruba Society.* Chicago: University of Chicago Press.

————. 1999. "IBB=419: Nigerian Democracy and the Politics of Illusion." In *Civil Society and the Political Imagination in Africa: Critical Perspectives,* ed. John L. Comaroff and Jean Comaroff. Chicago: University of Chicago Press.

Apter, David. 1955. *Ghana in Transition.* Princeton, N.J.: Princeton University Press.

Asante, Clement. 1996. *The Press in Ghana: Problems and Prospects.* Lanham, Md.: University Press of America.

Asare-Addy, Nii. 1992. "Ghana: Ready to Go." *Index on Censorship* (July 1992): 27.

Austin, Dennis. 1964. *Politics in Ghana, 1946–1960.* London: Oxford University Press.

Barber, Karin. 1991. *I Could Speak until Tomorrow: Oriki, Women, and the Past in a Yoruba Town.* Edinburgh: Edinburgh University Press for the International African Institute, London.

————. 2000. *The Generation of Plays: Yoruba Popular Life in Theater.* Bloomington: Indiana University Press.

————, ed.. 1997. *Readings in African Popular Culture.* Bloomington: International African Institute in association with Indiana University Press.

Barton, Frank. 1966. *The Press in Africa.* Nairobi: East African Publishing House.

Bastian, Misty. 1993 "'Bloodhounds Who Have No Friends': Witchcraft and Locality in the Nigerian Press." In *Modernity and Its Malcontents,* ed. Jean Comaroff and John Comaroff, 129–166. Chicago: University of Chicago Press.

Bayart, Jean-François. 1986. "Civil Society in Africa." In *Political Domination in Africa,* ed. Patrick Chabal. Cambridge: Cambridge University Press.

————. 1993. *The State in Africa: The Politics of the Belly.* London: Longman.

Bayart, Jean-François, Stephen Ellis, and Beatrice Hibou. 1999. *The Criminalization of the State in Africa.* Translated from the French by Stephen Ellis. Bloomington: Indiana University Press.

Bhabha, Homi, ed.. 1990. *Nation and Narration.* London: Routledge.

Blay-Amihere, Kabral. 1994. *Tears for a Continent: An American Diary.* Accra: Trans Afrika News.

————. 1996. "Preface," "Editorial Introduction," and "State of the Media in Ghana." In *State of the Media in West Africa, 1995–1996,* ed. Kabral Blay-Amihere and Niyi Alabi. Accra: Friedrich Ebert Foundation, Ghana Office.

Blay-Amihere, Kabral, and Niyi Alabi, eds. 1996. *State of the Media in West Africa, 1995–1996.* Accra: Friedrich Ebert Foundation, Ghana Office.

Bloch, Maurice, ed. 1975. *Political Language and Oratory in Traditional Society.* London: Academic Press.

Boafo, Kwame. 1985. "Utilizing Development Communication Strategies in African Societies: A Critical Perspective." *Gazette* 35:83–92.

Bourgault, Louise. 1995. *Mass Media in Sub-Saharan Africa.* Bloomington: Indiana University Press.

Bourdieu, Pierre. 1984/85. "Delegation and Political Fetishism." *Thesis Eleven* 10/11:56–70.

Boyer, Dominic. 2000. "Spirit and System: Mass Media, Journalism, and the Dialectics of Modern German Intellectual Culture." Ph.D. dissertation, Anthropology, University of Chicago.

Bratton, Michael. 1994. "Civil Society and Political Transitions in Africa." In *Civil Society and the State in Africa,* ed. John D. Harbeson, Donald Rothchild, and Naomi Chazan, 51–81. Boulder: Lynne Reinner.

Busia, Kofi. 1951. *The Position of the Chief in the Modern Political System of Ashanti.* London: Oxford University Press.

Calhoun, Craig. 1993. "Civil Society and the Public Sphere." *Public Culture* 5 (2): 267–280.

Callaghy, Thomas M. "Civil Society, Democracy, and Economic Change in Africa: A Dissenting Opinion about Resurgent Societies. In *Civil Society and the State in Africa,* ed. John W. Harbeson, Donald Rothchild, and Naomi Chazan. Boulder: Lynne Rienner.

Casely Hayford, J. E.. 1903. *Gold Coast Native Institutions.* London: London, Sweet, and Maxwell.

Chazan, Naomi. 1983. *An Anatomy of Ghanaian Politics: Managing Political Recession, 1969–1982.* Boulder: Westview.

———. 1991. "The Political Transformation of Ghana under the PNDC." In *Ghana: The Political Economy of Recovery,* ed., D. Rothchild, 21–48. Boulder: Lynne Rienner.

———. 1992. "Ghana." In *Handbook of Political Science Research on Sub-Saharan Africa,* ed. M. DeLancey, 299–328. Westport, Conn.: Greenwood.

Codjoe, Frank Kwaw. 1988. *Elites, Ideology and Development Problems of Ghana.* Hamburg: Verlag an der Lottbek Jensen.

"CHRAJ Report" and "President Accepts Resignation of Two Ministers." 1996. *Home Front* (October–December): 21, 29. Accra: Information Services Department.

Comaroff, Jean, and John Comaroff, eds.. 2001. *Millenial Capitalism and the Culture of Neoliberalism.* Durham, N.C.: Duke University Press.

Comaroff, John L., and Jean Comaroff, eds. 1999. *Civil Society and the Political Imagination in Africa: Critical Perspectives.* Chicago: University of Chicago Press.

Commission for Human Rights and Administrative Justice. 1996. "Report on Investigation into Allegations of Corruption against Col. E. M. Osei-Owusu, Minister for the Interior." Accra.

Curriculum Research and Development Division, Ghana Education Service. 1989. *Cultural Studies for Junior Secondary Schools, Pupil's Book 3.* Accra: Adwinsa.

de Graft-Johnson, K. E.. 1975. "Corruption and Modernization in Ghana." *Conch* 7 (1–2): 165–183.

Deleuze, Gilles, and Felix Guattari. 1977. *Anti-Oedipus: Capitalism and Schizophrenia.* Translated from the French by Robert Hurley, Mark Seem, and Helen R. Lane. New York: Viking.

Denkabe, Aloysius, and Audrey Gadzekpo. 1996. *What Is Fit to Print? Language of the Press in Ghana.* Accra: Friedrich Ebert Foundation, Ghana Office.

Domatob, Jerry, and S. Hall. 1983. "Development Journalism in Black Africa." *Gazette* 31 (1): 9–33.

Durham, Deborah. 1999. "Civil Lives: Leadership and Accomplishment in Botswana." In *Civil Society and the Political Imagination in Africa: Critical Perspectives,* ed. John L. Comaroff and Jean Comaroff, 192–218. Chicago: University of Chicago Press.

Ebo, Bosah. 1988. "Newswork: Negotiating Professional Reality: A Study of a News Organization in Nigeria." Ph.D. dissertation, Mass Communication, University of Iowa.

Eickelman, Dale F., and Jon W. Anderson. 1999. *Media in the Muslim World: The Emerging Public Sphere.* Bloomington: Indiana University Press.

Ekpu, Ray. 1992. "'We Have Democratised the News.'" *Index on Censorship* (February): 26–27.

Ellis, Stephen. 1999. *The Mask of Anarchy: The Destruction of Liberia and the Religious Dimension of an African Civil War.* New York: New York University Press.

Fair, Jo Ellen. 1989. "29 Years of Theory and Research on Media and Development: The Dominant Paradigm Impact." *Gazette* 44:129–150.

Faringer, Gunilla. 1991. *Press Freedom in Africa.* New York: Praeger.

Fatton, Robert, Jr. 1992. *Predatory Rule: State and Civil Society in Africa.* Boulder: Lynne Reinner.

Ferguson, James. 1990. *The Anti-Politics Machine: "Development," Depoliticization, and Bureaucratic Power in Letsotho.* Cambridge: Cambridge University Press.

Ferme, Mariane. 1999. "Staging Politisi: The Dialogics of Publicity and Secrecy in Sierra Leone." In *Civil Society and the Political Imagination in Africa: Critical Perspectives,* ed. John L. Comaroff and Jean Comaroff, 160–191. Chicago: University of Chicago Press.

Finnegan, Ruth. 1976. *Oral Literature in Africa.* Nairobi: Oxford University Press.

Folson, Kweku. 1993. "Ideology, Revolution and Development—The Years of Jerry John Rawlings." In *Ghana under PNDC Rule,* ed. E. Gyimah-Boadi. Wiltshire: CODESRIA.

Foucault, Michel. 1970. *The Order of Things: An Archaeology of the Human Sciences.* London: Tavistock.

———. 1972. *The Archaeology of Knowledge.* Translated from the French by A. M. Sheridan Smith. New York: Pantheon.

———. 1978. *The History of Sexuality.* Translated from the French by Robert Hurley. New York: Pantheon.

"The Friedrich Ebert Foundation in Ghana: A Partner in Development." Brochure. Accra: Friedrich Ebert Foundation, Ghana Office.

Furniss, Graham, and Liz Gunner, eds.. 1995. *Power, Marginality and African Oral Literature.* Cambridge: Cambridge University Press.

Geekie, Russell. 1994. "A Symbol of Repression." *Africa Report* (May/June): 44–45.

Geschiere, Peter. 1997. *The Modernity of Witchcraft: Politics and the Occult in Postcolonial Africa.* Charlottesville: University Press of Virginia.

Ghana Journalists Association. 1994. *Code of Ethics.* Accra: Ripples Ads Productions.

Ghana Journalists Association, in cooperation with Friedrich Ebert Stiftung. 1994. *State of the Media in Ghana.* Ghana: Anansesem.

Giddens, Anthony. 1990. *The Consequences of Modernity.* Stanford, Calif.: Stanford University Press.

Gilroy, Paul. 1993. *The Black Atlantic: Modernity and Double Consciousness.* Cambridge, Mass.: Harvard University Press.

Goankar, Dilip Parameshwar. 1999. "Editor's Comment on Alternative Modernities." *Public Culture* 11 (1): 14–34.

Graham, Yao. 1996. "Facing Up against Lawsuits." *Media Monitor* (July–September): 7–9.

Gramsci, Antonio. 1971. *Selections from the Prison Notebooks.* New York: International.

Gupta, Akhil. 1995. "Blurred Boundaries: The Discourse of Corruption, the Culture of Politics, and the Imagined State." *American Ethnologist* 22 (2): 375–402.

Gyekye, Kwame. 1997. *Political Corruption: A Philosophical Inquiry into a Moral Problem.* Accra: School of Communications Press–Legon/Sankofa Publishing.

Gyimah-Boadi, E.. 1994. "Associational Life, Civil Society, and Democratization in Ghana." In *Civil Society and the State in Africa,* ed. John Harbeson, Donald Rothchild, and Naomi Chazan, 125–148. Boulder: Lynne Rienner.

Habermas, Jurgen. 1989. *The Structural Transformation of the Public Sphere: An Inquiry into a Category of Bourgeois Society.* Translated by Thomas Burger with the assistance of Frederick Lawrence. Cambridge, Mass.: MIT Press.

Hachten, W. A.. 1971. *Muffled Drums: The News Media in Africa.* Ames: Iowa State University Press.

Harbeson, John. 1994. "Civil Society and Political Renaissance in Africa." In *Civil Society and the State in Africa,* ed. John Harbeson, Donald Rothchild, and Naomi Chazan, 1–29. Boulder: Lynne Rienner.

Harbeson, John, Donald Rothchild, and Naomi Chazan, eds.. 1994. *Civil Society and the State in Africa.* Boulder: Lynne Rienner.

Hardt, Michael, and Antonio Negri. 2000. *Empire.* Cambridge, Mass.: Harvard University Press.

Harvey, David. 1989. *The Condition of Postmodernity: An Enquiry into the Origins of Cultural Change.* Cambridge, Mass.: Blackwell.

Hasty, Jennifer. 1999. "Big Language and Brown Envelopes: The Press and Political Culture in Ghana." Ph.D. dissertation, Department of Cultural Anthropology, Duke University.

———. 2001. "From Culture of Silence to Culture of Contest: Hegemony, Legitimacy, and the Press in Ghana." *Journal of Cultural Studies* 3 (2): 348–359.

———. 2003. "Rites of Passage, Routes of Redemption: Emancipation Tourism and the Wealth of Culture." *Africa Today* 49 (3): 47–78.

———. 2003. "Ghana." In *World Press Encyclopedia,* ed. Amanda Quick, 368–377. New York: Thompson Gale.

———. 2004. "'Forget the Past or Go Back to the Slave Trade!': Trans-Africanism and Popular History in Postcolonial Ghana." *Ghana Studies* 6:131–157.

———. 2005. "Sympathetic Magic/Contagious Corruption: Sociality, Democracy, and the Press in Ghana." *Public Culture* 17 (3). In press.

———. 2005. "The Pleasures of Corruption: Desire and Discipline in Ghanaian Political Culture." *Cultural Anthropology* 20 (1). In press.

Haynes, Jeff. 1991. "Human Rights and Democracy in Ghana: The Record of the Rawlings Regime." *African Affairs* 90:407–425.

Haynes, Jeff. 1995. "Ghana: From Personalist to Democratic Rule." In *Democracy and Political Change in Sub-Saharan Africa,* ed. J. Wiseman. London: Routledge.

Herbst, Jeffrey. 1993. *The Politics of Reform in Ghana, 1982–1991.* Berkeley: University of California Press.

————. Herbst, Jeffrey. 1994. "The Dilemmas of Explaining Political Upheaval: Ghana in Comparative Perspective." In *Economic Change and Political Liberalization in Sub-Saharan Africa*, ed. J. Widner, 182–198. Baltimore, Md.: The Johns Hopkins University Press.

Herzfeld, Michael. 1997. *Cultural Intimacy: Social Poetics in the Nation-State*. New York: Routledge.

Ivy, Marilyn. 1988. "Tradition and Difference in the Japanese Mass Media." *Public Culture* 1 (1): 21–29

————. 1995. *Discourses of the Vanishing: Modernity, Phantasm, Japan*. Chicago: University of Chicago Press.

Jackson, Robert, and Carl Rosberg. 1982. *Personal Rule in Black Africa: Prince, Autocrat, Prophet*. Berkeley: University of California Press.

Jameson, Frederic. 1991. *Postmodernism; or, The Cultural Logic of Late Capitalism*. Durham, N.C.: Duke University Press.

————. 1998. Preface to *The Cultures of Globalisation*, ed. Frederic Jameson and Masao Miyoshi, xii–xvii. Durham: Duke University Press

Jameson, Frederic, and Masao Miyoshi, eds. 1998. *The Cultures of Globalisation*. Durham: Duke University Press.

Jeffries, Richard. 1991. "Leadership Commitment and Political Opposition to Structural Adjustment in Ghana." In *Ghana: The Political Economy of Recovery*, ed. D. Rothchild, 157–172. Boulder: Lynne Rienner.

Jones-Quartey, K.A.B.. 1975. *History, Politics, and Early Press in Ghana: The Fictions and the Facts*. Accra: Assembly.

Kaakyire, Kwasi. 1998. "Ordinary Talk." *Media Monitor* (January–March): 22.

Karikari, Kwame, and Kwasi Ansu-Kyeremeh. 1996. "Who Reads the Graphic: Profile of Readers of the *Daily Graphic*, Report of a Readership Study of the *Daily Graphic*." Study Conducted for Graphic Corporation. Legon: School of Communications Studies.

Kimble, David. 1963. *A Political History of Ghana: The Rise of Gold Coast Nationalism, 1850–1928*. Oxford: Clarendon.

Klein, Martin A. 1992. "Back to Democracy: Presidential Address to the 1991 Annual Meeting of the African Studies Association." *African Studies Review* 35 (3): 1.

Koomson, A. Bonah. 1997. *Journalism and Ethics*. Accra: Friedrich Ebert Foundation, Ghana Office.

Kraus, Jon. 1991. "The Political Economy of Stabilization and Structural Adjustment in Ghana." In *Ghana: The Political Economy of Recovery*, ed. D. Rothchild, 119–156. Boulder: Lynne Rienner.

Lardner, Tunji. 1993. "Democratization and Forces in the African Media." *Journal of International Affairs* 47 (1): 89.

Le Vine, Victor. 1975. *Political Corruption: The Ghana Case*. Stanford, Calif.: Hoover Institution Press.

Lukacs, Gyorgy. 1971 [1916]. *The Theory of the Novel*. Cambridge, Mass.: MIT Press.

MachLachlan, Elizabeth. 2000. "National Television News in Japan: A Production Study." Ph.D. dissertation, Anthropology, Columbia University.

Maliqualim Simone, Abdou, and Edgar Pieterse. 1993. "Civil Societies in an Internationalized Africa." *Social Dynamics* 19 (2): 41–69.

Malkki, Liisa. 1995. *Purity and Exile: Violence, Memory, and National Cosmology among Hutu Refugees in Tanzani*a. Chicago: University of Chicago Press.

———. 1997. "News and Culture: Transitory Phenomena and the Fieldwork Tradition." In *Anthropological Locations: Boundaries and Grounds of a Field Science,* ed. Akjil Gupta and James Ferguson, 86–101. Berkeley: University of California Press.

Mamdani, Mahmood. 1995. "A Critique of the State and Civil Society Paradigm in Africanist Studies." In *African Studies in Social Movements and Democracy,* ed. M. Mamdani and E. Wamba-dia-Wamba, 602–616. Dakar: CODESRIA.

———. 1996. *Citizen and Subject: Contemporary Africa and the Legacy of Late Colonialism.* Princeton, N.J.: Princeton University Press.

Mankekar, Purnima. 1999. *Screening Culture/Viewing Politics: An Ethnography of Television, Womanhood, and Nation in Postcolonial India.* Durham, N.C.: Duke University Press.

———. 2001. "Television Tales and a Woman's Rage: A National Recasting of Draupadi's 'Disrobing.'" *Public Culture* 5 (3): 469–492.

Mbachu, Dulue. 1992. "Owners and Censors." *Index on Censorship* (February): 28.

Mbembe, Achille. 1992. "The Banality of Power and the Aesthetics of Vulgarity in the Postcolony." *Public Culture* 4 (2): 1–30.

———. 2001. *On the Postcolony.* Berkeley: University of California Press.

McCaskie, T. C. 1983. "Accumulation, Wealth, and Belief in Asante History I: To the Close of the Nineteenth Century." *Africa* 53 (1): 23–43.

———. 1995. *State and Society in Precolonial Asante.* Cambridge: Cambridge University Press.

Mensa-Bonsu, H. 1997. *The Law and the Journalist.* Accra: Friedrich Ebert Foundation, Ghana Office.

Meyer, Birgit. 1999a. "Popular Ghanaian Cinema and the African Heritage." *Africa Today* 46 (2): 93–114.

———. 1999b. "Blood Money, Nigerian Movies and Debates about Morality in Ghana." Paper delivered at the Ninety-eighth Annual Meeting of the American Anthropological Association, Chicago.

Migdal, Joel. 1988. *Strong Societies and Weak States: State-Society Relations and State Capabilities in the Third World.* Princeton, N.J.: Princeton University Press.

Monga, Celestin. 1995. "Civil Society and the Democratisation in Francophone Africa." *Journal of Modern African Studies* 33 (3): 359–379.

———. 1996. *The Anthropology of Anger: Civil Society and Democracy in Africa.* Translated by Linda L. Fleck and Celestin Monga. Boulder: Lynne Rienner.

Newell, Stephanie. 2002. *Literary Culture in Colonial Ghana: How to Play the Game of Life.* Bloomington: Indiana University Press.

Nketia, J.H.K.. 1971. "The Linguistic Aspect of Style in African Language." *Current Trends in Linguistics* 7:733–757.

Nonini, D., and A. Ong. 1997. "Introduction: Chinese Transnationalism as an Alternative Modernity." In *Ungrounded Empires: The Cultural Politics of Modern Chinese Transnationalmism,* ed. A. Ong and D. Nonini, 3–33. New York: Routledge.

Nugent, Paul. 1996. *Big Men, Small Boys and Politics in Ghana.* Accra: Asempa.

Nukunya, G. K.. 1992. *Tradition and Change in Ghana.* Accra: Ghana Universities Press.

Ogbondah, Chris. 1994. "Press Freedom in West Africa: Analysis of One Ramification of Human Rights." *Issue: A Journal of Opinion* 12 (2): 21–25.

Oquaye, Mike. 1980. *Politics in Ghana, 1972–1979.* Accra: Tornado.

———. 1993. "Law, Justice and the Revolution." In *Ghana under PNDC Rule,* ed. E. Gymimah-Boadi. Wiltshire: CODESRIA.

Owusu, Maxwell. 1989. "Rebellion, Revolution, and Tradition: Reinterpreting Coups in Ghana." *Comparative Studies of Society and History* 31 (2): 372–397.

Pellow, Deborah, and Naomi Chazan. 1986. *Ghana: Coping with Uncertainty.* Boulder: Westview.

Pieke, Frank N. 1995. "Witnessing the 1989 Chinese People's Movement." In *Fieldwork under Fire: Contemporary Studies of Violence and Survival,* ed. Carolyn Nordstrom and Antonius C. G.M. Robben, 62–79. Berkeley: University of California Press.

Piot, Charles. 1993. "Secrecy, Ambiguity, and the Everyday in Kabre Culture." *American Anthropologist* 95 (2): 353–370.

———. 1999. *Remotely Global: Village Modernity in West Africa.* Chicago: University of Chicago Press.

Price, Robert. 1974. "Politics and Culture in Ghana: The Big-Man Small-Boy Syndrome." *Journal of African Studies* 1 (2): 173–204.

———. 1975. *Society and Bureaucracy in Contemporary Ghana.* Berkeley: University of California Press.

Puri, Shamlal. 1992. "Ghana: Private Press Shaken to the Core." *IPI Report* (May): 13–14.

Rattray, Robert Sutherland. 1929. *Ashanti Law and Constitution.* Oxford: Clarendon.

Rimmer, Douglas. 1992. *Staying Poor: Ghana's Political Economy, 1950–1990.* Oxford: Pergamon.

Robben, Antonius C.G.M. "The Politics of Truth and Emotion among Victims and Perpetrators of Violence." In *Fieldwork under Fire: Contemporary Studies of Violence and Survival,* ed. Carolyn Nordstrom and Antonius C.G.M. Robben, 81–103. Berkeley: University of California Press.

Rofel, Lisa. 1994. "Yearnings: Televisual Love and Melodramatic Politics in Contemporary China." *American Ethnologist* 21 (4): 700–722.

Rogers, Everett. 1976. "Communication and Development: The Passing of the Dominant Paradigm." *Communication Research* 3 (2): 213–240.

Roseberry, William. 1996. "Hegemony, Power, and Languages of Contention." In *The Politics of Difference: Ethnic Premises in a World of Power,* ed. Edwin N. Wilmsen and Patrick McAllister, 71–84. Chicago: University of Chicago Press.

Rothchild, Donald. 1994. "Structuring State-Society Relations in Africa: Toward an Enabling Political Environment." In *Economic Change and Political Liberalization in Sub-Saharan Africa,* ed. J. Widner, 201–229. Baltimore, Md. : The Johns Hopkins University Press.

———. 1995. "Rawlings and the Engineering of Legitimacy in Ghana." In *Collapsed States: The Disintegration and Restoration of Legitimate Authority,* ed. W. Zartman, 49–65. Boulder: Lynne Rienner.

———, ed. 1991. *Ghana: The Political Economy of Recovery.* Boulder: Lynne Rienner.

Rothchild, Donald, and Letitia Lawson. 1994. "The Interactions between State and Civil Society in Africa: From Deadlock to New Routines." In *Civil Society and the State in Africa,* ed. John Harbeson, Donald Rothchild, and Naomi Chazan, 255–281. Boulder: Lynne Rienner.

Saah, Kofi. 1986. "Language Use and Attitudes in Ghana." *Anthropological Linguistics* 28:367–377.

Sampson, M. J.. 1969. *Gold Coast Men of Affairs.* London: Dawsons of Pall Mall.

Sandbrook, Richard. 1993. *The Politics of Africa's Economic Recovery.* Cambridge: Cambridge University Press.

Sarpong, Peter. 1974. *Ghana in Retrospect: Some Aspects of Ghanaian Culture.* Tema: Ghana Publishing Corporation.

Schatzberg, Michael G. 2001. *Political Legitimacy in Middle Africa: Father, Family, Food.* Bloomington: Indiana University Press.

Schein, Louisa. 1999. "Performing Modernity." *Cultural Anthropology* 14 (3): 361–395.

Schulz, Dorothea. 1997. "Praise without Enchantment: Griots, Broadcast Media, and the Politics of Tradition in Mali." *Africa Today* 44 (4): 443–464.

Shillington, Kevin. 1992. *Ghana and the Rawlings Factor.* London: Macmillan.

Shope, Ronald. 1995. "The Patron's Press: An Examination of Broadcast Press Freedom in the Republic of Liberia between 1976 and 1986." Ph.D. dissertation, Pennsylvania State University.

Spitulnik, Debra. 1993. "Anthropology and Mass Media." *Annual Review of Anthropology* 22:293–315.

———. 1993b. "Mediating Communities: Nation, Locality, and Public Moralities in Zambian Radio Broadcasting." Ph.D. dissertation, University of Chicago.

United States Information Agency. 1997. "Stormy Weather Ahead for Ghana's Independent Press?" Unclassified Document. Accra: USIA, Ghana Office.

Van Dijk, Teun A. 1991. *Racism and the Press.* New York: Routledge.

Widner, J., ed. 1994. *Economic Change and Political Liberalization in Sub-Saharan Africa.* Baltimore, Md.: The Johns Hopkins University Press.

Wilks, Ivor. 1975. *Asante in the Nineteenth Century: The Structure and Evolution of a Political Order.* Cambridge: Cambridge University Press.

———. 1993. *Forests of Gold: Essays on the Akan and the Kingdom of Asante.* Athens: Ohio University Press.

Wiseman, John A. 1991. "Democratic Resurgence in Black Africa." *Contemporary Review* 259 (1506): 7–14.

Wolfe, Thomas. 1997. "Imagining Journalism: Politics, Government, and the Person in the Press in the Soviet Union and Russia, 1953–1993." Ph.D. dissertation, Anthropology, University of Michigan.

"World Press Freedom Review: Ghana." *IPI Report* (December): 30–31.

Yang, Mayfair Mei-hui. 1994. *Gifts, Favors, and Banquets: The Art of Social Relationships in China.* Ithaca, N.Y.: Cornell University Press.

Yankah, Kwesi. 1989. *The Proverb in the Context of Akan Rhetoric.* Bern: Peter Lang.

———. 1995. *Speaking for the Chief: Okyeame and the Politics of Akan Royal Oratory.* Bloomington: Indiana University Press.

———. 1996. *Woes of a Kwatriot: No Big English.* Accra: Anansesem.

———. 1997. "Nana Ampadu, the Sung-Tale Metaphor, and Protest Discourse in Contemporary Ghana." In *Language Rhythm and Sound in Black Popular Cultures into the 21st Century,* ed. Joseph K. Adjaye, 54–74. Pittsburgh: University of Pittsburgh Press.

Young, Crawford. 1994. "Democratization in Africa: The Contradictions of a Political Imperative." In *Economic Change and Political Liberalization in Sub-Saharan Africa,* ed. J. Widner, 230–250. Baltimore: The Johns Hopkins University Press.

Yurchak, Alexei. 1997. "The Cynical Reason of Late Socialism: Language, Ideology and Culture of the Last Soviet Generation." Ph.D. dissertation, Cultural Anthropology, Duke University.

Zartman, William. 1995. "Introduction: Posing the Problem of State Collapse." In *Collapsed States: The Disintegration and Restoration of Legitimate Authority,* ed. W. Zartman, 1–11. Boulder: Lynne Rienner.

Ziegler, D., and M. K. Asante. 1992. *Thunder and Silence: The Mass Media in Africa.* Trenton, N.J.: Africa World Press.

Ghanaian Newspapers

Ashanti Independent
Daily Graphic
Free Press
Ghanaian Chronicle
Ghanaian Times
Guide
Independent
Public Agenda
Statesman
Weekend Chronicle
Weekend Statesman

INDEX

Numbers in *italics* refer to illustrations.

JENNIFER HASTY is Assistant Professor of Anthropology
at Pacific Lutheran University.

DATE DUE

OCT 18 2010		
APR 05 2013		
APR 23 2013		

Demco, Inc. 38-293